LOOKING

LOOKING FOR AMERICA

AVIROOK SEN

HarperCollins *Publishers* India
a joint venture with

New Delhi

First published in India in 2010 by
HarperCollins *Publishers* India
a joint venture with
The India Today Group

Copyright © Avirook Sen 2010

ISBN: 978-81-7223-982-4

2 4 6 8 10 9 7 5 3 1

HarperCollins *Publishers*
A-53, Sector 57, NOIDA, Uttar Pradesh – 201301, India
77-85 Fulham Palace Road, London W6 8JB, United Kingdom
Hazelton Lanes, 55 Avenue Road, Suite 2900, Toronto, Ontario M5R 3L2
and 1995 Markham Road, Scarborough, Ontario M1B 5M8, Canada
25 Ryde Road, Pymble, Sydney, NSW 2073, Australia
31 View Road, Glenfield, Auckland 10, New Zealand
10 East 53rd Street, New York NY 10022, USA

Typeset in 10.5/15 Adobe Caslon Pro
Jojy Philip New Delhi 110 015

Printed and bound at
Thomson Press (India) Ltd.

For my son Agastya,
may you explore and discover

Contents

Preface

The first time I visited the United States was in September 2002 on assignment to cover the United Nations General Assembly. On the evening of the first anniversary of 9/11, I went to visit a friend in Brooklyn, across the bridge from downtown. You couldn't see the New York skyline from his terrace (from most terraces in Brooklyn you usually see more of sprawling Brooklyn). But he told me that until 9/11 the previous year, you could just about see the tips of the Twin Towers from there.

He also narrated a rather haunting incident. The day after 9/11, a burnt fragment of paper, some kind of office memo, had wafted across the river and landed on his terrace. I am sure that many terraces in the neighbourhood provided resting places for similar morbid leaflets—the fliers of the times. We sat and speculated idly about which firm in the World Trade Centre the fragment might have flown from. Whose desk was it on? On which floor? Did this person survive...? After a few beers, it was agreed that the world would not be the same again.

The germ of the idea for this book gestated in the back of my head from the time I heard the story of the burnt office memo. But it was when I went back to the States in May 2008 that I felt the time was right. For me, personally, it sure was. A few months previously, I had been fired from my job as executive editor of a yet-to-be-launched English news channel. It was a rather public firing, made more ugly by all manner of accusations hurled at me by the shysters who masqueraded as the channel's promoters.

I decided to fight them and sent a legal notice for defamation. The odds weren't that great, my friends constantly reminded me. Well-funded corporate entity vs journo—there could only be one winner. This is exactly what I believed as well—the difference was I thought the winner had to be me.

In the end my former employers admitted they had lied, and they did this with their wallets. This made me richer in excess of rupees two crores—an unheard of settlement in Indian media terms. I decided that this was the perfect time to write my book.

But back to that trip in May. I spent my time largely in Texas, visiting my sister. She lives on the outskirts of Dallas, in the sort of modern community that tends to come up around a golf course. It is an idyll of a certain kind—with street names like 'Fresh Meadow Drive'—but once you are outside, the world can appear very different. In the malls—those great monuments of modern America (and now Gurgaon!)—the big stores were closing by May. Shops selling Texas boots and hats resembled ghost saloons after the gold rush. Even cut-price clothing seemed to have no takers.

In New York, I met nervous financial market executives who were getting to work by 7 a.m. to demonstrate to their equally clueless employers that what was happening couldn't be their fault—they were working too hard. Local retailers complained of increasing credit card declines;

people were losing jobs, and homes... something was wrong. The following months would proclaim the exact extent to the world loudly, clearly, and very cruelly.

✧   ✧   ✧

The list of authors who have written about their travels in America is long. There is the classic *Travels with Charley* by John Steinbeck. More recently, Bill Bryson has made this genre a sort of cottage industry. Stephen Fry has visited every state in the US in a London black cab, and journalists Peter Jennings and Todd Brewster have a volume of essays in words and pictures on the subject. I have no hesitation in admitting that I had read none of these books when I undertook my trip, and it was humbling (for different reasons in the case of different authors) to read some of them later. My book is a small addition to an already robust collection of work, but I would hope that it has its own voice, and I know that it records an interesting time. These attributes make it different.

As Indians, our relationship with America and Americans is quite complex. We hate the visa queues at the consulate, followed by the harrowing interrogations at immigration. But we lap up Hollywood, rock, soul and blues, and more often than not, the chance to live and work in America. We vacillate between liking and disliking America for secular reasons, because the bottom-line is, whatever the US does— from selling fraudulent mortgages to going to war, to mass-producing batter-fried chicken—we are affected in measurable ways. And since we have to live with that, I figured why not get to know who these people are? And what better time to do it than when the country was in transition?

This book doesn't make any claim of providing a comprehensive understanding of the United States. The need to satisfy personal curiosity (some of it trivial, or at least to do with trivia) had a lot to do with the trip. Why, for instance, did it take this friend of Cathy's in the Simon and Garfunkel song *America* 'four days to hitch-hike from Saginaw?' Where was this place anyway? Did anyone actually live there? On the subject of songs, what was Salinas like? That town near where Bobby McGee hopped off to find love and a home.

There were reference points outside the realm of popular culture. I remembered the images of the classroom in a Sarasota school where George Bush was listening to kids reading when 9/11 was taking place. The flight training schools where the terrorists became pilots (skipping the landing lessons) were conveniently located in nearby Venice, Florida.

There were two much broader subjects that also fascinated me. The first was that 'Christian' America was getting quite vocal since the events of 9/11 (apart from waging war, of course). The racket was directed mainly at the Muslim world, but it didn't take very long to create a 'with us or against us' situation with wider implications. The tag 'pro-abortion' and 'pro-terrorist' meant the same thing to a sizeable number of people ('pro-life' is used to describe those who oppose abortion; implying those who don't are 'anti-life').

A similar polarization was taking place over a number of other issues. As in the teaching of evolution—as opposed to that wonderful story that the earth was created in seven days. Or the concern over global warming—an act of God; humans are too insignificant to give Mother Earth a fever. While a lot of this could be attributed to on-the-ground nutcases, plenty of it could also be traced back to the very top—the White House. It is no secret that Bush the younger was under the influence... of several prophets of Armageddon. It is also no secret that the staunchest evangelical belief in the US—ranking alongside immaculate conception—is that if the evangelicals vote, the Republicans win. This was to be tested in the 2008 election, except that the economy came in the way.

There was yet another delicious prospect to writing my book—Barack Obama's candidacy opened up a discussion on race, not just in print and television, but in people's drawing rooms. All in all, the months between October 2008 and January 2009 were a great time to observe America and to converse with Americans. So that is what I set about doing.

Choosing where to go was easy, getting there a little tougher. Just to illustrate—Dinosaur, Colorado. This is not a made-up name. My son Ogu and I were going through a map of the States when we spotted it. He insisted I go there and I readily agreed. Had it not been for my brother-in-law Basudeb Ghosh, who drove me up from Denver, I would probably have become a fossil trying to get there. There is NO public transport.

I would like to clarify that my stops were not all chosen by throwing darts at a US map. Popular culture and/or zeitgeist pointed me in the direction of most of my destinations. I chose to go to places that would faintly ring a bell—Malta,

Montana sounds very unfamiliar, until you connect it to the fact that the Sundance Kid once robbed a train there.

For transport, I depended on Greyhound buses and Amtrak. My sister Indrakshi's American Airlines passes often came to the rescue—but there is nothing like a long road or rail journey when it comes to striking up conversations. This book records the more interesting of these conversations— and the 'cultural learnings' (and other education) that I gathered. Along the way, I had several sobering experiences that let me know how uninformed I was.

On a train to Dearborn, Michigan (where Ford is headquartered), I was surprised to meet an Arab passenger, a recent immigrant with no English at all, who was completely lost through the journey but came into his own at the station—a place as unlike his native Yemen as any I could have imagined. I learned later that about a third of Dearborn's population has Arab ancestry and speaks Arabic. The town is one of America's assimilation successes.

Each encounter I've described in this book was enriching. Some were strange, others were funny, and a few lay somewhere between disturbing and dangerous.

I enjoyed the ride. I hope you do too.

AVIROOK SEN

May 2010

1

• Chicago
ILLINOIS

Change, Hope; Meanings of

I haven't made an appointment. I walk over to meet him on the corner of Rush and Oake Streets, in downtown Chicago—he's seeking change.

I get straight to the point.

'So who's it going to be, man?'

'You mean, for Prezeedent?'

'Yeah.'

'Oh, Obama, man. Obama. Do you have some change?'

There is that distinctive sound of metal-on-coffee-cup that you will only find in the begging bowls of the West, disposable receptacles for disposable income, as he shakes his chalice of change. And then he says to someone else, 'Don't be sad, man.'

I had just got out of a jazz bar called the Back Room. (Don't be fooled by the name. Not much politics here, just a cover charge and the J.W. Williams Blues Band with Patricia Scott, but we missed her playing stuff like *It's a wonderful world*.)

'Don't be sad, man,' says my man, smiling from his wheelchair, his folded jeans, thighs downward, swinging ever so slightly in the light autumn breeze and grazing the top of his footrest. There are no feet on it.

A man—a black man in a good suit—the kind you saw on TV perhaps, walking out of Lehman Brothers carrying a cardboard box a week or so ago, but unattached to a box here, strides by. He is forced, much the way many others are, to stop and stick out a fist. It doesn't unclench to release change. It just meets the one that's pointed in his direction from the wheelchair in polite acknowledgement.

I begin to think about the fuss that was created after just such a handshake a few months ago, when the fists that met belonged to Barack and Michelle Obama. I think this because the well-heeled black man reminds me of Obama. He is made to look even better by his middleweight boxer's gait (most other men on Rush and Oake this midnight are oscillating between a light sway and stagger). The few words the faux Barack says to my man, he says coherently. This is more than can be said of several people who articulate a response to 'Don't be sad, man.'

Even though the man in the suit doesn't offer any change, I ask my man if he reminds him of the future 'prezeedent'.

'Who? That guy? No man, he's two shades darker than me. And I'm 'bout three shades darker than Obama. Know what um sayin'?'

It's either the street lights, or it's just me. But I tell him I don't get it, that I don't know what he's saying—on the basis of empirical evidence. I saw the man in the suit; I can see my man in his wheelchair; and I have watched Barack Obama without adjusting my television set.

'He's not so black. Know what um sayin'?'

Now if I got that right, what he means is that his support will go to a 'white' black guy (visions of Michael Jackson invade my already addled brain). I feel sorry for Obama. I mean, here's a guy trying his damnedest to knock a country semi-conscious about race and colour, and this is what he gets? Being called whitey by the brothers? But what the hell, he's ahead in the polls, so something must be working.

I change the subject to my man's personal situation.

'Lost ma legs 31 years ago. Shootout. Yesssir. Got 16 bullets in me. Here.' To back this claim, he lifts his Tommy Hilfiger T-shirt to expose enough craters on his stomach and back for me to be embarrassed into saying, 'I believe you.'

I ask what happened to the shooter.

'Oh, he's dead. But I like to give back, you know what um sayin' ... How your night been, baby? Don't be sad.' (Some change gets into the coffee cup) ... 'Know what um sayin'?

'I do volunteer work with people who are in bad situations. At the hospital. (And now, he invents a beautiful word.) I mean, my situation was "uncopable", man. I tell them, if I can make it...'

We are interrupted by possible donors coming our way... 'How your night been, baby? Had a good time? Don't be sad...' They give it a pass.

'Know what um sayin'?'

'If you've coped, why do you sit here every night?' I ask. (I cannot get myself to be more direct, as in 'Why are you begging?' He seems to know what I mean.)

'I try and make people feel good man. And get some of their change if possible. Heh, heh. Anything's possible, know what um sayin'?'

His soliciting style isn't that different from Obama's. It differs only in the details. At a base level, both try and make you feel good. After that, one takes the coffee cup route and goes solo on a street corner, with relatively low expectations. The other takes the Internet highway, with an army of subscribers to the cause, who in turn ask for an expected minimum from those who *want* change.

I got one of these in my mailbox a few days after I met my man.

Avirook

I've never asked you to make a donation before.

But I'm about to make some major decisions about deploying field staff and volunteers to key battleground states.

The resources we have on hand going into October will directly impact our voter registration and Get Out The Vote operations. And now that early voting has begun in eight states including Ohio as of today we need to move as quickly as possible.

Please donate $5 or more before the deadline to help register voters, get out the vote, and win this election.

We're stretching every dollar and doing everything we can with what we have. But every day I see firsthand

how much more we could do and how far your donation will go.
Thanks for your support,

Jon

Jon Carson
National Field Director
Obama for America.

Everyone's seeking change. Know what um sayin'?

✧ ✧ ✧

A drunk white bum walks up and, without bothering anyone else, asks my man for alms. He gets the fag end of a cigarette, still good for at least three quick puffs. My man, like he said, he likes to give back.

'I got to sit here man. I get $562 from welfare. I stay round here at the YMCA, that's $390 in rent. Know what um sayin'?'

'What changes for you if Obama is elected?'

'Issues, I mean health care man. Like right now, I could go to any of the fine hospitals in Chicago and they'd see me and all, but they won't *admit* me. 'Coz I don't have proper insurance.'

My man and about 47 million people in the States have this in common: they can be diagnosed, but not treated in a hospital. They don't have insurance, and 8.6 million Americans are recent inductees to this unfortunate club. The Bush administration accounted for them. One reason was that insurance costs rose by nearly five times the rate of incomes in the Bush years. A family health-care plan costs about a thousand dollars a month.

Universal health care is one of Obama's issues. In theory, if you are an American citizen, you will get treated, no matter what, under President Obama.* I am about to ask my man what has convinced him (beyond Barack's oratory) that this would indeed happen, but he is gone.

I turn and see a stationary cop car and a wheelchair exiting at top speed. The officer has evidently told my man that he should seek his change elsewhere in Chicago, if at all. Certainly not around the Magnificent Mile.

Know what um sayin'?

❖   ❖   ❖

Imagine cooking a meal. Nothing elaborate, but something original. Something that you've never tried before. Imagine also, that you are cooking this meal for the most discerning group of people that can possibly exist: people who pay good money for it.

---

* Health-care reforms were initiated by Obama within a few months of his taking over. Most of the 47 million left out are expected to gain coverage through a system that taxes the rich and subsidizes the poor. This is, of course, an oversimplification. The kind of bill 'Obamacare' rests on is a complex creature that America has been grappling with for a hundred years. The opponents of state-sponsored 'universal health-care' have a tradition of fighting and winning. Previous efforts failed after opponents shouted 'Prussianization!' in the early twentieth century, since the Germans had implemented a programme that covered everyone well before the nineteenth century was out. ('Pre-existing Condition', *New Yorker*, December 2009.)

The current bill was passed through the American legislative process with some difficulty, and there is no guarantee that it will work. Among the arguments against it were a few hilarious ones: that under Obamacare, the elderly would be counselled on a regular basis as to when they should die. Among the accommodations the Democrats had to make (for other

Now, imagine sipping a tablespoon of the gravy you've prepared. Rolling it on your tongue, gulping it down—and feeling nothing but a flavourless liquid of a certain consistency go down your throat. You cannot answer the simple questions, 'Does it need more salt? Is it too sweet? Are the spices overdone?'—because you don't know.

Imagine being a chef who cannot taste.

I met one in North Halsted, a tony part of Chicago. There was no sign at the grey entrance of No. 1723, just a notice for package delivery people on when packages were received. The cream curtains were drawn, and you could peek in only through a sliver of a window on the side. The pizza guy next door, like most people in the neighbourhood, would have no clue that this repurposed Chicago brownstone housed Alinea, one of the best restaurants in America, and was the thriving workplace of one of its most celebrated chefs.

Democrats mostly) was keeping abortion away from government money; and in the case of a recalcitrant Louisiana Democrat, the carrot of a 100 million dollars was pledged to her state, for her support. This was dubbed by clever Republicans as the 'Louisiana Purchase'.

In December 2009, I got an email from President Barack Obama:

Avirook,

As we head into the final stretch on health reform, big insurance company lobbyists and their partisan allies hope that their relentless attacks and millions of dollars can intimidate us into accepting the status quo.

So I have a message for them, from all of us: Not this time. We have come too far. We will not turn back. We will not back down...

Please donate $5 or whatever you can afford today...

Obama's search for change hasn't ended.

Grant Achatz, 35, was diagnosed with tongue cancer in 2007. The doctor said, 'Remove a large part of your tongue or die in six months.' Through all this—the radio and the chemo that is a cancer patient's lot—Achatz lost hair, weight and, crucially, his sense of taste.

For a man who said his mission was to make the argument for 'food as art', it was a Beethovenesque disability. But even though he could taste nothing and survived on liquids through his illness, he never stopped composing food. (He prefers the word 'composition' to recipe, and always uses it when he talks about his work.)

One such dish was a study in how to deal with adversity. It was smoked beef 'tongue' with morel—a bunch of different lettuces, arugula, romaine and watercress, with a piece of actual rib-eye beef made to look like tongue. It was just a composition that played off the tongue.

'We cut the rib-eye in such a way that it looks like the silhouette of a tongue. Like, if you cut it breadth-wise, it just looks like a chunk of meat. But if you cut it length-wise, it looks like—a tongue! So we cut it like that—so everybody knew what it was. You know, it was just fun. And it tasted good!'

It also forced everyone in Alinea to allude to Achatz's cancer. To say the word 'tongue' every day it was on the menu.

'People approach adversity and difficult times in different ways', he explained to me. So some people close up, some people lash out and become aggressive. Some people laugh! And you know, some people do a combination of all of these.

'For me, I'm this guy that 52 other people look at to lead this thing. They work an incredible amount of hours (70 in a Wednesday-to-Sunday week), they don't get a lot of money (Alinea cooks get $26,000 a year, though the service staff make more). They're here because they believe in it. And I felt that it was my responsibility as the leader of that group to show some light-heartedness.

'Like you know what, I'm really sick. I could die. But come on, the world is not going to end if I die. This restaurant might close. Maybe it won't. So what?'

Achatz told me that he worked through his two-year illness, so I thought I might as well ask him the converse question.

'You took eight days off. Why was that?'

'I looked very sick.'

'What did you look like?'

'What did I look like? I weighed 129 pounds (he'd lost about a third of his weight). My eyes were very sunken in and very dark. I had a rash, a very bad rash, all over my body from the chemo. I didn't have any hair. I looked very sick….

'I mean who wants somebody that's very, very sick cooking them dinner? People can get scared. They might go, like, you know: can I get cancer if he cooked my food? It was like AIDS in the 1980s…. We don't want to make people uncomfortable.

'A lot of people come to the kitchen and ask to see me. So if they see me back there, I have to go and talk to them even though I look very sickly. But if I'm not here, at least the staff can say that.'

He said this evenly, with no drama. But it was more than I could take. I groped around for a question and lowered my eyes to avoid his, but there was no escape. He was a member of a cancer support group and wore a T-shirt that said 'Still in the Fight'. Twenty-four maudlin questions formed themselves before my mind's eye. I felt like a rookie TV reporter.

Then the book came to my rescue. I had seen it on the way up. A slick 2-kg glossy that was a compilation of Achatz's work at Alinea. Achatz and his partner Nick Kokonas, a genuinely evolved gent who was like a brother to the patient, had put this book together after hours.

'The book... emm, you had discussed the possibility that this was the legacy... this was what would remain....'

'Right. Always wanted a book.'

'And along the way you figured you didn't have that much time...?'

'Well, that's part of it, you know....'

'So was it a rush job?'

Achatz laughed out loud. 'No! No! Took two years! You know part of it was, I always wanted a book, and then we started it, and then I got sick. You know, it was like, yeah, I wanted something to leave behind. I wanted people to... I feel awkward saying this... but I feel that this restaurant, it's important. In this country and maybe even in the world.

'Alinea is very important to the United States, because it legitimized modern cooking. There had been attempts to open restaurants in this country that were cooking in this avant-garde, molecular gastronomy* or modern way, whatever you want to call it. That failed, and they got

---

* Molecular gastronomy is a fairly recent phenomenon, pioneered in Spain by a Catalonian called Ferran Adria, in which kitchens might resemble laboratories; liquid nitrogen could be used to freeze potatoes, for instance, and butter might be served in toothpaste tubes. Surprise and novelty are priorities. Taste? Yes, that too.

pushed out… people didn't like it. We were the first one that they embraced. They said, you know what, "They're cooking in this genre—and it's really good."'

Bookings now have to be made a couple of months in advance. But nobody greets guests as they first enter Alinea. Many of them wonder, 'Am I in the right place?' Then a door opens dramatically to the left of a dark, narrow corridor and patrons, pre-googled by the staff, are ushered in to sit at tables that have nothing on them but napkins, and perhaps an intriguing piece of ginger in the middle.

As they settle down to their meal they might, for instance, be given a bowl that they can't set down—it's got a perfectly round bottom—so they are forced to hold what they are eating. Or they may be served squid tempura on a little steel contraption that prevents the crust from getting soggy (it would sweat on the plate). This contraption, with its flexible wire arms, clasps the squid exactly right—not too loose, not too tight—and it doesn't keel over because it's got a low centre of gravity. According to those who believe in Alinea, the food tastes better for all of this: you wouldn't want your tempura to keel over, would you? Certainly not at $300 a head.

Last I heard, Grant Achatz was getting his sense of taste back. But 'taste' is such an abstract thing, you never really know. When I asked Achatz about it, he said, yes, his taste buds had started working again, but they were probably working in new and different ways.

In the meantime, two abstract words that hit my eardrums with irritating regularity because of the elections had revealed their meaning to me in Chicago, through two people at opposite ends of the American rainbow:

Change: metallic, drops into your cup; the more frequently, the better; makes a difference.

Hope: useless emotion on its own; it works against itself—as in 'hoping against hope'; has remarkable effects when combined with resolve.

❖ ❖ ❖

I had arrived in America in late September 2008, my battered Samsonite full of extra warm clothes (Indians never learn) and books that I would not read (I never learn). The last time I was here, in May, the battle for the Democratic nomination was still in progress. It had all the negative energy of a full-fledged presidential race—and therefore, great drama and suspense.

Obama vs Clinton, as everyone will recall, was way closer than Obama vs McCain. One of the races that made it so close was the Indiana primary. It was decided, eventually, in Clinton's favour, despite the best efforts of a town called Gary, where Michael Jackson grew up.

That primary night, as America stayed up listening to increasingly exasperated news anchors relaying excuses for why the result was held up, Gary kept hand-counting votes. Then recounting hand-counted votes. My kind of town, I'd thought then, well before I thought about this book.

I took the Greyhound out from Chicago—not the best way to get to Gary—and saw some of the chimneys of American manufacturing that had breathed their last, either side of the road. They stood quietly in the distance, well back from the casino billboards that had come to the fore, advertising the 'loosest slots in the Midwest'.

The ride was less than an hour, just about right for a Greyhound virgin like myself. As the bus pulled out of 95-Dan Ryan, the driver made a few polite requests: do not talk loudly on the cellphone or play music loudly, do not assault a fellow passenger or the driver, and so on. Even as the poor man spoke, a foot appeared on the empty seat next to mine, belonging to a man across the aisle, who was not only blasting music in his ears, but also singing along. Any protest on my part may have led to the 'assaulting a fellow passenger' rule going out of the window as well. Along with me.

On the seats in front and across, there were two single moms, also bound for Gary. The labour and stress involved in parenting alone had aged each of them by about ten years, I thought, while keeping an eye on the unpredictable jerking foot next to me. And so, not knowing quite what to expect, I was on my way. Gary, I was told, wasn't America. But if you believed the fine crop of pessimists that the Bush years had produced, America could be Gary in a short time.

2

● Gary
INDIANA

Somethin' Wrong with the Picture

I was on a wide and weird street when a beat up old Ford stopped noisily on the other side. There was no one else within a 100 yards of either of us.

'Yo!'

This was sharp and it was meant for me. It pierced through the din made by the part of the car that worked best—the sound system playing hip-hop.

'Look in that shop... Tyrone there?'

Whatever it is that was going on was well beyond my understanding. I found myself responding robotically, first looking up, then turning my head, seemingly without the function of several joints, towards 'that shop'.

It was right next to me—an old furniture store of some sort. So old that it was certifiably dead: dust sheets covered the wares, the glass entrance had to make do with cobwebs. Was Tyrone a skeleton in one of the store's cupboards?

'Tyy-rooaane!'

Nobody had been shot. This was not an anguished cry, just a reminder from across the street. A prompt to knock on the glass door and ask for the wanted man.

There was only one sensible thing for me to do: walk on along the sidewalk as if I hadn't heard him. But how could I? As I looked across the street again, I saw the man holding something in his free hand, which he seemed keen to conceal. A gun? So I took the even more sensible option two.

I went close to the door, knocked lightly twice, whispered 'Tyrone, Tyrone', turned around, forced the ball-and-socket joint in my shoulder into a telling shrug and whispered, 'No one here.'

The driver made a sharp U-turn right after, not wasting time on courtesies. He passed in front of me as R2D2 ceded control of my body and I saw the concealed weapon. It was a hot dog.

I was too embarrassed to berate myself. Why was I afraid? Why did I suspect this man might hurt me and so pretend to help him find this Tyrone? But on that subject, why would anyone be looking for Tyrone at that joint unless he was a skeleton? Why wasn't there anyone else around?

The last question was easy to answer: this was Broadway, Gary, Indiana.

✦ ✦ ✦

Every shop on the west side of Broadway was shut. Or had been shut for the last quarter of a century. At the Palace Theatre, a short distance away, it said the Jackson Five was playing tonight, but that was a lie. The Jackson Five lived here (Michael was the youngest of them), but they beat it a long time ago.

Nobody had played at the Palace Theatre since 1972. It had been ruined in instalments since then. Its Italianate tower was vandalized, the terracotta ornamentation stolen. The big hole the thieves left exposed the interiors to the elements which peeled the frescoes from the walls, rusted the ornate seats and gave the stage the look of a stalactite cave. Someone should have had the courtesy of bringing the curtain down.

That was the inside. In 2001, when the Miss America pageant was held in Gary, they painted a ticket agent on the boarded-up counter out front, and flower pots on the plywood-covered windows of the abandoned apartments above the theatre. This might have fooled some of the contestants, but that's about it. They also put up the Jackson Five sign.

This was part of Gary's effort to appear prettier for the pageant—the town had come into some money. The 'loosest slots in the Midwest', which floated on riverboat casinos on Lake Michigan because laws do not allow them on shore, had made it possible for Gary to spend on this bizarre face-painting. The gambling business gave Indiana close to $50 million a year, some of which went to the third-rate artists employed for the prettification.

There had been other attempts to revive the Palace Theatre, a building as important for its architecture as it was as a point of convergence for the townspeople. In1987, a troika of doctors—two of them of Indian origin—bought the building at an auction for a reported $30,000. They had plans to spend over half a million dollars on renovating the theatre itself, opening a restaurant on the storefront and make the apartments above habitable. The restaurant opened for a while, but like every other business on Broadway, shut down soon enough.

None of the storefronts were spared the makeover. The artwork on the boarded-up windows had that unintentionally perverse quality which only carpenters who try their hand at painting can achieve. Men and women looking onto the street with curious perspective, painted salesmen in stores that hadn't sold a thing in decades—their necks twisted at unlikely angles, their faces a litany of deformities. Everything was in two dimensions, because there was nothing below the surface. Who were they trying to fool (apart from the Miss America hopefuls)? And now, even that coat of paint was peeling, the painted people aging poorly.

I said every shop on Broadway was closed, but this was inaccurate. Payday Loans was open and doing great business offering advances for a small price—about a dollar on the hundred that you might not earn. There was a queue at the place. Cars lined up outside, their occupants nervous—twitching like drug addicts waiting for a slightly overdue fix.

Two old men in wheelchairs discussed welfare on a side street. Across the road from them was the shabbiest 'Upscale Convention Centre' sign that you would ever see—with no trace of the actual centre anywhere.

✧ ✧ ✧

At 85%, Gary had the highest percentage of African Americans in cities with a count of 100,000 or more people. The man who presided over this town sat in City Hall, built in the 1920s when Gary was an artificially settled boom town. The waiting area on the second floor was quiet. The front desk had a couple of things to deal with—unseasonal floods, an unfairly towed car...

I asked to use the washroom before I went in to meet the mayor and was directed across the hall. As I entered the first stall, I was hit by one of my lasting images of Gary: a massive floater in a yellowing commode. One of those that needed a stick of dynamite to send down.

I leaped back, did my business elsewhere, but the image refused to leave my head, even as I met the mayor and talked politics, race and stuff. It was an effort to keep from asking, 'Who's responsible for that? What do you mean you don't know? You're the mayor, aren't you?'

The fact of the matter was that you could never tell by the size of one of those things. The unlikeliest people—women and children included—could leave them behind. I found myself making a list of suspects as I was called into the office. That's the kind of effect an outsize floater can have. The security guy? The lady whose shift just changed? The man with the car complaint... ?

Mayor Clay had those 1970s-type sideburns that linked up with the moustache. His white shirt had shiny white polka dots on it, the large circles making a failed understatement. His cuffs had his name embroidered on them.

'When all the votes are counted up and *iss aaalll* even, and you add Gary, where Obama gets 95% (this was a fair estimate), that's when you win the state,' he said from his rather nice office in City Hall, a few buildings down from the boarded establishments, and just across the street from a perforated ghost: the old Sheraton, a hotel that stayed on because it was too big to move.

Clay had effectively just said that Gary would be the last to turn in the results. Just like on primary night a few months ago, when there was some suggestion of foul play. Obama may have lost Indiana to Hillary Clinton despite Gary's overwhelming support, but the town had slowed the game down enough to ensure a more important victory.

Two states held primaries that day. The results for North Carolina, which Obama won comfortably, came in time for prime-time news. And, thanks to Gary, news of Clinton's victory in Indiana came in too late to make a difference in public perception.

The mayor's explanation for the slow count was that it took his town that long because 11,000 early voters had cast their votes. That's all there was to it.

'We're going to win (in November),' he said. 'In fact, we should have won that primary. In 2007, we only had 2,000 early voters; 2008 we had 11,000 early voters. State law says you can't start counting them before noon that day. And we count ours the ol'-fashioned way... by hand. So it took us longer to count those than it did before.

'And the CNN people went "gimme a number, gimme a number"... Holy! Wait till we count them! Know what um sayin'? Once we count them, you got it.

'But we're doin' it a different way now. We'll have more people counting and a bigger space. So, in November, it'll go faster.' (In the end, Gary's vote just added to the momentum of the landslide; it wasn't decisive, as the mayor had predicted.)

✧ ✧ ✧

The pace of the vote count in Gary was an inescapable metaphor. This was a town that had got left behind just when it thought it was blazing a new trail—at the very front of a movement for equality among races. It had elected the country's first black mayor and held the first National Black Political Convention.

'I was there. I was running for state senate at the time… 1972.' The large antique clock behind Mayor Clay is stuck at five to eleven.

'I'll tell you what's changed from then to now. Then, we had only approximately 800 African-American elected officials. Now we have almost 8,000. So that's a big change, in terms of the numbers. Now you got Barack Obama knockin' on the door… got his foot in the door really, to become the first African-American president of the *United* States of America. (The stress on United is Clay's.)

'The people are going to vote for him because we need a change in this country and he represents that change. Now there's gonna be a few people who're going to vote against him because of his colour. And there's gonna be some folk who'll vote for him—a few (he adds quickly) *because* of his colour. But the majority of the people in this country are voting for Barack Obama because we need a change in the *United* States of America.

'Give you a good example. Right now, in *Eyeraq*, the cost of a gallon of gas is a dollar and 36 cents. In the *United*

States the cost of a gallon of gas is almost five dollars. Somethin' wrong with the picture.

'We're spending almost 12 billion* a month in *Eyeraq* and here in Gary, Indiana, we can't get 12 dollars to fix a pothole. Somethin' wrong with the picture.'

Clay would know about screwed up pictures—he saw them every day on the shuttered shops of his town.

'Do you know Mr Obama? Are you friends… ?' I enquired.

'Oh yeah, we're friends.' The mayor got up to fetch a postcard-type flier that showed him and Obama together. Both sported the sort of wooden smile that gets chiselled into publicity material like this with unerring consistency.

'Me and *Buhrrrack*!' he said with a flourish as he showed it to me.

The mayor returned to the subject of Gary. Earlier in 2008, he had visited Gary's sister city, Fuxian, China, to solicit investment. There were indignant murmurs on the Internet about this: it was insult to injury, couldn't America take care of the cities it had built?

Relying on the hopes of a bailout from someone—the Chinese, the new administration, God—Mayor Clay said, 'Gary is going to be a bustling city, we have a lot on the drawing board.' He reached over to a light pile of papers on his desk—architectural plans for the buildings, which, according to him, would change Gary.

'Dat's a great place to eat,' he said, pointing to Dustie's diner. 'Just opened. Right across from the baseball stadium. It's a buffet—eat all you want, man.

* The mayor's estimate, approximately true for the time he said it (varying between 10 and 12 billion dollars), has gone down since.

'This one, right here. It's the Michael Jackson Museum and Performing Arts Centre. You know Michael Jackson? He was born in Gary. The house that he was born in—2300 Jackson—we're going to lift it up, put it on the highway and build this museum around it.'

Many things have happened since I met Mayor Clay. In June 2009, Michael Jackson died. Gary held a memorial service for its most famous son in early July. It had the usual suspects in attendance: members of the Jackson family, chief among them Michael's father Joe, the Reverend Jesse Jackson, an old schoolteacher of Michael's who told stories about his energy and enthusiasm ('Michael was always the first to volunteer') and, of course, local admirers.

Michael himself came back to Gary only once after becoming famous. The first record label to sign him (as part of the Jackson Five, in 1967 when he was just nine) was a local venture called Steeltown. But the company, like so many other businesses in Gary, shut down soon after. Jackson's music moved to Motown Records—to add to the body of exciting new sounds coming out of Detroit which, at the time, was still successfully making large cars and adventurous music.

While reading the copious coverage of Jackson's strange death, it was impossible not to think of Gary. The shifting of the prodigy's interests to more happening towns started at almost exactly the same time as Gary's decline began, in 1968.

One fact that emerged in the aftermath of Jackson's death was that he had two voices: the public falsetto meant for fans, and a gruff, barking intonation reserved for those who served him. To live a whole life like that required a bizarre self-discipline, but this was a part of him.

The paradox was that no matter who he was, Michael Jackson always wanted to be somebody else. And high on the list of people he didn't want to be was Michael Jackson of Gary, Indiana.

For this, you couldn't really blame him. His dad may have been up on the stage at the memorial function, but Joe Jackson regularly beat Michael during his childhood.

Michael moved away from his days in Gary, but Gary wasn't going to let go so easily. His teachers clung to the memory of the dark-skinned bubbly boy, hard as it was to reconcile this with the frail white recluse always hiding his eyes. The mayor wanted a museum (and, in small print, an entertainment centre—it would be very close to the casinos) to attract attention and money. Gary wanted to be something else too.

The mayor's plan became more relevant with Jackson's death, but six months after the event, it was not clear how and when the centre would actually be built. No one knew where the money was going to come from.

❖ ❖ ❖

Gary has a motto: We are doing great things. The mayor's office insisted on listing Dustie's all-you-can-eat diner as one of those, so it was easy to forget the town had done a few great things in the past. It *was* the first major town in the United States to elect a black mayor, Richard Hatcher, in 1967. That said something about the town. What happened immediately after made a much broader point: it said something about America.

White people fled Gary after that election, hitting the gas even harder after the National Black Political Convention of 1972. They took all their money and their business and went down to Merrillville, 22 miles south, to entrench themselves in a town that once belonged to the peace-loving Potawatomi Indians. (Merrillville's approximate demographics: 70% white; 22% black, 0.33% American Indian.)

Gary, once a market where shampoos and lotions were tested by the likes of Lever Brothers before being sold in the big cities, turned into a place where detergents were hard to find. This happened quite rapidly. After years of steady growth in population, helped by the then competitive steel mills that offered decent blue-collar employment at the very least, the South (and south of) Chicago steel mills that Barack Obama recalls from his youth started shutting down in the 1960s and 1970s.

Broadway, a picture dated 1923 hanging in City Hall told you, was a bustling street. Dr Eurit the dentist was clearly extracting some business. The theatre poster did not lie when it said 'Tonight: Dorothy Philips stars in *Slander and the Woman*'. Most of all, there were people. People who occupied the marvellous buildings that had come up through the first 30 years or so of the twentieth century. Once Gary, with its proximity to Chicago, its connect through railway lines, its abundance of water and a great lakefront, was officially a boom town.

A list of historic buildings that were vacant and in poor condition could be found in the town's comprehensive plan for 2008. It made depressing reading: at least eight out of ten major buildings in the city centre were vacant and in really poor shape. Among them were the once stately Methodist church and the post office.

Gary's striking Union Station, the vital node along the artery that kept the city's robust circulation going, was now an unstable pile of rubble, designated as one of the most dangerous buildings in Indiana. The Steel City building on Broadway still sported a sign proclaiming itself as such, but it looked like a dead animal that had had its eyes gouged out.

The thing about Gary was that its decay hit you in the face. There were a fair number of towns in the USA which were similarly depressed. But Gary, through the dereliction of its downtown and its *vacancy*, said to you: 'Look at me, I'm dying.'

The inescapable conclusion was that it paid the price for its role in the civil rights movement of the 1960s. Gary's glory days were when hierarchies were set. The election of a black mayor was an act of defiance that upset the order. It was punished with an economic lynching. A crime in which the fingerprints of the culprits were too many to count, although the pieces of evidence, the spectacular ruins of the town, were open for inspection.

Some consequences were inevitable. By the time Michael Jackson was recording *Thriller* (1982), Gary had one of the highest crime rates in the country. With 71 homicides in 2007 (a bad year) and another 49 in 2008, among a host of other crimes, it remained in statistical terms exponentially unsafe among American cities.

✧ ✧ ✧

'I'm the king of business in Gary. That's why I'm celebrating my twentieth year in business. I had a newspaper out when I was nine years old, when the city was full of businesses everywhere.' Dr Guy Spencer, doctor of business and humanities, radio talk show host, model and printer, told me this as I sat in his office. It was a chaotic place, in keeping with his multiple professions: paper everywhere, his little daughter doodling on the floor, old posters and signs laid to rest against walls, and an unkempt counter behind which, on his swivel chair throne, sat Gary's king of business, dressed in T-shirt, shorts and sandals.

'The thing about Gary,' said Spencer, 'is that its decay is telling.' That's why I call Gary the test-tube baby. For everything that happens in urban areas (like a depression or a breakdown of law and order), there's usually one spot in the country that shows the symptoms. You just happen to be in the city where it shows on Broadway.

'Gary, Indiana, was actually known for testing a lot of products, soaps and everything. We had such a diverse community, it was a melting pot. We even had the first black mayor in the whole of the country... that tells you something.'

Spencer recognized that Gary paid for that last test. 'The businesses decided, since they couldn't work with this new mayor who wanted equality for every citizen, that they would move out of the city. So over the next ten years, huge anchoring stores like Sears, Goldblatt's, Montgomery Ward, you name it, left.'

The 'summit', or the National Black Political Convention of 1972, was held across the street from where Spencer ran his printing business. He went there holding his dad's hand and he has a briefcase from it as a keepsake.

The summit was important, of course. But in Gary's context, it did very little to cure what Spencer called the black people's 'crabs in the bucket disease', which read:

'If one of us tries to improve our lives, we will pull him down.'

'People commuted here to work in the steel mills, but they wouldn't shop here. That still hasn't changed. There's still 20,000 people coming out here to work, but they spend their money in other places,' he added.

Across the lobby of the office building where Spencer ran his business, was a little place that demonstrated this fact. As the nationwide 'Yes we can' chorus grew louder, it was easy to forget the people who threw up their hands and said that, in fact, they *couldn't*.

Along with a really good corned-beef sandwich (the bread was deliciously deep-fried), the Eat Your Heart Out deli cafe on Broadway passed me a little note: 'Due to the slowing economy and rising food costs, we regret to inform you that (we) will be closing this location effective 17 October.'

What a shame they couldn't hold on for a couple of weeks more. The man who could solve all problems would be elected. But while the heart might have wanted that, the head told the proprietors that cutting losses was a better move.

Towns like Gary led the way in placing a crippling burden of expectation on Obama. They would be intent on collecting on every promise and some that were never made. This set him up for failure like no Clinton or Republican could.

Dr Spencer advised me to leave Gary before dark. I took the South Shore line, carrying away images of those strange painted facades and (despite my best efforts) the stubborn floater in the City Hall toilet. That about summed it up.

On the platform, there were quaint wooden stalls for seats. Somebody (on his way out, I suspect) had scrawled 'Fuck Gary'. To which someone had responded: 'But he's a man.'

I boarded a quiet train, barring a neurotic woman sitting in front of me. She spoke about her many problems incessantly for an hour, not a second's rest, to the hapless stranger next to her. She had lived in Gary all her life.

AN ASIDE

My friend told me this story from Gary. He had developed the beginnings of a gambling addiction a few years ago. That was what took him to Gary. There were about five casinos that floated on the lake shore there. Tenuous ramps, from land to water, made them legal.

Said my friend, 'I used to go there often. They were the closest casinos from Chicago. The clientele was really strange. One night I saw a woman at the Blackjack table who collapsed in tears. The dealer told me that she had just lost $10,000. She had started by losing a few hundred she had borrowed from her boyfriend. She then used the rent money she was supposed to have given the landlord a few days earlier, but hadn't. After that she dipped into her boyfriend's checking account (which he had trusted her with). That was a life destroyed right there.

'I made friends at the casino, even though I went there maybe a couple of times a month. People recognized me. I guess that's probably because *they* were always there. This spectacled black guy, John, actually became quite fond of me. I noticed that he always bet in hundreds. Very brave, but you can even out every forty hands or so if you're smart.

I played with $25 chips. This made us the biggest punters at the table and we developed this strange bond. He would encourage me, and I him.

'I got over the gambling thing and didn't go there for a bit. About six months after my last trip, I went again. And that's when I heard the story. Something improbably fortuitous had happened to a man at the poker table. If you threw in an extra dollar with every hand, aside from your bet, you could win a jackpot that went into hundreds of thousands. What you also needed was a straight flush: Ace to 10 of the same colour. This was a rare hand—one in several hundred thousand, if not more.

'This man got one of those—$180,000. And that was it. He decided that he'd just use thirty grand from his money for future gambling, put the rest away, and not work—because he was invincible at poker, you see. Good plan, but the thirty grand was gone in no time. Then he started drawing on the capital at about $5,000 a day.

'I was having a drink when someone narrated the story. He never mentioned a name. But I couldn't help asking him if the man's name was John, and if he was likely to show up that night. "You didn't hear?" the storyteller said. "In three months or so, he'd lost the $180,000, and everything he owned. He blew his brains out last month."'

3

• Dayton
TENNESSEE

The Main Things Are the Plain Things

'I'm a red hatter,' said Mrs Karen Black, talking about a constituency that I had not heard of, as we sipped sweet tea in the Dayton Coffee House. She explained, 'There is a poem that says, "When I grow old I shall wear purple/ With red hats that do not match and do not go/ I'll learn to spit on the sidewalk and spend the grocery money for brandy/ And tell the family that we have no money for butter..." And the poem goes on... all these things that we're never allowed to do as proper ladies. And then at the end it says, "So that my family won't be too surprised/ I think I'll start practising now."

'And so—you will see this throughout the United States—there are gatherings of ladies, 50 and older who, regardless of what life has thrown at them, whether it's widowhood, cancer, loss of a child... regardless of what life has done to them... they choose joy. The red hatters are all about choosing joy. And you will see them with feathers and glitters and red hats and purple outfits...'

I had been watching quite a bit of American television and I couldn't help thinking what a fine red hatter Bill O'Reilly of Fox News would make. O'Reilly's 'Factor' is the modern Bible, with ratings that match (according to him). That he might have shaped (or at the very least, shared) Mrs Black's views, was very apparent. So I thought of O'Reilly in a purple dress and glitters, with a red hat, feathers and all. That tall figure, prancing at the front of a merry bunch of red hatters, leading them on a happy shopping expedition on his day off—there would be no need to preach, because these were the converted.

For the record, I did spot some 'possible O'Reillys', but could not get a confirmation that any of them was the 'one'.

Mrs Black was 58. She was wearing a green floral outfit, without any sort of hat, but I had no reason to believe she was not a red hatter. We did not, however, get off on the best possible note. While I addressed her as 'ma'am' at all times, there was a short discussion on appropriate appellation before we began talking in earnest.

'When I call the bank, and someone from *your* country answers and says, "Hi Karen", I always let them know it is "Mrs Black"... you may come in, but only if I invite you.'

This was probably good feedback for call centre training back home, where bumbling undergrads with little English were doing their best to appear warm and friendly. So I nodded in agreement.

My friend Budhu Bhaduri, who worked at the Oak Ridge Labs in Knoxville, had driven me to Dayton. He was a US citizen and had spent enough time in the South to call himself 'from the South as well', meaning that he understood.

'Oh no,' said Mrs Black, with emphasis, '*you* will never be from the South, no matter how hard you try.'

I liked her. Most of all because when she said she 'chose joy at all times', she meant it. In the context of our meeting, choosing joy would mean going with the McCain–Palin ticket in about a month's time.

She was a good Christian, Mrs Black. I asked what denomination she belonged to and she laughed and said, 'I'm a methabaptapristacostal... just a Christian.' Then, assuming the air of someone who is about to reveal a secret, she looked me in the eye and said, 'The main things are the plain things.'

She began counting the main things on her fingers: 'Was He born of a virgin; was He crucified; did He die; was He raised from the dead; had He ascended to the right hand of the father... the main things are the *plaayne* things. And you can put any label you want to put on it, but the main things are the plain things. And they are true. They are true.'

Faced with these profound and totally sincere beliefs, I couldn't help turn the conversation towards other countries and other faiths. We began with Iraq, where the plane things would be those that dropped death from the sky.

Mrs Black paused a bit to take in the question. 'I think about the bigger picture, I think that politicians will come and go and do whatever it is that they have to do. I think the truth is that God is in control. And the truth is that this is going to play out how He wants it to play out.'

She continued, 'Things that are meant for evil, God has a way of turning them into good in the bigger picture that we don't even see. I do know that the end-time war, Armageddon in Revelation, is going to be somewhere in the east. Somewhere, Iraq, Iran... somewhere there. I think it's a fool's game not to keep that firmly in mind.'

Right there, I thought, in succinct, easy language, was Bush's foreign policy. Had Mrs Black ghostwritten it?

'But what about good, young American kids going out there and dying?' I asked.

'Good young American kids died for the revolution. Good young American kids died for World War I, for World War II, for Vietnam. Do I *like* good, young American kids going to die? Absolutely not,' she said.

'Wouldn't you want to stop the war right now?' I asked.

'All wars. The-o-ret-ically,' she draws the word out deliberately, 'in a perfect world... that would be wonderful. In a perfect world, there would be no sorrow. In a perfect world, we wouldn't have people trying to come over and kill us. In a perfect world we wouldn't have to have a bigger stick than the other guy to make them behave. In a perfect world...'

She was clearly not ghostwriting Dubya's speeches—they had nothing of the lyrical quality of her extempore. (A few years ago, some twit had said that Bush's rhetoric had a Hemingwayesque quality. I was gratified to know that at least one person had objected. Norman Mailer had written to the publication to say it was like comparing Jackie Susann to Jane Austen.)

Mrs Black continued, 'People have died for the rights that we have. To go to the churches we go to, or not. To pray when and where we choose... people have died for these rights that we have to make this country what it is.

'We have more of a sense of "I appreciate that", and clearly the rest of the world thinks that, because they're pouring into our shores legally and illegally by the millions. Clearly, other people think: "We see that, we like that, we want a piece of that." We think that's good.

'And our boys think that's worth dying for. And the mothers send them off... to die for it.'

Two teardrops rolled down Mrs Black's pink cheeks as she said this. She looked away, her lips quivering. I asked if I had upset her.

'No, no, no, no, no! Honey, I'm Southern. We cry as easy as we laugh. We'll probably hug when we're through,' she said, wiping her tears.

'I was saying that if a ship is moving, God can turn the rudder to change the direction of the ship, but if it's just sitting there stagnant, ain't nothing gonna happen. So we're moving, and if we've made mistakes, God can alter and change them. Whether it's through who gets in office or whatever he uses. Yes, I vote—but I also pray.'

That this conversation was taking place a hundred metres from the site where some of Mrs Black's fundamental beliefs were contested more than 80 years ago—the Dayton courthouse, where the Scopes or 'Monkey Trial' took place in 1925—seemed a bit ironic to me.

We parted with the promised hug—one for Budhu too—because, Mrs Black said, she was an 'equal opportunity' supporter. And as she embraced me, she whispered, 'You're a liberal, aren't ya?' I came up with an 'it depends on your perspective' answer, which only confirmed to her that I was a socialist.

But we did agree on something. Mrs Black really fancied my brown leather Converse shoes. 'I should get a pair of those,' she said. I wondered how well they would go with a red hat, but I quickly reminded myself of the essence of red hatter philosophy: to do the things you're not supposed to do as a fine lady. The shoes would look good on Mrs Black—and on Bill O'Reilly too, with the right dress.

✧ ✧ ✧

In the fall, if you travel over the hills near the Smoky Mountains and roll along smooth, broad highways that bend and weave through forests of maple trees, which seem to turn from green to red even as you pass them mesmerized, it is easy to miss anything made by man—houses, gas stations, McDonald's signs and more. But you cannot miss the churches, there are too many of them. People here will point out, however, that these are works of God.

Would such a country initiate a debate on whether man descended from apes or was made in God's image? Yes, in 1925, with *State of Tennessee vs Scopes*, Dayton did exactly that.

Tennessee is in the Bible Belt—a group of states, strapped tight across the middle of America, which has historically done a terrific job of concealing, or at least pushing north or west, an annoying liberal belly which, nevertheless, seemed to be getting a little out of hand this election year—what with the release of films like *Religulous* so close to election day. The very title (a fusion of religion and ridiculous) was abhorrent in these parts.

Comedian (and stubborn marijuana-legalization activist) Bill Maher's film wasn't playing in Dayton, although there was a lone theatre in Knoxville, 100 miles away, screening it. (May the Lord forgive it.)

These were communities whose foundations lay in the literal interpretation of the Bible. They were easy to mock—they believed in a talking snake, and that dinosaurs roamed the earth alongside man. But their persuasions were not always religious. The best example of this, ironically, is the Scopes 'Monkey Trial' of 1925.

This trial kicked off the debate on whether God made man, and took his rib to make woman, or whether there was any truth in what this chap called Darwin was saying. But Dayton didn't host the trial to champion either cause. It had the most secular motive there can be—money.

The story goes back to 1885 when coal was discovered in the area. A boom followed, but after 30 years and three accidents in quick succession, the mines were closed. The town went into decline and was fumbling around for life support, when townspeople read an advertisement in the *Chattanooga Times* published nearby.

On 13 March 1925, the Tennessee General Assembly had passed the Butler Act. The Act made it unlawful to 'teach any theory that denies the story of the Divine creation of man as taught in the Bible, and to teach instead that man is descended from a lower order of animals'. Breaking the law meant a fine ranging from $100 to $5,000.

The American Civil Liberties Union (ACLU), head-quartered in New York, wanted to challenge the Butler Act. To do so, it needed a teacher who was willing to break the law and be tried. All expenses would be paid by the ACLU, said the ad.

An engineer from the sick Cumberland Coal and Iron Company saw the potential of hosting such a trial right away: the attention the town would get would surely revive it. Soon, the whole town was conspiring to make it happen. The 'hustling' drugstore owner, the superintendent of schools, the barber, even—according to some accounts— the judge who would hear the case were in on it.

They called in John T. Scopes, 24, a man with classic 'teacher' looks, complete with horn-rimmed glasses, and asked him whether he would be willing to be prosecuted. Scopes had just one problem: he was a teacher but had never taught evolution. An added complication was that all this was taking place during the summer vacation. The conspirators worked around these difficulties by summoning a few boys and getting Scopes to talk with them in a nearby meadow, since school was closed. Scopes was then formally charged.

In New York, ACLU members, unaware of most of this, thought they had it made. Clarence Darrow, one of the top defence lawyers of the time, volunteered to defend Scopes. His opposing number would be the prominent Democrat and lawyer William Jennings Bryan.

The (general and very loose) modern view is that Democrats are liberal and secular, while Republicans are conservative and 'more Christian'. The southern view is a bit different. Liberalism or conservatism are subsets of the superset of fundamental Christian beliefs. Bryan, a leading intellectual of his time who ran for president thrice, was a Democrat from that stock. A later, more notorious and less intellectual version of Bryan would be George Wallace, whose constituency Nixon strategists would refer to as 'Wallace Democrats'—a support base that they would successfully prey upon and break from the Democratic fold.

It is because of the continued presence of a large constituency that no Democrat running for high office will come out clearly in support of, say, gay marriage (e.g., Joe Biden pussy-footed around this and made it a 'civil liberties issue' in the vice-presidential debate against the formidable Sarah Palin).

But back to 1925. By the time the trial began in July, the town's plan was working so well that Divine intervention was the only explanation. Dayton, where only a few thousand ragged people lived, suddenly had 200 journalists descending upon it, using 65 telegraph lines to file their stories. A future Supreme Court chief justice attended the proceedings, as did prominent individuals from the church and public life. Joe Mendi, the famous trained chimpanzee, came as well. It was an 11-day carnival.

Outside of Dayton, the interest was huge. For the first time in its history, America would hear the court proceedings live on the radio (the O.J. Simpson trial is a descendent of the Scopes Trial). Thinkers like George Bernard Shaw and Albert Einstein responded to the trial proceedings. Dayton was booming again.

As for the trial itself, the judge, probably keeping public sentiment in mind, stuck only to whether Scopes had broken the law or not, rather than begin the larger debate. Clarence Darrow got around this, to an extent, by asking Bryan to take the stand as an expert. The prosecution lawyer was made to look somewhat foolish and pedantic (he insisted that a 'big fish' rather than a mere whale swallowed Jonah, the prophet who spent three days floating in digestive juices to escape a storm). Bryan also conceded an important, but quickly forgotten point: that the Bible cannot always be interpreted literally.

Nevertheless, the judge found Scopes guilty and fined him $100. This was okay with the ACLU, because the real debate would take place in the Tennessee Supreme Court during the appeal. But the Supreme Court was too clever to allow that. It dismissed the case on the technicality that the judge set the fine, and not the jury, as required by law.

The swarms that had descended trooped out, but the positive economic impact of the trial on Dayton was lasting—and it's probably why the town exists today. Bryan died shortly after the trial, but Bryan University came up in 1930 and now forms the core of the town.

And what of the impact on religion and belief? Well, God willed that it remain exactly the same in election year 2008, as it was in 1925. If there was a winner in *State vs Scopes*, it was Dayton.

✧ ✧ ✧

Miss Eleanor would have been three when the 'Monkey Trial' took place. She spent her life as a math teacher. One math problem that she and the several generations of teachers in Tennessee (including the present one) haven't posed to their students is: If a boat were to accommodate a pair of animals of every species, how big would it need to be?

It would have to be a little bigger than Dayton (10,000 people) and, in fact, all of the Bible Belt, I suspect. But why recalculate when Noah's done all of that already? And it has now been vindicated by scientists from the Institute of Creation Research (ICR)?

In the Museum of Earth History at Santee, outside San Diego, which showcases the ICR's work, there is a little model of Noah's Ark, accompanied by FAQs. Here is an excerpt from that exhibit:

Q: Could the ark have housed 50,000 animals?

A: On the whole, most animals are quite small—very few are large—the average size being no greater than a sheep.

Noah also did not need to take the largest individuals. Instead, young virile specimens could have been collected for the ark.

Dimensions of the ark: 450 ft × 75 ft × 45 ft = 1,518,750 cubic feet.

This volume is equal to 569 railroad stock cars; one standard stock car handles 240 sheep.

Therefore, all animals on board the ark could have been housed in:

50,000/240 = 208 stock cars.

or

208/569 = 36.5% of the ark's capacity.

This would give everyone a bit of elbow/knee room—not bad in a time of dire contingency. The animals were, from all accounts, impeccably behaved—hunting rights had presumably been rescinded.

This was the only way I could explain to my son why the lion wouldn't eat the zebra. But ICR scientists have noted that predator and prey tend to 'mingle together' in the face of danger, assuming a laudable, though rare 'Buddy, I will eat you only after we get through this' attitude.

The exhibit offers an even more plausible explanation for the conservation of the precious couples on the boat: 'God could have instituted a state of hibernation, estivation or relative dormancy in the animals he sent to the ark, so that the need for animal husbandry would be minimized.'

I felt a little sorry for those that didn't make the boat—especially the fat ones—and someone might do a paper at some stage, tying modern aesthetics to the ark's deep sociological impact. But there were other exclusions as well: the poor insects and arachnids and suchlike were left to drown.

I can understand 20,000-odd species of fish being left out (why would you want a fish out of water?), but couldn't a few of the close to a million other species have been included at the expense of the 2,500 amphibians (known swimmers) who got berths?

To me, some of the questions and answers on display fell into the category of:

Q: Why didn't rats leave the ark?
A: Because it didn't sink. Dumbass.

It is scary to look at the formidable resumes of the scientists who put all of this together. There are scholars from Ivy League colleges (Harvard, Cornell, you name it) and other fine institutions—people who have collaborated with Nobel laureates on other (non-Bible) projects.

Against so much gravity, my scepticism is frivolous and obvious. I am sure they have excellent explanations for anything thrown at them (these parts were evidently left out of *Religulous*, deliberately, by the 'pothead' Maher). But they should have the answers since millions of dollars have been spent in the last 30 years, financing and promoting their research.

Is it research, however? Or does it fall more in the category of work done to propagate beliefs? In the second case, it helps to firm up a political constituency, and that, I would say, is its primary use.

Miss Eleanor planned to vote early—a wonderful system that allows senior citizens to avoid the queues on election day—and she would vote Republican. Her decision had a lot to do with John McCain's vice-presidential choice. 'Long before she became a running mate... when everybody wanted her to have that abortion (Palin's fifth child has Down's Syndrome, a condition that affects both physical and intellectual growth)... and she said that the Lord had given her this baby and she certainly wasn't going to get rid of it... Oh! I hope she wins this election.'

And with that, she left the Dayton Coffee House. It was her birthday and she had come in for lunch—as she did often, sitting at a table from where you could read the Ten Commandments on the wall.

On the streets, people wore badges that said: 'I'm voting for Sarah Palin... Oh yeah, and that old guy too.'

The Alaska governor is anti-abortion; her views on gay marriage are that the only union sanctioned by God is one between man and woman; and she is a believer in the biblical version of the origin of man and the world (created in a week).

What more proof did Dayton need that she would make a fine vice-president? Even the dominant Baptists grudgingly set aside their belief that the woman's place was in the home, for Sarah's sake—as long as, I guess, she set aside enough time to make a quota of moose steaks for the family, which she did.

People like Sarah Palin would prefer if creationism was taught alongside Darwin's theory as an *alternative* theory, but tough luck to them. Or is it? In practice, schools and teachers in places with the same beliefs as Dayton have got around the problem quite easily—they simply make an error of omission, by not teaching evolution. Result: there are kids who have never heard of Darwin, leave alone the Galapagos Islands.

There is one cost that these towns incur for doing this, which they refuse to account for. The Advanced Placement exam that high schoolers take to go to college has a curriculum where evolution is a central theme. If you fail the test because you haven't heard of natural selection, or cannot answer questions on the evidence in support of evolution, your chances of going to college are reduced.

Moreover, if you do well in these tests, you get credits to take with you to college. Which means you can graduate in less than four years. For parents who have to pay exorbitant fees, every semester gained is several thousand dollars saved. One would have thought that Dayton, which so cleverly brought money back into town with the Scopes Trial, wouldn't mind sitting through a few evolution lessons if it saved a few thousand bucks. But no, that's asking too much.

✧ ✧ ✧

I was looking for someone who could help with a telephone number I needed, when I strayed into the only occupied office I could find in the Dayton courthouse.

A plump, elderly gentleman was sitting at 45 degrees to his chair, his body a hypotenuse of sorts. He was almost hidden by a high counter at the entrance to the room and was speaking casually to two ladies sorting papers behind him.

'Could you help me find a number, sir... for a Baptist priest... his name is...'

He said sure, and whisked a directory off one of the ladies' desks and found it right away.

'Do you work here, sir? May I ask what you do?'

'I'm the judge.'

This was how I met Judge McKenzie, the man who now held court in that historic building. He was a jovial man and came from a family which was involved in the trial that made Dayton famous—on the prosecution side. We got talking, and I learned that his favourite word was 'jail' and his least favourite word was 'atheist'. Neither he, nor his kids, had read anything about evolution.

Nor had his convicts. Natalie Burke Reed was doing time. Tammy Lynn Wilson had done hers, and was now on probation. Both had to put in a few hours cleaning the court premises each day. I met them when they were going about their chores. Had they heard of the theory that made this court—and town—famous?

Tammy said, 'I heard about evolution. When we were in middle school, they taught about the Scopes Trial. You know, you could learn about the history of Dayton, but not the theory of evolution.'

'So what did they teach you about the origin of man, then?' I asked.

She started laughing. 'That he didn't come from monkey.'

'So they taught you that man was made in the image of God and that woman was created from Adam's rib… ?'

Natalie interjected, 'That's all I ever heard. That's what I believe and I don't care nothin' bout the Monkey Trial.'

When they were in jail, preachers came in three times a week. I asked whether that helped. Natalie was irritated at the embedded suggestion. 'I don't have jailhouse religion, if that's what you mean. I don't believe in God when I'm in jail and not when I'm not in jail. I didn't find religion in jail. I've been raised in the church,' she said.

I retreated quickly to the math problem mentioned earlier, and took the added precaution of directing the question at Tammy. (Natalie was now glaring at me.)

'Would it be possible to fit all the animals of the earth onto one boat?'

Tammy said, 'Yeah. I believe not all of them. Two of each. Yeah.'

'But there are so many species. Would that really be possible?'

Natalie was irritated and aggressive by now. 'Is it possible that we come from monkeys?' she challenged.

They both loved the word 'home' and hated the word 'jail', but on one subject they agreed with the judge: the Bible. And why just the judge? Pretty much everybody in Dayton. And all those scholars from Harvard and Cornell and Berkley and Ball State and who knows where else.

I experienced the strength (and stamina) of this Sarah Palin constituency almost everywhere I went in America (but not from everyone, I must make clear). I would have to stall an attempted conversion (on an Amtrak train) and clarify that I was not one of the people 'discovered' that very day (i.e., who had found God during the service) in an Alabama church. With each encounter, I understood a little better how the thread of religion was woven into the patchwork quilt of America. In one sense, it held it together, linking it with knits and knots of core values that made this country great. In another, its patterns marked boundaries of constituencies that had to be respected if you wanted to win elections.

The man I was interested in meeting on my next stop was a product of the South's value system. It didn't win him an election (although he tried). But his face was more readily recognized the world over than any on Mount Rushmore. And the recipe for his success was to be found in the town of Corbin, Kentucky.

4

• Corbin
KENTUCKY

• Haslet
TEXAS

• Knoxville
TENNESSEE

And They Fed Us

The first word I heard in Corbin, Kentucky (population 8,000), was 'deerekson'. This is Gujarati for 'direction', as articulated by the clerk at a gas station on the edge of town. I wanted to know how I could get to one of the temples dedicated to American global dominance. That I should have to do this through a Gujarati is ironic, but not unusual, because it can happen all the time in the US. No matter what it is you are looking for, there's usually a Gujarati middleman (or shall we say facilitator) handy.

Nevertheless, it was a little odd to ask this particular species of vegetarian how to get to the place that began the war against the chicken—a bird he probably had no quarrel with, unless it owed him money. I had bet on his general awareness, because the war against chicken was the only recent war that America had won outright. I assumed it must be common knowledge.

Well, I was wrong, but not entirely. 'Deerekson' pointed me first in the direction of a bona fide consumer of Kentucky Fried Chicken—a man with thick glasses, wearing jeans and a flannel shirt draped over a live, hairy basketball. He was very helpful. So we went north, past Main Street with its little nail salons and florists, to where it all began. It was just about lunchtime.

Sanders Court and Cafe opened in 1930, during the Depression. By 1935, Harland Sanders was made a 'colonel' by the Kentucky governor for his services to Kentucky cuisine, which one would presume was in dire need of both recipes and role models at the time. By 1940, the colonel had worked out a way to pressure-fry chicken so that it would be ready in nine minutes, making it possible to serve real fast.

But the big step forward was prompted by adversity. In the early 1950s, a new interstate highway bypassed Corbin, hurting business brutally. Sanders packed it in, collected a $105 social security cheque, and hit the road trying to franchise his original 11-herb-and-spice recipe.

He did this so successfully that by 1964 he'd sold out for $2 million, although he remained the face of the business. Recent surveys have shown that 98% of Americans recognize him. What McCain or Obama would not do to get that rating! (Sanders himself once ran for the state senate as a Republican—but lost.)

KFC is now owned by Pepsi (do not ask for a Coke at KFC), under the umbrella of Yum! Brands, which also owns such fine dining offerings as Taco Bell and Pizza

Hut. They sell over a billion portions of chicken annually. Statistically, this means every sixth person in the world has been subjected to KFC once a year.

At the restored Sanders Court and Cafe in Corbin (also a museum of sorts, with Sanders' kitchen in its original condition), a middle-aged couple said grace before they settled down to their fried chicken. I tried to work out why they were thankful (even given faith, the food crisis and all). Maybe it was because they did not have to eat at McDonald's. This was the only reasonable explanation.

I could knock KFC from this safe distance. I would not dare do this at home. There are KFC maniacs out there (like my wife Suparna) who would choose a bucket of legs over a bucket of water if both were offered to them in the Sahara. Such is the power and global reach of the original recipe.

Every aspect of the business had been perfected over the years. When they hired employees, for instance, they tried to avoid the free-range variety. One of the service staff at Corbin told me her favourite word was 'chicken'. And that what she enjoyed most was 'serving customers'. She had been in the coop for 18 years. The assistant manager (26; nine years in KFC) did not have a favourite word because, he said, he didn't 'have much of a vocabulary'. They were both Corbin locals.

The staff was extremely courteous, however, and served us an awful meal through no fault of theirs: shrivelled, depressed chickens that would have probably committed suicide had KFC not offered the more humane mass slaughter option; fried in oil that would surely have thrown up intriguing results if carbon-dated, with coleslaw which was sugar-bombed to disguise the many failings of Walmart cabbage.

Had KFC won the war with just these weapons? Yes, and no. Most of the civilized world had recognized its suzerainty, but not always without voicing protest. In Vietnam, which was very sensitive about anything to do with Ho Chi Minh, an American attempt at serving 'Uncle Ho's Hamburgers' was thwarted by the government before a single bun could be warmed.

The crack Kentucky Fried Force, however, infiltrated the territory, even if they were reminded where their limits lay. A casual remark about the striking similarity between the iconic Uncle Ho and Colonel Sanders was met with total disapproval by KFC's Vietnamese joint-venture partner: 'Ho Chi Minh was a general.' Still, the generation that survived on tapioca in tunnels through the 1960s and 1970s did not grudge their children a tub or two.

But one outpost that had held out was Iraq. In late July 2008, the excitable twits at Fox News celebrated that the recipe had worked in that country too. They reported that a KFC outlet had opened in Fallujah. General Tommy Franks, who directed the overthrow of Saddam Hussein, could be seen salivating during his interview to Fox as the story broke. Chicken wings had achieved what the air force couldn't.

Alas, this was not a bona fide KFC joint. Ingenuous Iraqi entrepreneurs had opened such an obviously fake outlet that anyone who wasn't blind could have told the difference. The assumption of this impairment was fundamental to their business model. It worked. US soldiers were seen paying $3.50 for dinner anyway. As the colonel would say: 'Not worth it—but mighty good food!' Hmmm.

❖ ❖ ❖

The colonel's secret 11-herb-and-spice recipe is protected against proliferation, but here's a handwritten 1950s vintage recipe from the cafe at Corbin. Cook at your own risk:

Colonel's Mock Oyster

Peel and dice eggplant. Soak overnight in salt water. Next day, boil till tender. Alternate (i.e. put one after the other) eggplant, crumbled crackers, oleo, salt and pepper, finishing off with crackers.

Before placing in the oven, fill with '1/2 and 1/2 cream' (somewhere between milk and cream). Bake at 350 degrees till brown.

Voila.

✧ ✧ ✧

There was another recipe, a close contemporary of the 'original', that had been guarded as zealously as the colonel's. Not far from Corbin was Knoxville, Tennessee. It was here, at the Oak Ridge National Laboratory that Enrico Fermi and his colleagues developed the world's first sustained nuclear reaction as part of the Manhattan Project. Hiroshima and Nagasaki were to feel the immediate consequences of this work. The world, its prolonged aftermath.

Experiments at Oak Ridge were conducted under aliases (the scientists were given code names) in a 'secret city' that had come up almost overnight just outside Knoxville.

And now, a couple of months from the November 2008 elections, the opening arguments in a debate on whether America required another Manhattan-type project were being made. Of course, it wasn't about a bomb (the US has at least a thousand of those). It was about the scale of effort needed to overcome adversity.

There were two common factors: as in the early 1940s, the country was at war (albeit not on the grand scale of World War II) and this was breaking the back of an economy struggling to survive the Depression. The answer *then* was to bring the war to a swift end. The solution *now* was to invest—for the long term—in energy security. Everybody agreed that this was the key to national security. America consumed a quarter of the world's oil, and although most of it came from Canada, higher prices meant more dollars and leverage, direct or indirect, to countries that weren't exactly friends (Russia, Venezuela and Iran, for instance). The question was whether any modern-day government would be able to pull off what President Roosevelt had: set a goal and orchestrate the most concerted effort in American history to achieve it.

The Manhattan Project started as a reaction. In August 1939, Albert Einstein sent a letter to Roosevelt warning of the possibility of a German nuke. 'A single bomb of this type, carried by boat and exploded in a port, might very well destroy the whole port together with some of the surrounding territory,' he wrote. Einstein asked that experimental work be speeded up and funds be made available so that an American bomb could be built.

But the world's greatest scientist had been grossly conservative about the bomb's destructive power. A few weeks after I left Knoxville on a train to Toledo, I met Corporal Howard Patterson. Born in 1923 and raised through the Depression, he was drafted into the army at 19 at a salary of $18 a month ('and they fed us', he added).

'I was in the Philippine Islands when the bomb was dropped. We were readying the boat and then we got a message. Then they signed the treaty and everything, and we went right in.

'Hiroshima. That's where we went... buildings many storeys high just vanished and nothin' to clean up on the ground. Destroyed... all dirt, like sand.

'No people... they'd cleaned them out before we got there...'

Patterson's thoughts wandered off. 'Ohio River, goes right on down to the Mississippi. I knew that the river was here and there it is!'

❖ ❖ ❖

In 1939, Franklin D. Roosevelt took Einstein's advice (even though the letter actually reached him two months later). A small project was launched right away. Oak Ridge was born in 1943: a town hidden from view by ridges on either side, with abundant water supply from the Clinch River—critical for the lab's uranium enrichment work—and easy access to cheap hydro power from one of FDR's pet projects, the Tennessee Valley Authority.

The area's former inhabitants were given as little as two weeks to vacate, and soon a 75,000-strong community was driven in by bus. Everyone knew their job, but hardly anyone knew exactly why they were doing it. (Incidentally, President Truman, who pushed the button, so to speak, knew very little about the Manhattan Project when he was FDR's deputy.)

But a whole city is a tough secret to keep. Over a billion dollars worth of building materials had to be shipped into surrounding towns. People were asking why Elza, Tennessee (population 151), needed 15,000 toilet fixtures. And it was extremely difficult to convince a mattress manufacturer that 15,000 mattresses were required in Clinton (population 4,820).

More than all the secrecy, it was about the reallocation of resources, and this didn't only mean money. At one time, for instance, the Oak Ridge facility, which produced the Uranium 235 required for the bomb, was using up to one-sixth of the country's power supply.

❖ ❖ ❖

'Did you want to go to the war?'

Corporal Patterson had simultaneous coughing and laughing fits: 'Oh no! They drafted me. They sent home a letter saying I had to go.'

'But they fed you.'

'Oh yeah. Yeah. I went hungry once in a while… but I gained weight. I went from 150 to 180. We'd get 'C' rations and 'K' rations. C rations was in a can and there was beef and vegetables and stuff like that. K rations was in a box. You opened them up and there was… three cigarettes… *three* cigarettes and sandwich meat.' He trailed off, as if humming a tune, like aged people often do, and then remembered more about his diet while growing up.

His dad was a truck driver who transported coal. 'We raised pigs and had a thousand chickens. Ate chicken every day till the Depression changed everything. Seven of us… eight of us. One died. Born right here in Pennsylvania. Couldn't buy nothin'.'

'And the chickens?'

'Gone, had to sell 'em. But we still got no money.' He sounded amused. 'Been to the soup kitchen. Many times. You know what dandelion is? Dan-de-lions? We used to pick 'em off the street and cook 'em.'

FDR's government led the Pattersons and millions of other American families through these times. It spent the $24 billion (in today's money) the Manhattan Project required to solve its immediate problems by forcing an end to the war.

In 2008, proponents of a similar project to secure America's future pointed to the $10 billion a month being spent on the war in Iraq and argued the money would be much better spent on energy research at labs like Oak Ridge.

Although there was no sign of a Manhattan-type push (this would have required an FDR-type will, in addition to cash), alternative energy was high on Barack Obama's agenda. Which was, most people agreed, a more thoughtful approach than the three-word McCain plan: 'drill baby drill'.

In Knoxville, even if you didn't get past the signs that said 'Y-12 Security Complex, non-badged personnel must stop…', you could tell from the local mood that nuclear science was experiencing a revival of sorts after a longish period, during which it languished under the burden of environmental and efficiency concerns.

One urban legend in Knoxville recounts the 'attack of the radioactive frogs'. In order to protect birds who might be tempted to dip their beaks in a cooling pond (into which nuclear waste was being poured) the lab decided to cover it with wire netting.

This saved the birds, but it disturbed the food chain and caused a frog population explosion. Finding it too crowded in the pond, the frogs hopped out and hit the road. The less fortunate were squashed under wheels that carried bits of their radioactive remains to various parts of Tennessee and beyond, causing a clean-up problem and a half. Those that survived allegedly begot progeny that glowed in the dark. At least that's what the children said.

I could not confirm whether this episode occurred before or after the time when members of Bush the elder's security detail backed their official car into the same cooling pond, while on a recce before his visit. The car was never recovered, but the geniuses survived unhurt.

Perhaps it was a cumulation of events such as these that led to the deflation of the nuclear sciences boom of the 1970s. But a revival is under way. You can discover this anecdotally. Scientists (many of them Indian) who were out of jobs and went into such professions as running nutrition stores in malls, had been getting offers over the last year. Some of them were in their seventies—talk about renewable resources.

At Oak Ridge, they were trying to solve the 'big problems', as they put it. One of the items on the list was a 'zero energy home', which they hoped to develop by 2012. That was already about four years too late. The department of energy had predicted that the 2008 winter would be 2.7% colder, and cost Americans 15% more in fuel bills.

And Corporal Patterson? He would feel the (lack of) heat. He led a subsistence existence in Florida, though his house was paid for. After the war he drove a truck, like his dad.

'Hauled coal in the wintertime, and asphalt in the summer... But coal died out here. And then I had to haul steel. But that went, and I moved down south and hauled sand and gravel for all the construction.

'It was cheap. It was cheap down there... We took a hell of a cut going down south. But we had no work here. See this, it used to be all steel in here (pointing outside as if towards Pittsburgh), every place... '

I told him a story I had heard in Knoxville. Apparently, a Japanese delegation that had come visiting Oak Ridge was bizarrely gifted some bomb memorabilia.

'Ne'er heard that. But they were nice, the Japanese. I was in hospital there after the surrender, and the Japanese ladies would bathe us and clothe us and bow to us... '

Corporal Patterson began humming again.

✧ ✧ ✧

Like the years in Corporal Patterson's life, the miles rushed by. I made my way back to Dallas for some home-cooked food at my sister's. But KFC, K rations and soup kitchens occupied my mind. It turned out that there was a man who was serving not just wholesome but delicious food to those in the know, in the Dallas area—at very moderate rates.

There was one little catch. He was known as the 'Barbeque Nazi'. So off I went to Haslet, across the Texas Plains (most of which appeared to be owned by former presidential candidate Ross Perot).

The tycoon's choppers hovered overhead, and on one of his neat green ranches, there was the baffling presence of a solitary camel, an animal that must regard his life as an unending mirage.

At first sight, Lee's Barbeque—a lone concrete and asbestos structure near the railway tracks in Haslet—seemed as out of place as Perot's camel. The difference was, people passed the camel by.

The people who stopped at Lee's did so despite the Barbeque Nazi's fierce reputation. He liked to do things only one way: his. To find someone like him, you would have to watch old episodes of *Seinfeld*.

Several years ago, Jerry Seinfeld had created a character called the 'Soup Nazi' for his show. A man who quickly achieved a cult following, partly for running the best soup stall in New York, and partly for grabbing bowls back from paying customers, barking 'No soup for you!' because they didn't follow the house rules.

Rule 1 was that you should not protest any of the soup vendor's actions—your job was to pay, receive your soup exactly as it was served, eat, and get out. Deviant behaviour had a terrible consequence: denial of soup.

Seinfeld based the character on a real soup vendor called Al Yeganeh, who ran a place in midtown Manhattan till 2005 and then shut it, hoping to open a soup-stall chain.

Even though he had the best barbeque in the state, Lee had no such ambitions. Also, he would never say 'No barbeque for you!' to his patrons. On the other hand, no one who came into Lee's seemed to fall foul of the unspoken laws that may or may not have been laid down. The house rules got magically hardwired into the brains of customers. Besides, Lee was 6' 5" and 250 pounds. So perhaps he hadn't been tested...

His clients stood in orderly queues watching him slice meat, dice potatoes and pour sauce for those ahead of them.

He (often) worked alone and did not multi-task: it was one order at a time. When, and only when, he gave you a nod and made eye contact was it time for you to swallow the juices playing high-tide low-tide inside your mouth and place your order, coherently. And then you waited.

'You want fries with that?'

'Yes.'

Now he got a potato and started hand-cutting it. (This is rare and worth the effort. But if you were someone in queue behind a guy that just ordered 11 portions, it can be very, very, frustrating).

Lee would not do it any other way. 'Fries don't sit very well. After 15–20 minutes, they're not a whole lotta good. They're nothing like they would be if you just fried them for somebody and put 'em on their plate.

'It won't back up everybody—unless they're waiting on fries too! And you can really get into trouble skippin' over people… you know. So it's best to get everything that the person who you're waiting on wants, and then go on to the next person.'

You would think this is hardly the way to run a business in these blighted times. But not if you were Lee. He spoke of his work as if it were art (and it was); something that required a special talent.

Behind the shop, under a tin shed, was his real kitchen. Vertical green ovens that looked like safe deposit boxes stood in a room over which a permanent haze of aromatic smoke seemed to hang. Inside the ovens were meats at various stages of cooking, helped along by fragrant woodchips that burnt to impart flavour, slow and even. Hickory-smoking meat is a precise business, but Lee's way was different.

'I don't smoke by time. I smoke by sight and feel... don't use a clock.'

He seldom ate what he made, but this was for a reason. 'If I sit down to eat a plate like ya'll are eatin', usually somebody will come through the door. By the time I'm waitin' on the second or third customer, everything is cold. Frustrating. So I don't put myself through that.

'I try very hard not to do bad work. For as long as I've been doin' it, I think people have the right to expect more than ordinary.'

In 2003, Lee was faced with a problem similar to Colonel Sanders' 50 years ago.

'They closed this road, to build that bridge over there. And that almost put me out of business. That year I lost $51,000. You had to take a detour and come all the way around to get here. It was tough, man. Meant I had to come here into this place knowing that I had to put money—and take nothing out.'

He survived for one reason: give it a shot, but you will not get a better barbeque meal for $10 anywhere in Texas. You could pay five times that, and there were still no guarantees. Yet, even at Lee's, in the latter half of 2008, there were 'Fewer people with cash. Fewer people writing cheques. More people using credit cards. More declines—I don't talk to them, just show them the slip.'

Lee started 20 years ago in South Lake, not far from Haslet, but the place got too busy for his liking. Before that, he inspected aircraft engines: 'No business background, no business education, no experience.'

Add to that, formative years in a really rough South Dallas neighbourhood. 'Most of the guys I grew up with,

they're either dead, ex-cons, you know, that kind of thing.'
There was hardly any contact with white people. 'In South
Oak Cliff, that's all that were there, people of colour. So
if we saw someone that didn't look like us, they were
misplaced. Wasn't us.

'I don't think people understand that I still have that
mentality! My territory. I'm not out of place—which I am—
but I haven't got around to that yet. And it looks like I'm
not going to.'

Every afternoon, the scene at Lee's arranged itself as
follows: his daughter, 10-year-old Chloe, would be in the
restaurant doing her homework as a snowy television
set played in the background, while customers came and
went—at Lee's pace.

They usually took away, but a few settled down to eat
at tables draped with red check cloth. By the evening, when
Chloe was a little sleepy, the furniture was rearranged to
make a bed. The television spat out static as Lee tidied up
before shutting at 8 p.m.

'Then,' said Lee, 'I get home. Put her to bed, put me to
bed, get up in the morning and do it all over again.'

I concluded that Lee's formidable reputation had been
exaggerated by fretful customers who could not accept that
you had to be patient to get the good stuff in life. For real
Nazis I would have to dig into a bit of history, which was
what I hoped to do at my next stop.

5

• Stone Mountain
GEORGIA

Let Freedom Ring—Turn Off Your Phones

As you took the cable car up to the top of Stone Mountain, Georgia, they told you all about the rock's volcanic origins. That it took about 120 million years to take the shape we saw it in now; that it was 825 feet tall and a five-mile walk around the base; that a variety of lichens and mosses grew on the top of this apparently bald heap of granite, quartz, feldspar and mica; and that the massive carving on the side, of Confederate heroes who lost the civil war, took 60 years to be completed in 1970.

What they didn't tell you was that it was on top of this mountain that the Ku Klux Klan (KKK) was reborn in 1915.

What they also didn't tell you was that in the goosebump-inducing crescendo of Martin Luther King's 1963 'I have a dream' speech, he wanted 'freedom to ring from Stone Mountain of Georgia'.

Stone Mountain Park seemed to offer lots of freedom and 'some of the best facilities for hiking, golf, tennis and biking in America', according to park announcements. It was a place where families went to picnic and children went on excursions to marvel at the sight of the huge carving on its side—a six-foot man could fit inside the mouth of Robert E. Lee's horse. Wow.

Lee, Jefferson Davis (the president of the Confederate states) and Stonewall Jackson had always been considered heroes in the South for their valour during the American Civil War. They lost, but some of the values they fought for (specifically white supremacy), survived for generations to come—and do so even now. Barack Obama referred to places 'where the Confederate flag still flies', when talking about racial inequalities. Stone Mountain was one of those places.

Brian Bowers, 41 and black, said everyone knew what Stone Mountain stood for, but no one talked about it. 'In the actual town of Stone Mountain (close by), there's a city square where the KKK have a march every year.'

'They still have that march?' I asked.

'Yeah. Every year. I don't know if they do it under the name of KKK, but I know that's who are doing it. Because they have their Confederate flags and everything. It still happens. Every year.' Then he shrugged his shoulders and said, 'It's freedom of speech, I guess.'

This was exactly the kind of place that black America looked at to measure how far they had come in their journey towards King's dream: 'A dream deeply rooted in the American Dream.'

The South knew a thing or two about the subject. It was in Mobile, Alabama, where Michael Donald, a 19-year-old black, was killed and hanged from a tree by the KKK (in its signature style) in 1981—the last lynching in America. That incident led to the prosecution and eventual bankruptcy of the United Klans of America. They had to surrender all their assets, including their headquarters in Tuscaloosa, Alabama, to pay the $7 million awarded to Donald's mother.

A quarter of a century has passed since those events, and it is fair to say that Ameirca has moved on. The Klan still exists, and reportedly has about 5,000 members who have now turned their hatred towards immigration and gay marriage. However, lynchings by a hooded mob carrying flaming crosses are almost inconceivable.

But just pure racism? Bowers and I talked on the train towards downtown Atlanta—the outline of which you could see if you looked west from the top of Stone Mountain.

'Our values are so screwed up,' he said. 'Let me give you an example that really bothered me. When Palin got nominated, her daughter was pregnant, and she was 17 years old. Let's flip that around, let's say that that was Barack Obama's 17-year-old daughter. An African-American girl pregnant, can you imagine the fallout? Can you imagine what would have been said about her? Our values are buried in so much hatred. This is not a free country. It's not.

'And if we elect another Republican, we're doomed. We have a hothead, McCain who's ready to fight Korea, who's ready to fight all of these countries. Nobody's going to take it any more. People are looking at America and laughing at us now. Look at the state that we're in.

'So rather than have four more years of the same thing

that we have now, I would be willing to go ahead and vote for Barack Obama and hope that his vision can change at least the course that we're on. 'Coz I think we're on a course to nowhere...'

The best indicator of that rudderless mess was the economy. And its impact was being felt by ordinary Americans in whatever they did. Bowers said this was only his second ride on the (excellent) MARTA trains—he didn't even know how to buy a ticket.

'I'm on the train today, because I don't want to fill up gas and drive all the way downtown. (He jangles his car keys.) I drive an SUV—by the time I drive all the way downtown, park my car, drive all the way back over to this side of town, I'm on half a tank of gas. I can just pay the four dollars, ride the train, go down there, walk a couple of blocks, get back and... everything is good.

'We are the fattest country in the world, so maybe something good comes out of this. 'Coz I'm not a walker. (He looks very fit and slim, however.) A lot of people have started taking the trains.'

✧   ✧   ✧

Bowers spoke in a soft, collected sort of way. He had gone to Tuskegee University and was conscious of history and his community's place in it.

'Back during the civil war, even the Union soldiers, I mean, they didn't know what they were fighting for. Abe Lincoln was not the man who wanted everybody freed. He just did it because it was the political thing to do at the time. He wasn't so visionary that he wanted black people to be free. I don't buy that.'

Bowers' suspicion of motives extended to respondents in opinion polls as well. He, like many blacks and genuine white liberals, felt that people lied in polls because it was politically correct.

'How many people will tell you to your face that they don't like Indians? And what do they say behind closed doors?'

He did have faith, however, in the simple emotion of fear. The lost jobs and homes had got the American people scared.

'People are so fearful now that they go... you know... we're going to give the black man a chance. Fear makes you do strange things. Fear makes you act differently.'

Ironically, that was the exact emotion that the McCain campaign was trying to tap into. At every opportunity that presented itself (or didn't), the attempt was made to paint Obama as somebody America didn't really know at all. Ergo, he must be extremely dangerous, that is, either a socialist or a terrorist, possibly an Arab. Wasn't that approximately what Sarah Palin was saying? That Obama was 'dangerous'?

The mention of Palin was an assault on Bowers' otherwise admirable composure. Now his nostrils flared, his pitch got sharper and his head moved about dramatically.

'How so? That's what I would ask them, how so? With a woman who's been a governor for a year (two, actually) and who walks around shooting bears and wolves or whatever. And McCain is not a picture of health... and, God forbid, he dies in the first year of office, is she ready to run the country? No, *she's* dangerous for me.

'And... she... is... an idiot. If she could answer *one* question for me, I think I might have a different view of her, but she goes all around in a circle and the questions are still not answered.'

I mentioned that one commentator found a good reason for this: How could she have the answers if she didn't understand the question?

'I don't get it with her. And I think what McCain did was that he saw the reaction that people were having to Hillary. And he says, well, if I get a female, then that's the answer. That's all I need, is a female. Who cares whether she has a brain or not? And I think that's so degrading to women that it's almost like he's a pimp and he says, let me just go get a prostitute and put her on my ticket to see if I can get some votes. That's my opinion.'

Bowers regained his composure and returned to his message. 'I'm hoping that people will use their fear to make a rational choice to fix the mess we're in. For the last eight years, we've been fed a bunch of crap about what was going to happen and why it was good for us to be in Iraq and why this was good or that. But if you keep doing the same thing, you always get what you always got.'

We arrived at our destination, Five Points station; he left me with the thought that black America had still some distance to go before a 'more perfect union'.

On Forsythe Street, dusk's shift was just about ending. You could tell—the big CNN neon sign was getting progressively brighter at the channel's headquarters and the crack cocaine dealers were out. But how was I to know that I would meet someone once closely associated with this trade almost immediately?

❖ ❖ ❖

CIA Awkwardly Debriefs Obama on Creation of Crack Cocaine

WASHINGTON—In his first meeting with President Barack Obama, CIA crime and counter-narcotics analyst Timothy R. McIntire haltingly explained to the nation's first African-American commander-in-chief the highly classified origin of crack cocaine and the resultant epidemic that swept across US inner cities. 'Well, you see, sir... thing is, we needed money to help those Contras back in 1985, and we never really expected... so we distributed it, and... short-sighted... and, ha, well, Christ—is it hot in here?' McIntire said between exaggerated coughs...

Posted on *Onion.com*, 26 February 2009.

This post appeared in 'America's finest news source' several months after I met Rick in downtown Atlanta. He caught my arm as I was about to cross a street—an act that probably prevented my being run over by a bus that was determined to climb the sidewalk.

He was on his way back from a visit to the hospital. As we walked towards the tube station, I noticed he had a limp. 'Was it about your leg?' I asked somewhat undiplomatically. He said yes. And then he told me a set of seemingly unconnected stories which, like it happens more often than we realize, added up to a biography.

'I have very bad pain in my legs. This leg, I need knee replacement. I got shot... We were coming out of a concert, up on North Avenue at the Fox Theatre, and this guy wanted to steal my car. I didn't know he had a gun, so I pushed him. My wife was in the car and I was worried about her. And he pulled the gun out and shot. Twice. He tried to shoot her and he missed.

'She got out of the car and ran toward me. And he and some others took off with the car, but they got caught. They got caught very soon, like 20 minutes later they were caught. They get caught, eventually. You always get caught.'

He said this with such conviction that I suspected there was something there. We walked along, Rick limping rapidly in his shorts, me soldiering on with my backpack and a laptop bag that swayed, protesting the pace.

'I was born and raised in Michigan and I came from a pretty nice family and I played sports. I played hockey and I had the opportunity to go to university and play hockey. And I was injured, and I got introduced to drugs while I was injured... painkillers... and I became a heroin addict. And I went to rehab and bounced from place to place and steadily I went back to heroin.'

I didn't ask any questions.

'Then I was introduced to a channel where I could transport drugs. Move drugs from Canada to United States... Michigan. And I got caught doing that by the federal government. It's a lot of trouble. I got in *laaawwt* of trouble.

'And from there, off and on I'd be clean and sober for some time, but eventually I'd find my way back to it. I've been to prison five times. I never had a chance to go into serious rehabilitation until this one. I was caught selling drugs... three times. When I was out on parole I would do it again. And they would catch me and send me back to jail... California, Texas, South Carolina...'

Here, I couldn't help myself and asked whether he was 'wanted' all over the United States or something.

'Never really "wanted" because I did my time. Moved on, got in trouble somewhere else and moved on from there... I spent 12 years in all. Twelve years in prison. Several prisons in California and Texas. Louisiana, Marion, Illinois... they shipped me through different prisons around the federal system.'

Marion prison rang a bell. It once held the mobster John Gotti and was a maximum security facility for a time, built in 1963 to replace Alcatraz that was now a museum.

'I'm 49 (which meant he spent about a third of his adult life in prison)... I'll never get it back.'

Again, there was that absence of regret.

'But at the same time I had a very, very adventuresome life... I made the choice to do what I did. And I made a lot of money. And when I wasn't in trouble... I lived a very... lot of men, women... I lived a very, very decadent lifestyle...

'I was making $35,000 a trip to Mexico and I was making this twice a month at least... so I was making about a million dollars a year, close to.

'I was bringing 400 pounds of heroin into the United States each time I did it. In the trunk of the vehicle I was driving—and I got caught. Eventually I got caught. Somebody told. Somebody in the organization that I worked with got caught... and I was set up.

'It was a Sunday, we always came through on a Sunday. And I always had on a Hawaiian shirt and carried beach balls, like I'd just been down to Mexico on the weekend, and they would look at me and wave me through.

'This time, they were waiting. There was around 20

police with dogs and they saw me... they didn't even look and say 'yeah, maybe we'll check him'... they were waiting for me. And they found the dope—I didn't even know where the dope was.

'My instructions were to go to Rosarita Beach, pick up a vehicle, drive to San Diego, California, where there would be another vehicle in the parking lot at a grocery store. I would park the car—I had the keys to the other vehicle—and drive off. I would see nobody, talk to nobody and the next day they would come and pay me my money. Mexican mafia... that's who it was.'

Rick's story was incredible. Very few people in the drug business made that kind of money. An Indian social scientist called Suresh Venkatesh had established that. Drug dealers, Venkatesh said, made about $3.3 an hour as foot soldiers—the guys who stood in street corners selling the stuff. They were so poor, said the economist Steven Levitt, picking up on Venkatesh's work, that they couldn't afford their own places—they lived with their moms.

But that wasn't Rick's gig. He was hired to do something else altogether. Something that black boys from the inner city, typical foot soldiers, could never do: avoid suspicion at a border gate and bring in the goods. Just another sphere of American life where race plays a part.

'They needed a white guy, clean-cut, college-educated type. I was younger then, had a very straight all-American look. I was doing this when I was between 25 and 30. But I looked much younger at the time. Now I'm 49, but I look much older—from the stress of the life, you know...

'I was married, I was straight for six years... I lived a clean life... beautiful woman, beautiful, beautiful woman.

Very hardworking. We ran a successful lawn care business, very successful down in Hilton Head Island, South Carolina. I have a degree in turf grass management from Purdue University.'

But the happy ending was postponed. He went back to it again.

'The lure of it, the money, brought me back. But then I started using... do you see the marks? I got to the point where, here in Atlanta, I would sell myself... for $20, prostitute with men. My level of degradation was—not that I am against homosexuality, I mean it's no problem for me—but it was *baaad*.

'Just like these guys (he points to a few dazed, dishevelled male prostitutes), well, maybe not that bad, because I was always clean, but yeah, $20 for the next hit of crack cocaine, I would do it.'

And the money he had made?

'Well, the federal government took a lot of it. And I blew a lot of it. I lived the lifestyle, went to the club, bottles of champagne, many women, men. You know, sleep all day, party all night.

'The job was one day every two weeks, five hours a day. Very easy. I work for my sponsor right now, and I only have money for my bus pass... and my vices are cigarettes and ice cream. I can't vote, but I'm for Barack. And I hate George Bush. I think he's a war criminal. I think he should be hung. I do.'

And with that, he walked me to the 'Underground', a mall-type complex of shops, stalls and bars where you could have your fortune told, get a manicure, or pose for pictures with exotic birds. You could also grab a bite to eat.

I was hungry and ordered a beer and roast beef. A man with a heavy bandage around his right arm came and sat on the bar stool next to mine.

'Wassup?'

I smiled and nodded in acknowledgement. This seemed to be enough for Michael Johnson (that was his name) to wave to the waitress and order a drink—on me.

Michael was a musician, and the second victim of armed assault whom I had met in the space of two hours. He was black, 6' 4", and had droopy eyes, in the corners of which there seemed to be permanent teardrops.

'I got robbed, man... it's rough everywhere.' It happened in DeKalb County, which is the second richest African-American majority county in the US. I felt sorry for the man—a bad cut on the hand is hardly what a pianist wants.

Turned out that Michael *used* to have a band. Now, he said, he was unemployed and performed with gospel groups. I might have wanted to continue the conversation had he not waved to the waitress once again.

'That one's not on me,' I said. Michael smiled the guilty hustler's smile and switched to another mode.

'Man, I'm hungry.'

My food had just arrived. A few slices of roast beef, bread and a pile of vegetables. I told him he was welcome to some of it.

'Naww man, I couldn't do that.'

'Up to you,' I said.

A few seconds passed before I heard an 'okay', and saw a bandaged hand pick up some beef and a piece of bread off my plate. Michael wolfed the food down and said he had no money to pay the rent either.

He then made a very convoluted pitch for ten dollars. This included offering to open up his bandage and showing me his cut, to convince me that he really couldn't work. I said I believed him about the injury, but I wasn't going to give him money.

Instead of ten dollars, he now wanted five. And then two. America was in a deep recession.

✧ ✧ ✧

Greyhound buses have a special place in American life. Thousands of them roll along the neat grid of American highways every second. They carry people who're usually too poor to fly, cheaply across the vast expanse of America, sometimes for days. Over the years, they've popped up in songs and books—even as vehicles of protest during the civil rights movement.

The Greyhound experience is different in different parts of the country. Up North, the drivers are somewhat harried, even apprehensive—behaving like schoolmasters on their first day, taking charge of a notorious class. They would like to be firm, but aren't quite sure where that would lead. They make bland announcements—expressionless readings from route maps and rule books—and I suspect they constantly have one eye on the mirror, looking out for the assault or robbery that is destined to take place.

In the South, the drivers seem much more in control. They are usually portly, smiling black men who do not take any nonsense. When they take the microphone, they do it like professional MCs introducing an evening's line-up at a concert, not a cheap bus ride.

'This is schedule 1245. We got an 8.15 departure, we are 25, maybe 30 minutes late. I'll try and make a little bit of time up by squeezing some stops together and *keepin' it movin'*...

'This bus makes stops at Haightville, Georgia; Opelika, Alabama; Tuskegee, Alabama; Montgomery, Alabama; final destination for me is Mobile, Alabama.

'This bus continues on further, south...

'If anyone needs to use the restroom, please hold on to the overhead luggage racks as you make your way to the back. *Please do not play with the handle once you get inside there.* Those handles are known to come off. If it comes off, you'll have to wait till we get to *Mobile* to get out. *That's where the mechanic is.* So don't play with that handle once you get inside there.

'Please turn all cellphones off at this time. Please turn all cellphones off. So you won't disturb either your neighbours or the driver. Don't turn the ringers off, turn the *phones* off.

'Federal law prohibits smoking or drinking on a motor coach, that includes the restroom. No smoking, or drinking of alcoholic beverages, or smoking anything else you might want to smoke. So sit back, relax and enjoy the ride.

'But, first, there are some things that the family tells you, you never do in public. And one o' them is: take your shoes off. If you're part of a family that told you never to take your shoes off in public, you already know not to do it.

'Sit back, relax, and thank you for riding Greyhound. Let's raaaaide.'

I was off to Montgomery, in my shoes.

6

Montgomery
ALABAMA

Questions for Mama

The only time through my four months in America that I had an aggressive racist taunt directed at me, was on the bus to Montgomery. It came from a black woman.

She was in the seat behind me and was annoyed that I had pushed my reclining seat back.

'Don't you fuckin'…'

Fine till there. I turned around and in order to avoid a pointless confrontation, let the profanity pass and politely told her that I'd adjust the seat so that neither of us would be uncomfortable. This I did. But the spirit of accommodation was totally lost on her. She muttered more profanities to the black man sitting next to her. This man found the situation mildly funny.

Next, a Hispanic family got on, adding to the numbers

on board, although there were plenty of seats vacant. This was when my antagonist let fly: 'So fuckin' crowded! So fuckin' crowded with all these fuckin' *mixtures*!'

The emphasis was entirely hers, and directed towards me. The man next to her let out an approving laugh. The Mexicans or Puerto Ricans were too busy arranging their luggage and their children to pay any attention, and would have likely ignored the remark anyway.

As for me, I chuckled inwardly, thinking this was a bus in the South. Where the right of everyone—blacks, whites and 'mixtures'—to ride equally was won after years of sacrifice and protest. To top it all, it was bound for Montgomery, Alabama, where the most famous bus ride in American history took place. And just incidentally, a 'mixture' between a Luo tribal from Kenya and a Caucasian from Kansas was running for president. This was genuinely funny.

I mean, imagine Rosa Parks telling the driver that she was not budging from her seat, and when a 'mixture' hopped on board she went, 'Hey! Off! You're crowding this thing.'

But Rosa Parks wasn't sitting behind me.

✧ ✧ ✧

I took Route No. 1 from Zelda Road to downtown Montgomery, the city where a black seamstress had, in 1955, refused to give up her seat in the front section of a bus to a white man and move to the back, where the coloured folk were supposed to sit. I sat in the front.

Our driver was a black woman, Miss Pat, who told me the story: 'She was just so tired and fed up that when that driver told her to get up, she just wouldn't.' The rest is fairly well known: Rosa Parks was arrested, the black population of the town boycotted the buses and the civil rights movement was born.

But there were a couple of myths that have been hard to dispel. One, that she was an old lady (she was 42); the other, that the action was totally spontaneous because she was tired that day. Parks had been an active member of the National Association for Advancement of Coloured People (NAACP) and plans for a protest were at least a few months in the making.

Also, what hastened a compromise was the fact that the boycott was costing the city bus service $3,000 a day. Blacks had to stand or sit in the back of the bus, but they paid the same fare. There was no better metaphor for segregation than this bus ride: you gave the same, but you received less.

After paying a dollar, I rolled along in Miss Pat's bus to downtown Montgomery where Rosa Parks had hopped on in 1955—an impressive museum had been built there in her honour.

The well-preserved colonial architecture of Court Square was filled with history, if painted over by a coat of charm to hide warts, old and recent. In the mid-1800s Court Square was a thriving slave market. Now it was the town's WiFi hotspot. A century and a half ago, the slave trade was deeply entrenched because it was so lucrative. In the 1860s slaves cost upward of $1,500 and up to $3,000—a hell of a lot of money for the time. But slaves provided what was perhaps the scarcest resource in America in those days—labour.

Their fortunes—and those of their masters—fluctuated for various market-driven reasons from changing crop patterns (the demand for cotton, for instance, made slaves dearer), to the ban on slave trade elsewhere in the world (the scarcity of new supplies made slave owners' net worth go up). On an average, slaves as an 'asset class' provided returns to the tune of 10% a year on investment.

The fact that profit was the prime motive to keep slavery alive (rather than soft cultural arguments such as southern prestige/way of life) has now been fairly well established—even if it took about a hundred years to see what was blindingly obvious.

The slavery-supporting South had sound economic motives behind that position—always a clear disincentive to act fairly, justly and with a conscience. In fact, when the Confederate Army, desperate for personnel, tried to recruit 'overseers' (the white men who herded slaves together and kept them working and in line) during the civil war, the South resisted vigorously. The war was important, of course, but not at the cost of all the slaves who would make a run for freedom once the overseer went off to battle.

I took in the neat columns and archways of downtown Montgomery at a time when America was asking the question: are we ready for a black president? And the McCain campaign, primarily through a single-brain-celled organism called Sarah Palin, was saying that it was not. ('He is Barack *Hussein* Obama, an Arab, a terrorist, who *is* he?' and so on could be heard at her rallies.)

A (probably apocryphal) story about Palin surfaced later: she thought that Africa, where most slaves came from, was a country. Her handlers apparently tried to convince her that the landmass was, in reality, a continent comprising *several* countries, but she was unable to grasp the concept.

The kind of currency the story gained was a measure of how credible it must have been to the ears of the American public. But it would take some virtuoso displays of idiocy from the former Miss Alaska runner-up, to get to that stage.

When I visited Montgomery in October 2008, that stage hadn't arrived. In the South, Palin's questions (and incredibly, her answers) on all subjects, from the origins of Obama to the origins of dinosaurs, were being taken very seriously indeed by evangelical whites.

But blacks?

I met Coleman Smith, the tough security officer at the Montgomery Area Transit System (MATS) bus terminus. He said he had been following this election more closely than any of the others he had seen in his 63 years. Why was that?

'Because of Obama, I guess.'

'What's special about him?'

'He's black.'

Forget running for president, it is easy enough to overlook the fact that blacks got the unfettered right to vote in the world's greatest democracy less than 50 years ago, in 1965 (they were kept out by devices like a literacy test). They have voted 'freely' only in the last 11 of the country's 56 elections so far.

But standing in Montgomery, which played a pivotal role in winning that right, I wasn't about to let Smith go. I told him about this black guy who (literally) begged McCain to take over the country at a public meeting.

'Is one o' them Uncle Toms', he said. 'Like in *Uncle Tom's Cabin*, when the white man say "I'm sick", the black man say "we sick". Know what 'um saying. That's when the white man ask the black man to lay on his feet. And then when the white man say "I'm feelin' better" the black man say "we feelin' better". Brainwashed, man...'

He made a point right afterwards: it isn't the white man who keeps the black man down, it's other black men. That is a recurring theme, no matter where you travel in the US.

✧   ✧   ✧

A man's colour was such an obvious marker that the very clever people in the Obama camp postulated that it didn't require stating. And with that single piece of reasoning, they pushed the Obama campaign in a different direction from all the other major campaigns run by people whose colour we will not state.

This was not something that Obama simply dreamed up one day. And there was nothing half-baked about it—the dough was kneaded through his formative years, and was leavened by his later electoral experiences.

Perhaps what made his final position easier (or more difficult?) was that he was much more than just black. This was a circumstance of history. His dad was Kenyan; his mom was a white girl from Kansas; he went to school in Hawaii, which is hardly the South Side of Chicago; his stepdad was from Indonesia, a country he lived in for a while; his white grandmother was probably his soundest support system during his childhood, and black people sometimes made her uncomfortable.

Barack Obama had probably asked the question 'Who is Barack Obama?' well before any Republican campaign strategist thought it up. It is quite certain that he thought of himself as 'much more than black' even at an early age.

When he was growing up, well-meaning, if unintended, reminders that he was black made him wince. Like when white girls told him that they liked Stevie Wonder. (This is a bit like telling a Muslim in India 'I just love biryani' with the intention of making him feel more comfortable, without considering that this person might much prefer a ham-and-cheese sandwich.)

But growing up in general is very different from growing up in Chicago politics. Obama tried his hand at the 'conventional' approach in the city. He did social work in the rough South Side, shooting hoops with young black men to gain their confidence, and won a seat to the Illinois state senate in 1996.

Okay till there, but for a very ambitious man—somebody who wrote his autobiography in his early thirties—the next step would be a character-building experience. In 2000, Obama took on Bobby Rush in a race for a Democratic nomination to the House of Representatives. In the 1960s, Rush was an active student campaigner of civil rights and later a Black Panther. Obama got 'whupped' as the brothers would say.

He came across as 'insufficiently black' according to a seminal piece on race in the *New Yorker* by David Remnick. Rush, the seasoned 'black' politician, knew his constituency and knew that painting Obama as a 'pretending' black would go down well. That he went to Harvard made him 'less black' in that race, and an 'educated fool' according to Rush.

Obama lost the primary by a landslide.

During the Democratic primaries for the presidential nomination in 2008, the Clinton camp searched for ways to portray a man who would seldom state his colour as someone who was not black enough. They came up with the fact that Obama ate arugula. Real blacks don't eat arugula!

By any measure, this was kind of weak. (Arugula, or rocket leaves, is described as an easy green to grow at home, but is expensive for some reason, and you may not/cannot order an arugula salad at a Burger King.)

The loss to Rush would no doubt have shaped Obama's strategic thinking. He wasn't born when Rosa Parks rebelled. He was four years old during the march from Selma to Montgomery—his legs were too short to do the distance. The civil rights road had been travelled by those who came before him. His path would have to be different.

Besides, the Clintons had cornered the market on the hardcore civil rights types, well before the primaries. Vernon Jordan was quoted by Remnick as telling Obama before he announced his candidacy: 'Barack, I am an old Negro who believes that for everything there is a season—and I don't think this is your season... I was so wrong. Anyway, I said, if you do run, as I think you will, I will be with Hillary. I am too old to trade friendship for race.'

There was one other problem. Obama appeared uppity to the civil rights veterans who held important office, or had tried to. His observations that the black community (like everybody else) should be more responsible were seen by these men as sermons from an impostor.

Reverend Jesse Jackson, not knowing that the tapes were rolling, said Obama was talking down to black people and he wanted to 'cut his nuts out'. He later apologized. Jackson ran for president in 1984 and 1988. While he made a reasonable initial run each time, he presented black voters with a dilemma: should they invest in him? After all, he wasn't going to win. In the end, they did the pragmatic thing and didn't.

But here's the difference: Jackson 'spoke the language' with blacks, who therefore knew that while he was on their side, he would not win. Obama, who spoke a more inclusive tongue, was perceived by some as talking down to blacks and raising suspicion in the community. White voters quite liked this: it made Obama more electable for them, and therefore America. Black people now had both a racial and a practical reason for voting Obama.

This was why the lasting image of Jesse Jackson was likely to be that of the man standing behind Oprah Winfrey in Grant Park and shedding more tears than her. And that of Obama would be him saying 'Yes we can' from the podium at the same victory rally.

There were two key things that had to be done, or avoided, in order to accomplish the task of becoming America's first black president. The first was to find a space in which to operate, and the second was to perfect the rhetoric. Both would take a degree of 'delinking', if that's the right word, from the civil rights movement. Obama took a position of gratitude to that struggle, and presented himself as a candidate who might actually win this thing, as proof of its impact.

The rhetoric was trickier.

✧   ✧   ✧

Questions for Mama

Mother, how come everything is white?
How come Jesus is blond with blue eyes?
Why's the last supper all white men?
Angels are white.

Miss America was always white
Miss World was always white
Miss Universe was always white

And the angel fruitcake was the white cake
And the devil fruitcake was the chocolate cake.

And the president lived in the White House.
And Mary had a little lamb his feet as white as snow

And if I threaten you, I'm gonna blackmail you.
I said mama, why not whitemail? They lie too!

This is when I knew something was wrong.

—Muhammad Ali, excerpt from an interview with
Michael Parkinson.

Obama's mama was white, and felt that every black man had the responsibility of growing up to become Sidney Poitier, so young Barack would probably not have had the same list of questions. Not in the same words, at any rate. (Barack may be a great speaker, but Ali was the greatest—and without a teleprompter.)

Ali's views were extreme. He had been radicalized by personal experience and by (often malign) influences. His stories were the stuff of folklore. But everyone knew 'something was wrong'. These stories swirled around in the 1960s and 1970s, and their pitch was impossible to ignore for blacks or whites—even if they were growing up in Hawaii or wherever. You couldn't ignore Ali or the Black Power Salute at the Mexico Olympics, even if you didn't hear much about a riot in a town near you. Ali was a member of the virulently radical Nation of Islam, but various shades of these views have survived among people of colour. The darker the shade, the blacker you are, apparently.

While none of the civil rights veterans would talk Ali's language, there were those who were more strident, or less inclusive, than others. These men, like Jesse Jackson or Al Sharpton (who wanted to run for President in 2004), were classified as 'radioactive blacks' by the Obama team. Through the campaign, every possible care was taken to avoid them. The price for not doing this, it seems, was the presidency.

But what did you do about a black madman whose church you went to, and who, as we heard ad nauseum, baptized your children?

The reverend Jeremiah Wright was a mentor to Barack Obama and that was good until the point that Obama wasn't running for a nomination. But 'God damn America!' on what seemed like every Sunday was hardly what the United States wanted to hear from a candidate's pastor.

In the end, with the nomination hanging in balance, the candidate spoke. And how.

In March 2008, in a speech that's now called the 'More Perfect Union' speech, delivered at the National Constitution Centre in Philadelphia, Obama spoke a set of words in lucid English that perhaps changed the language of discourse on race in the United States.

> I can no more disown him (Wright) than I can disown the black community. I can no more disown him than I can my white grandmother—a woman who helped raise me, a woman who sacrificed again and again for me, a woman who loves me as much as anything in this world, but a woman who once confessed her fear of black men who passed her on the street, and who on more than one

occasion uttered racial or ethnic stereotypes that made me cringe. These people are a part of me. And they are a part of America. This country that I love.

I tried, and failed, to calculate the distance between 'Questions for Mama' and 'A More Perfect Union'. But I clearly saw the road Obama was on.

✧ ✧ ✧

When it was time for me to leave Montgomery, I realized that I could not make the Greyhound bus that I was supposed to be on, because the city bus wouldn't get me to the stop. I took the problem to the information desk at the local bus terminus. There the clerk conspired to arrange an unscheduled bus, to take a solitary passenger, me, to the Greyhound station.

The bus wasn't anything like the one Rosa Parks rode. It was more like a van, seating just about a dozen people and it didn't have the mid-section door, which served as the racial boundary in the segregation-era buses.

Benny Jackson, the driver, had been in those buses. He was 14 when the boycott happened. 'We did a lot of walkin'… a laawt of walkin',' he said of the time. Many people 'had no money to afford no ride' in the carpools that were organized by the black community so that people got to work. The walking, however, got them further than most had imagined.

As we drove, I couldn't help wondering what the odds would have been for such a special ride for a person of colour (like myself) in Montgomery, circa 1955. And just by the way, I thought, where *was* the bus that Rosa Parks was arrested from? The town's museum had a wonderfully rendered model (this fools children and the naive, but anyone looking, well, not even very closely, would find that the bus on display is only *half* a bus).

To see the original Parks bus, you needed to visit the Ford Museum in Dearborn, Michigan.

A knowledgeable Ford Museum employee told me the details later, pointing to the yellow vehicle:

> The bus is used by a private company till a little bit after Mrs Parks is arrested. During the 381 days after her arrest that the community stayed off the buses, they are driving a bunch of empty buses around the city because they got a contract with the city, so they are losing money.
>
> It was the National Bus Lines, they were based out of Chicago. So this is a northern company, which to me makes it interesting, because they're following the rules of the South when this whole boycott thing is going on. But they got to run the routes...
>
> Shortly after the boycott ends, this becomes run by the city like most buses in the US are now. They use it till 1970. When the city's ready to get rid of it, a gentleman, local in town, wants a couple of storage sheds. He knows the city wants to get rid of this bus. He buys two buses for $500 each, this (the Parks bus) is one of them.
>
> He knows the history of the bus when he buys it. He takes everything but four seat frames out of this bus, he throws them down a hill on his property. He sells the engine, he sells the transmission. When we got the bus it had bullet holes in it, so it must have been used as a very large target.
>
> He tells his son-in-law and his daughter before he passes away that this is *that* bus. This is their chance to go make money. They put it up on e-Bay... I'm sure every museum in this country had a good laugh, there was no reason to think that this was the right bus.

Montgomery's museum and Memphis' civil rights museum are two that I know thought they had the right bus...

The research is done, after nobody bids on it. They figure out that the parent company was paying somebody to cut out newspaper articles on any bus that they have across the north and south of the country. The company that cut out newspaper articles for them, their manager hangs onto the three scrapbooks that have stories about Rosa's arrest.

When it goes up for sale (in 2000) and that research is done, you have forensic scientists looking at the scrapbooks to make sure you're dealing with 1955 glue, ink, paper, you know, all that... this would be a very creative way to make an awful lot of money... Once the research is in place, museums bid on it.

The final bidders are us, the city of Denver and the Smithsonian. We get the bus for a total of $750,000, including $300,000 to restore the bus and $75,000 for the scrapbooks, and stuff like a typical bus driver's uniform, a bus token of the time and so on.

Rosa Parks spent the last 50 years of her life in Detroit, not very far from Dearborn, where her bus is on display. She moved because she became a pariah in Montgomery and had lost her job, as had her husband.

In Detroit, she worked for US representative John Conyers, one of the early African-American congressmen. In 1987, a schoolteacher who wanted to familiarize his students with the civil rights movement cold-called Conyer's office and asked nervously if Rosa Parks worked there and what she was like. Mrs Parks answered the phone. She was just a 'normal person', she said. And could she be of any help?

7

Sweet Home Alabama

I arrived in Birmingham from Montgomery on a day when there was some kind of national nurses' conference. Apparently, more than 10,000 paramedics from across the country had descended upon the town—first-aid would not be a problem, but a hotel room would.

I had to settle for something in the suburb of Fultondale, but this, as I found out later, would not be without its rewards. On bus rides and walks in Atlanta and Montgomery, and travelling to Birmingham, I ruminated about what it might have been like in this part of the world 50 years ago.

At the museums I visited, kids invariably thought that drinking water fountains from that era, marked 'colored', must be special. That they would spout sweet, coloured water, rather than remind a person of his race as he performed an essential, mundane activity. But these were today's kids. An older generation, albeit shrinking, was well versed with the language of those times. In April 2008, a Tennessee lawmaker addressing a Republican gathering had instinctively said of the prospect of an Obama presidency: 'That boy's finger does not need to be on the button.'

The appellation 'boy' had too many resonances, over too many years, to be ignored. Half a century ago, a young pastor called Martin Luther King had pointed to it as a source of daily humiliation. The Negro's 'middle name becomes boy'.

Representative Davis, who made the remark, would have grown up with this language, and had not grown out of it. He apologized, but mainly, and oddly, for questioning Obama's integrity. But back in the day, there was no need for either an explanation or an apology. In 1963, Birmingham police commissioner Eugene 'Bull' Connor had fired water hoses and set dogs on protesters, many of them children. He claimed to have enjoyed 'watchin' the niggers run'. (Connor's life is full of 'nigger' quotes.)

In Montgomery, a similarly bigoted sheriff called Jim Clark had the first Selma–Montgomery marchers clubbed and beaten in 1965, on what came to be known as 'Bloody Sunday'. Giving men like Clark and Connor instructions and providing an uncompromising public face was one of the most prominent American politicians of the day— Alabama's Democratic governor George Wallace, who took on Washington for the South. He had won Alabama on a segregation plank in 1962, proclaiming '...segregation now, segregation tomorrow, segregation forever' in his inaugural speech.*

In June 1963, Governor Wallace had stood at the door of an auditorium in University of Alabama to prevent black students from enrolling. He was made to step aside by federal law enforcers. But in September he did the same thing in schools at Huntsville, Alabama, attempting to prevent four black children from enrolling.

During those times, a young folk singer was writing the words:

> Come senators, congressmen
> Please heed the call
> Don't stand in the doorway
> Don't block up the hall...
>
> ...There's a battle outside
> And it's ragin'
> It'll soon shake your windows
> And rattle your walls
> For the times they are a-changin'.

Bob Dylan's song was both document and prophecy. Apparently, when a friend of his first saw the words 'senators, congressmen' and so on, he asked, 'What is this shit, man?' Well, it was timely shit, and later, anthemic shit delivered by the flawed, real, rough-edged voice of

---

* In 1972, Wallace was the victim of an assassination attempt during a bid for the Democratic nomination for presidency, which left him paralysed. He also radically changed his views on race towards the end of his life, and repented his earlier position. The Birmingham strongman Eugene Connor, however, held on to his white supremacist beliefs without regret till his death in 1975.

that generation. The voice would be heard by a couple of hundred thousand people, black and white, who gathered at the Lincoln Memorial in Washington in August 1963. A Dylan performance set the stage, as it were, for Martin Luther King to deliver his 'I have a dream' speech at the culmination of the march to Washington.

✧ ✧ ✧

The days of standing in the doorway were coming to an end. Two historic legislations were passed by President Lyndon B. Johnson's administration. The first was the Civil Rights Act of 1964. This Act effectively ended the days of the 'Jim Crow' laws that sanctioned segregation. Jim Crow wasn't some lawmaker. He wasn't even a real person. He was a caricature of a black man, played by a white man with a blackened face, in entertainment routines. But laws defined by the name could be found everywhere in the United States and were enforced in everything from eating out and education, to where you could sit on a bus or whom you could marry.

But there was more legislative work to be done. Segregation was only part of the problem, because integration didn't mean equal rights, chief among them, the right to vote. That's how the march from Selma to Montgomery became a focal point of the civil rights movement in 1965.

The disenfranchisement of blacks was engineered in several ways. Many states required voters to be able to read the Constitution, which is a little difficult if you've worked on a farm rather than gone to school. Wallace claimed that Alabama was lenient with regard to the literacy clause: 'New York... requires the passage of a literacy test or an eighth grade certificate. We have registered many voters in Alabama with a fourth grade education.'

Nowhere was the problem of non-registration of coloured voters more acute than in Selma, part of Dallas County, Alabama. Blacks were in a majority there, but just about 1% of them were registered to vote. On the other hand, 99% of whites were.

Those responsible for registration of voters ensured that their office windows opened late on the two days in a month they functioned. And they were shut for interminable lunches so that those in the queue left in frustration. Officials would often reportedly 'test' the aspiring voter's credentials by asking such questions as, 'How many bubbles are there in a bar of soap?'

That Mahatma Gandhi's philosophy inspired King is well known. But King had also drawn on the great man's ability to find locations for his protests—to drop the stone where a wave would be created rather than a ripple.

To those without that vision, Selma might have appeared to be a local problem caused by racist individuals at the registrar's office, which locals would resolve, well, locally. This is exactly what the white establishment in Selma wanted.

> *Outside* racial agitators have chosen to make Selma what they call a focal point in their national drive to raise money, gain political power and to pressure the president of the United States and the Congress into enacting new and stronger civil rights laws... .
>
> We recognize the right of every *qualified* citizen to vote and give assurance that every citizen will have the opportunity to make application for registration.

Nevertheless, the *false* issue of voting rights is repeatedly raised and given as the reason for the present disorders… (emphases added)

> —Excerpt from a joint statement by Selma mayor Joe Smitherman and sheriff Jim Clark, *Selma Times Journal*, 14 March 1965.

The word 'outsider' acquired the much broader meaning of the 'other' during that time in the United States. Colour was a key marker of the 'other', but in all the ferment of those mixed up times, it wasn't enough. For the lack of anything more accurate, *hair* would have to do. A group of protesters singing 'freedom songs' at Brown Chapel had many 'out of state' students in 'beatnik attire' among them. 'Sharp March winds whipped their carelessly groomed hair into greater disarray,' wrote the *Selma Times Journal* on 17 March 1965.

The thing is, 'outsiders' answering to approximately the same description were stirring things up in the quest for freedom (of everything) outside Selma as well. At the University of California in Berkeley, there were protesters like 'Mario Savio, 22, a New Yorker with a wild mass of hair, and non-student John Thompson, 23, a long-haired New Yorker who has shoes but goes barefoot. Thompson paraded the campus with a crude sign. On it was an obscene four-letter word' (Associated Press, 26 March 1965).

George Wallace had a moment of inspiration in this regard. He said the only four-letter words these people didn't know were 'soap' and 'work'. With all these long-haired, goateed communist-types running amok all over the country, demanding the right to say 'fuck', the right to vote, jobs for the poor and so on, early 1965 was an interesting time.

President Johnson made it even more interesting by escalating the war in Vietnam at the end of January. The government announced the sending of 3,500 marines to Vietnam on 7 March. Within weeks of this, headlines such as '52 tons dropped into Vietnam' or 'North Vietnam hit fourth straight day' became a standard feature of newspaper front pages.

As if a battle at home and a war abroad weren't enough, there was a race in space as well which, much to the Americans' dismay, the reds were winning at the time. The US space programme had scheduled a 'walk around nothingness' by astronauts as part of their first group-manned flight into space on the *Molly Brown* spacecraft. But five days before the launch, the Russians sent one of their men for a 10-minute float-around, during which the space-suited Russian performed balletic somersaults on the vast dark stage of space with the curve of the earth serving as relief. This event was, of course, aired on television.

There was still the moon, however. At about the same time, the US sent the *Ranger* up there to transmit pictures—a precursor to the triumph of the first landing a few years later.

Back on earth, 'Dairy Princesses' were being crowned in Dallas County; the Tillman Drug company was hawking 'White Shoulders' perfume; school basketball games were degenerating into race riots in Detroit; white clergymen and activists in Selma were being killed by the KKK and allied groups for their role in the protests; Alabama state troopers were killing and injuring marchers, as local doctors objected to out-of-state medics treating them (these 'other' doctors didn't have valid Alabama licences). And amidst negotiations with Washington and confrontations with Wallace, the Selma marchers soldiered on.

It took King and his followers more than two weeks to finally complete the 50-mile obstacle course between Selma and Montgomery on 25 March 1965. Just hours afterwards, a white sympathizer who was ferrying marchers in her car was shot by the KKK. Within a day, Johnson announced the arrests of the four Birmingham area suspects and warned Klansmen that they should join 'decent society' before it was too late.

The president had primed lawmakers on the necessity of a Voting Rights Act during the unrest, and introduced the bill to Congress on 15 March. In August, he formally signed it into law. The one thing that stood out in the bill's passage was the Southern Democrats' opposition to it and the Republicans' support. This fissure in the Democratic Party would become permanent, and under President Nixon, the 'Wallace Democrats' became a strong Republican constituency that survives to this day.

❖ ❖ ❖

My visits to Stone Mountain and Montgomery had prepared me for Birmingham before I got there. In the 1950s and 1960s, they called the city Bombingham, for obvious reasons. Within weeks of Martin Luther King's speech, four little girls were blown up at the 16th Street Baptist Church, which had been targetted along with King's brother's home. Birmingham's history of bombings dated back to 1955. And in 1965, as the Selma–Montgomery march was under way, six bombs, made with a total of 300 dynamite sticks, were found in the area.

'The bombs, ticking in harmless looking green boxes, were spotted near the former home of a Negro leader, a Catholic church, a Negro attorney's twice previously bombed home, a funeral home and a Negro high school,' said the *Selma Times Journal* dated 22 March 1965.

Was I getting too caught up in all of this? Perhaps I was, I thought, as I made my way to a hotel that the nurses hadn't booked, from the Greyhound station in downtown.

At the check-in of the Days Inn, Fultondale, I found a fellow Bengali behind the counter. A squat, bald, somewhat nervous fellow, who told me he was from Jamshedpur and that he had an American wife. I was interested to hear more, but a little tired, so I settled into the standard room. A television with a faulty remote control, wallpaper peeling at the margins, a slightly damp carpet, a decent loo, a clean bed and an ashtray!

Sometimes you go to a town looking for one thing and get caught up in what you find instead. What I found in Birmingham was an angry Indian and a cleverer God.

✧ ✧ ✧

Rick, the weathered, itinerant fruit salesman from Oklahoma, told me about his sales technique, the 9/11 conspiracy, and his dad. When I walked out of my room that evening, he had thought I might be a radical Islamist, but got over this after we exchanged a few sentences. He looked rather old, but he liked talking about his dad.

'You know dawg, some time ago I told him, "Dad, Georgia's gone to war with Russia." And he said, "What?

And what about the rest of the United States?" ' Rick almost fell over laughing—partly because of the joke and partly due to the last Miller Lite he'd downed. (You need to drink the stuff in prodigious quantities for this to happen, which he was doing.)

We were sitting in the hotel parking lot, the fruit crew's pickup truck open from the back to show off cases sourced fresh from farms. A speaker tethered to the truck's CD player played Guns N' Roses or Hank Williams, depending on who got to it first.

There were five of them running this trip, going door to door selling grapefruit or oranges by the case to shops and establishments in different towns. It was Saturday and they had sold $3,800 worth of cases. It was time to party.

I asked Rick about all the 'No Soliciting' signs and how he got around them. 'Oh yeah, one time, there were these three huge signs on the same door, and it pissed me off. So I decided I just had to go in.

'The guy goes, "Didn't you read the signs?" And I say, "Oh, I wasn't smoking." He says, "That's a 'no soliciting' sign, can't you read?" And I say, "If I could read, would I be selling fucking fruit door to door?" I sold him a case alright.'

Part of the crew was JJ. He paced up and down a lot—long hair, tattoos on his bare body, jeans and a big old cowboy hat. He shook my hand, saying, 'I'm Indian, where you from, man?'

'India.'

'Oh yeah. I'm Cherokee-Chickasaw. Proud of my Indian heritage, man. Real proud.'

Stacy, one of the crew, said he wanted to put on some rap.

But JJ didn't like the idea. 'I don't want no nigger music, man. No nigger music around here,' he said.

Rick turned to me apologetically. 'He's just a redneck,' he said, smiling. Guns N' Roses kept playing.

The music from the truck attracted other guests. It was the only bit of life in an otherwise dismal setting, apart from the occasional group of bikers who came to the gas station next door with their brightly-lit machines, to fill up or get rubbery pizzas—$2.99 a slice; two for $5.

A large, young, black man came and joined us. If he hadn't said right away that he was a truck driver, I would have thought he was in the shrimping business—he was a carbon copy of 'Bubba' in *Forrest Gump*. So much so that I found myself humming *Sweet Home Alabama* and debated whether to ask the fruit sellers if they had the song, but decided against it mainly because JJ was prowling around.

Our 'Bubba' had the same, distended lower lip as his celluloid twin. The same sweet mixture of simplicity, pride and good manners—indicated in this case by his refusal to accept a beer. 'No sir, I buy my own beer.' The only difference that I could spot was his somewhat more urgent speech.

He ran trucks that had to be driven back after repairs ('Bam! We're off after it's done.') and he was stuck in Fultondale for some reason. I asked him what was keeping him, and he clapped his hands and answered: 'Bam! We're off after it's done.'

'So it's not done yet?' I enquired.

'Bam! We're off after it's done.'

Maybe he was in the shrimping business after all.

As Bubba inspected some fruit, another man joined the little Miller Lite and Coors party. He was a regular fellow in a neatly tucked yellow T-shirt. When he was 50 yards away, the fruit sellers had already spotted a Republican; this was not good, apparently.

He accepted a beer and entered into an edgy conversation about politics with one of the group. During the course of the conversation, he gratuitously used the word 'Injun'. JJ was within earshot. He walked up to where Rick and I were and in one smooth motion pulled out a slim switchblade. I could see its teeth glint under the neon light of the parking lot. Almost as if to make sure that I did, JJ brought the knife very close to my face. I could see that it would slice through a lot more than fruit, and was grateful it wasn't intended for me.

'I'm going to take the guy out. I'm going to slit him and watch him squeal,' JJ whispered to us. He then paced in a circle for maybe a minute. The others tried to use this time to lead the prospective victim away. It was no good. JJ rushed towards him, swinging wildly. He missed. The man retreated. JJ lunged again. Missed again. Then he turned around and strode back towards us, did a U-turn, and went back to look for the offender.

The little party was over. Bam! Bubba was off. Others dissolved into their rooms. JJ paced up and down the corridor on the second floor of the building. I heard him shout, 'Nobody insults my Indian heritage, man…'

In his little cabin at the front desk, my petrified Bengali friend watched all of this on closed circuit television. Wisely, he didn't come out to try and solve the problem. It was well beyond him. I was a little dazed, feeling as if·I had just come off a film set. But I could still hear JJ going at it—now threatening any guests who made the mistake of taking a peek to see what was going on.

I looked up 'Injun'. Noun. Redskin, red man. A term offensive to Native Americans. I wouldn't hear it again. But I would meet people like JJ.

✧ ✧ ✧

After the excesses of the night before, it was only fitting that I went to a church on an overcast Sunday.

If you looked left or right on any road, you'd find a house of God in Alabama. But I found myself stumbling into a pew at one of the biggest churches in the area. Gardendale First Baptist's modern building hosted the largest congregation in this Birmingham suburb. It was almost all white.

I was ushered in past a three-camera set-up, to a real good spot for a view of the 80-member choir that was limbering up, and the giant flat screen above, in case I missed anything.

The service had the ceremony of a full-fledged production, which it was. Pastor Kevin Hamm was a television personality as well—the show went out three weeks later to all of Alabama. He was 44. A slim, dapper, blue-eyed, well-spoken man who, in his beige suit, could have been collecting bonuses on Wall Street (well, maybe not this year), but seemed to be on to something better. I say this sincerely.

He made his entrance, like any star performer, after the supporting act, the choir, had got everyone's attention and the people had made the various necessary adjustments before seating themselves in God's House. No more shuffling or rustling or bottom scratching. Now the cameras had found their focus. So had Pastor Kevin.

'I don't know about you, but I'm believing that God's going to do something special in this service. And I hope that you came expecting to hear from God. You know, here's what I've discovered—if you're listening for God, you'll hear him.'

A soft chorus of 'Amens' went up.

Pastor Kevin continued to play on the theme: 'But if you're so busy with all the cares of this world... what should've been last week and what's going to be done this coming week... and what's gonna happen to our economy... and who's going to be elected president...'

(Was Alabama worried? About three weeks from election night, in this church they were, I figured. The McCain campaign was falling apart, which meant that they wouldn't get the vice-president they wanted.)

Pastor Kevin lifted the mood with a 'turn to your neighbours and introduce yourself' ritual. This had the desired effect. Riding the moment, the choir stepped in with a racy pop tune, which they claimed they hadn't done in a while. It was called *Faith*.

I began to get the cadence of the service now. Pastor Kevin had arranged it so that the congregation felt a number of emotions. In *Travels with Charley*, John Steinbeck wrote a memorable passage about a service he'd attended one Sunday in 1960 in Vermont. Describing the priest, he wrote:

> He spoke of Hell as an expert, not the mush-mush hell of these soft days, but a well-stoked, white-hot hell served by technicians of the first order. The reverend brought it to a

point where we could understand it, a good hard coal fire, plenty of draft, and a squad of open-hearth devils who put their hearts into their work, and their work was me.

That would have been a great service. Even being very far from a good Christian, I related completely to the sentiment that unless you take a good old-fashioned weekly whupping from God, administered through one of his messengers, life is incomplete.

I had found expressions of that feeling in many churches I visited in India. Once the customary (sometimes hilariously accented) hymn singing was over, I'd seen people kneel with more contrition than I'd ever mustered. The congregants' faces would be so intense and their brows so bunched that you felt they were seeing Hell right there, through their closed eyes.

I say with some regret that the twenty-first century has a different kind of God—even in Alabama. A cleverer God. One who, through his servants, takes you on a roller-coaster of emotions: joy, celebration, guilt... He reassures compassionately, suggests discreetly, advises judiciously, admonishes sternly and solicits shamelessly. He has mastered television for the family.

The next offering by the rather accomplished choir was the much slower:

> Lord reveal yourself to me, 'Coz you're all I want to see...

Which moved to:

> God is good, and his love is yours forever—more.
> God is good, he's so good...

Then Pastor Kevin took charge: 'Jesus paid a price he didn't owe, because we owed a price we couldn't pay...' He told the story of bread and blood and sins (briefly) as two little plastic cups—like cough syrup measures—one inside the other, a little cracker and some juice in them, were passed around.

I'd been part of this ritual before, but Katy Lewis next to me wasn't to know that. She said, helpfully, 'Baptist churches have this every week. Say "Lord, I'm sorry for what I've done," and his blood washes our sins away—but it's really just juice and bread.'

As the subdued organ played in the background, the guilt was chewed on and gulped down. Pastor Kevin announced a celebration: 'Jesus is alive!! Amen. Amen church. Jesus lives. Hallelujah.'

'You might have to wait for him, but he *will* come. He made Mary and Martha wait several days before he turned up to save their dead brother Lazarus. But when he came, he called out to Lazarus, and when the dead man walked out, Jesus said, "Take off the grave clothes and let him go."

'Some of you who've been set free, who've been resurrected... are walking around with grave clothes on. What has you tied up today?

'Maybe it's the cloak of bitterness. Maybe it's the cloth of anger. Maybe it's jealousy, I don't know what it is. But you're handcuffed, you're tied up, but Jesus came to set you free.

'Jesus didn't die so you could just survive. He didn't die just so you could breathe... and from looking at you, some of you are barely doing that!

'Maybe it's worry and fear. What's going to happen to the economy? What about Wall Street? Who's going to be elected president?

'Let me tell you something, my friends, I don't know what's going to happen to our economy, or who's going to be elected president, but I know this, God is still on his throne. And no matter what happens, He will see us through.'

There was a long round of applause, from an audience that was happy to hear that *someone* was in control.

'And before this world gets better, it's going to get darker. And Jesus is going to split the eastern sky and say, "Enough! Come up here, it's over."'

Whichever way you looked at it, it sounded like the solution to all problems. How did the economy matter once you were up there?

'Some of you really don't know Jesus. You know about him but you don't know him. You got a head know, not a heart know. Today is going to be a radical day in your life...

'I'm just asking you, whether you're in the balcony or on this main floor, I going to ask you to take a moment. Nobody's going to be looking, you're going to slip out by yourself, just get up and come to one of our staff and simply say to him, "I need Jesus, I know what the pastor's talking about." That's all you need to say. They'll understand your heart. They'll help you. It'll be the greatest decision you ever make. Won't take a long time.'

The organ filled the pause as the congregation took this in.

'We'll give you some information about your good decision and you'll be on your way. For some of you, God has led you to this place to join this church and God would love you to become a member. (And you say) "I don't know how to do that." Come to the staff and tell them. We have a welcome packet for you, it's very simple.'

The organ went to work, like a musical double space, after a terse bullet point. It faded as the next point appeared.

'Some of you need to be baptized. You've already been saved but you've never been baptized. Come and tell us, we'll schedule that for you.'

Another cue for the organ. And now, Pastor Kevin assumed a higher pitch: 'For others of you, you might just want to come to this altar and say, "God, deal with my heart about living below my privileges." Maybe you're carrying a burden. Come and lay it at this altar; lay it at the feet of Jesus...

'Here's what I'm going to pray. I'm going to pray that God will give you a holy boldness to respond. Because the Enemy will say to you, "Don't do it." There's too many people in your pew, it's too late, it's time for lunch. A hundred and one excuses. I'm going to pray that right now, in the name of Jesus, you will not listen to the Enemy's excuses, but *you* will respond this morning.'

The organ played, as the Enemy wondered why in hell he had got into this fight in the first place...

'And your life will never be the same again. And when I say Amen in just a moment, I'm going to ask you to get up immediately. Don't wait on somebody else. Don't worry about who's comin' and who's not comin'... I'm going to ask God to give you a holy boldness to respond immediately. No wait.'

The organ filled a truly dramatic pause.

'No wait. That's what the Enemy wants you to do—put it off, another day, another time. No! No! Don't listen to him!

'God, I pray right now, for an unusual boldness and courage. Lord, I know that you are speaking to people right now in this service, as you have in other services, and I pray right now that you give them the courage, in just a moment, to stand up—nobody's looking—and give their heart and life to Jesus, join this church, be baptized, whatever decision you want to make.

'I pray right now, in the name of Jesus, you will rebuke the Enemy, in stealing their victory right now. And I pray this in the name of Jesus... nobody lookin' around. Amen.

'Come on right now. Just get up. Come on, that's right. This is your day, come on...'

One by one, the pews began to ooze Jesus-discoverers. First a young lady, then a middle-aged man, then another woman wiping her tears came down from the balcony. The choir was on cue:

Jeeeesus, lover of my sooo-oul
Jeeeesus, I'll never let you gooo-oo...

Pastor Kevin went on, 'This is your moment, come on. From the balcony, come on. This is your victory...

'Aren't you tired of doing it your way? Come on...

'Aren't you tired of living below your privileges? Come on. Yes... that's right.'

A few more people walked up and were met by the staff.

'Yes, God is in the House today. Come on, my friends. Yes. Amen. Amen.' The choir sang:

My saviour, my closest friend
I will worship you until the very end...

'Come on. How about it, sir? How about it, ma'am? Teenagers, come on... It's your day...

You've taken me, from the night without an end
You've set my fears on the run
And now I'm whole...
I love you...

The flow of new faithfuls stopped—the pastor was now preaching to the converted. As the newly discovered were being given their information and their welcome kits, Dr Kevin Hamm brought his impressive service to a close.

'Lord, today we want to be faithful to you because we know that you will be faithful to us, regardless of what happens. With this economy, Lord, you're in control and you'll meet our needs. And so Lord, out of obedience and out of joy, we give you our tithes and offerings this morning. In Jesus' name, I pray, God bless you. We'll give. And then we'll go...'

The pastor had barely finished when it was time for promotional messages on the public address system:

A heavyweight boxing match... cannot be compared to a couple in conflict. Conflicts are a part of life, but how you handle them makes all the difference.

17 October, we'll watch five rounds of 'husband vs wife'. And our own expert panel will provide a blow-by-blow analysis of the fight. Learn to fight fair. 17 October.

I wanted to talk for a bit to Pastor Kevin, so I made my way towards the passage behind the stage, to find a staff member waiting there. He welcomed me with the proverbial open arms. 'I am glad you came,' he said, commending me on the discovery of my faith, and he was all set to give me my welcome kit and schedule a baptism.

He was bemused and disappointed when I said that it wasn't my day. 'Well, what faith are you?'

'I was born a Hindu, but I'm not religious... I want to interview the pastor.'

'You're not religious?' he said incredulously. 'Everyone needs a faith; maybe you'll change your mind after you speak to the pastor.'

But it really wasn't my day. Pastor Kevin and I spoke religion somewhat tangentially. He said that he didn't ask his congregation to vote one way or the other, but always emphasized that they vote according to their Christian values.

Not just that, they should make a checkbox of what weight they gave to positions on abortion, the economy, the war, gay marriage, the Word (creationist beliefs) and so on, and mark the candidates to see who came out on top. I thought that was a pretty decent way of going about it. A cleverer God would have expected no less.

8

Deer and Clothing in Colorado

Having heard that Sarah Palin was about to descend on Colorado after a week of poor ratings for the McCain–Palin ticket, I decided I needed to run to a place where she would definitely not find me. Looking at the perfect rectangle that is Colorado, I chose the top left-hand corner—a town called Dinosaur. (No, it is not named after John McCain.)

This town actually exists. You can even have a cappasaurus (the local version of cappuccino) at the Bedrock Cafe on Brontosaurus Boulevard. And one of the town's 350 people is always there in the 'welcome centre' at the corner of Brontosaurus and Stegosaurus Streets, to tell you about the attractions.

Local literature tells you that Dinosaur is at an 'excellent central location'. That's right. As central as the middle of nowhere. That's why, when they needed a mayor recently, they advertised the position in a paper in Grand Junction, four hours away. And at another local election, I was told, several voters chose Mickey Mouse.

You need to drive up to Dinosaur from Denver. A few hundred miles along rivers named after basic colours (Blue, Green, Red), past painted mountainsides, an endless number of seemingly deserted oil rigs and towns like Rifle and Rangeley. But be careful not to miss the sculpted Triceratops inside a fence to your right, somewhere on Highway 40, or you'll miss the town.

If you're enterprising, you can go down to nearby Vernal to look at dinosaur fossil bones found in the area. Or visit the Dinosaur National Monument, a few miles east, where hidden in the folds of the Rockies is a magnificent canyon at the confluence of the Green and Yampa rivers.

❖ ❖ ❖

At night, all you could see in Dinosaur was a green neon sign that had three words on it: Beer, Food, Pool. This was the Rainbow Tavern bar and grill, run by a self-confessed 'hockey mom' from Vernal. She opened every evening, shut at three in the morning and drove back.

She said she liked ice hockey (which is basically free-style wrestling in a rink), but conditionally. She fixed a Long Island Ice Tea the size of the Colorado River and explained her philosophy on contact sports (such as hockey or war) in the simplest possible terms: 'You touch my kid and I'll kill you. You like 'em in one piece, not two,' she laughed.

The kid mentioned was 6' 3" and a couple of hundred pounds. He was a fine track and field athlete, according to his mom, and aspired to be a brain surgeon, but a marine before that. Mom, however, did not like the idea.

'Why?' I asked.

''Coz I'm a mom.'

'But wouldn't going to college become much easier if he became a marine?'

'Well, yeah. But see, I have this thing about people hurting my kids. I get very mean. So I told this recruiter who had told Zack one thing (that college would be paid for)... I said, "Well, you sign this contract that you're going to do what you told him. Sign this piece of paper for me." And he says, "I can't do that."

'Zack wanted to study surgery, but they said they would pay for school, but not to study brain surgery. So I said, "If you do recruit him, I'll stick a note in his pocket saying, 'You mess with me, you mess with my mom'. And I don't care where in the world you are, I will find you." The recruiter said that it wasn't in either party's best interest for Zack to sign up.'

'But what of his brain surgery ambitions?'

'He decided to wait for a while. He wanted a car, so he went and bought himself a car. So now he's going to wait till he has his car paid for. 'Coz he had to have a fancy car. I bought him a Ford Escort, but it wasn't good enough. He had to have him a VW Passat.'

I thought about the curious choices Zack had made for as long as the Ice Tea allowed—which was not long.

✧ ✧ ✧

'I think the American people spend too much. I grew up in the 1930s—and it wasn't easy. And we didn't have a lot of money. We grew our produce and we lived on a farm, and money was almost non-existent. I don't think it hurt anybody to go through that.

'People have gotten too used to having everything, or everything at one time. They can't wait or save for anything. They have to have it right now. And that's what's wrong with this country, I think.'

I was talking to Vivienne Gabrielson, proprietor of the Terrace Motel, with a cup of regular tea in my hand. It was a sparkling morning, so bright that the pink facade of the motel's converted mobile home rooms seemed in danger of melting. Mrs Gabrielson has been a Dinosaur resident since 1959, when her husband came here to work for an oil company.

'When we came here it was called Artesia, because of the water wells. It looks real dry and rocky, but stick a drill in anywhere and you'll find oil or water. In 1965, the name was changed to Dinosaur—the town council at the time thought this would help tourism. It seems to have gone downhill. There's quite a bit of traffic down the highway, but not a lot going on.'

But this was the second day of the hunting season. Pickup trucks whizzed along Highway 40, the hoofs of some unfortunate elk or deer sticking out of the back. At the gas stations or at drive-by restaurants along the highway, there was the smell of coagulated blood. Towns like Maybell were festooned with 'Hunters Welcome' signs to advertise their meat processing units.

A chunk of Colorado's votes would be decided on who was the better president for hunters, and this was a no-contest. On hunting, the McCain–Palin ticket had all the experience, judgement and other ammunition required.

Palin liked shooting bears and wolves—especially from helicopters.

Two young men pulled their truck into the lot of Terrace Motel. A pair of beautiful horns stuck out from the back of the truck and when the vehicle swung around, you could see the animal, its blood, almost warm, leaching through its slashed stomach onto the truck floor.

The boys jumped off, beaming. Landon and Josh, from Craig (the elk-hunting capital of the world, a few hours east of Dinosaur).

'You got one!' said Mrs Gabrielson, her tone congratulatory. A bystander cracked a local joke: 'Sure you didn't just hit it with your truck?'

Landon was the one who 'got it'.

'We couldn't find any elk, so we started coming down and we saw about 15 bucks. So we jumped out and shot one... with a Roberts .257 at 250 yards.'

With its tongue limp and sticking out of one side of its mouth like a morbid caricature, it was difficult to imagine that just hours ago, somewhere in the vast surrounding hilly bush, the buck had put up a fight.

'I shot him in the shoulder,' said Landon of the first crack he took at the animal. 'He started moving, and we got up on a little cliff and we saw him lay down and we couldn't shoot him again... he was too far away. Then he ran off and we tracked him down some more. For about two miles... he wouldn't go down... and then I shot him in the spine. We went up on him and he was still alive; so we shot him one more time, thinking that he was going to die. Then I shot him in the neck. And then, that was pretty much about it,' Landon paused to catch his breath.

He had what is called a 'resident youth deer tag', which authorized a 'discount hunt'. Youngsters got to hunt a deer a season for $10.75, instead of the regular $45. The blue tag was now around the buck's left ear.

Josh, his hands bloodstained from hauling the thing, played with the tag, and then turned his attention to the dead animal's mouth, prizing it open with his fingers as if checking its dental health.

'He's decent. He's got a good body for a younger buck... he's probably about two or three years old. He was with two other really big bucks and there were about ten that went just before them,' said Josh. Too bad they didn't get one of those.

'The deer's about 200 pounds with hide and everything... They say that deer have about 30% guts, so you gut them out and field-dress them...' (which they had done).

'He's got about 75 pounds of meat... that we'll get out of him. That's a pretty good supply... That'll last the winter. It's like buying burgers from the grocery store, but it's just $10!'

And the rest?

'We'll skin it out, probably give the skin to somebody who wants it. Throw the bones... those are no good.

'A lot of people like to trophy-hunt, they like to shoulder-mount them... Like pretty much around here, like the big elk mounts and everything. But shoulder mounting, it's real expensive...

'So what you do is cut the head off right here (he points to the base of the neck), take all the fur off and everything, so you just get the skull. Then you boil it and the skull turns a bleached white, and then you have the dark horns and bleached white skull. That's a European mount. You can do it yourself for free… just a big pan and a stove put on the boil.'

That, in brief, was the buck's future. The boys jumped back in the truck and the animal was driven off to a processing plant, perhaps in Maybell. Its now irrelevant wounds were drying fast in the Colorado sun, and the whiff of death around it was getting staler. Its eyes were open, however.

✧ ✧ ✧

Few people have understood—and then articulated—what the West is about, better than Jack Weil who is credited with saying, 'The West is not a place, it is a state of mind.'

That is the kind of wisdom you will find if you look into the open eyes of a freshly killed buck, which is not to say that is how Weil came to attain it. The sociological discovery, along with a more mundane invention in the mid-1940s, made Weil rich, famous, and an institution. The invention was that of a shirt button.

Cowboys, he figured, wouldn't be particularly interested in sewing back buttons that were caught in the American West's ubiquitous sagebrush. His solution was to use a snap-fastener—it clicked a shirt front shut and was definitely less snag-prone than the ordinary button.

His LoDo (lower downtown) Denver company started manufacturing tight-fitting (therefore snag-resistant) denim shirts with their signature 'diamond' snaps and saw-tooth pockets that the boys in the country loved (Landon and Josh's granddads, for instance). The shirts were a fashion statement for a group of people who weren't exactly the best-dressed blokes in town.

It made cowboys 'stand apart from city slickers', and soon, the city slickers wanted Rockmount Ranch Wear shirts. Movies wanted them, movie stars wanted them, even presidents wanted them. In 2008, Democratic delegates at the August convention held in Denver, where Obama's nomination was formalized, wanted them. These shirts were specially designed with a red-and-blue patriotic theme, but the conservative Mr Weil did not live to see that event.

He passed away on 13 August 2008 at 107, still serving as America's oldest CEO, less than two weeks before the convention. Had I visited the Wazee Street warehouse of Rockmount Ranch Wear just a few months ago in July, in all likelihood, I'd have been met with a 'Where you from?' asked by 'Papa Jack' himself. He was coming to work until two weeks before he died, to sit at a desk positioned so that he was the first point of contact for anyone who walked in. His dog Wazee sat with him.

Wazee was there, however, looking a little lost. But instead of a 'Where you from?' I was met with a 'We're not that interested in promoting our work in India, China or Hong Kong.'

Welcome to the West.

The man who told me this was Steve Weil, the current president and CEO, Papa Jack's grandson. He was tweaking designs for the next batch of Rockmount shirts, from a desk that overlooked the shop floor and Papa Jack's empty desk. He had a great suspicion, even fear, of eastern rip-offs, and like his granddad, wished to see the business remain distinctly—and strictly—American.

Jack Weil's views on this were simple—for an American look, you needed American manufacturing. Besides, he would say, if he sent the work abroad, Americans wouldn't be able to buy his clothes because they'd have no jobs.

These are beliefs that are fundamental to Rockmount. As is the belief that discounts are bad for business, even if it means more shirts sold. So, while Rockmount— headquartered in a 90-year-old brick warehouse in whose bowels workers stitched shirts and stacked stock—sold to about 500 stores worldwide, Walmart was not one of them. Steve Weil was pestered endlessly by them, and essentially told them to piss off each time. The thinking was—if someone wanted the clothes enough, they would pay the price.

That applied to promotions as well. Rockmount provided shirts for *Brokeback Mountain*. 'But they bought the shirts,' said Steve. 'Sometimes movies approach us thinking it's an honour for us to be in their movie, even though their movie is costing tens of millions of dollars and we're a small family business. And they think we should treat them like a charity. We don't.'

Brokeback Mountain had about 30 Rockmount shirts in it, which were bought for between $25 and $35 apiece. Most were for the extras, but two, worn by the central characters, actually played a critical role. In the final scenes, the camera stays on them for long periods—draped one over the other, they are a very powerful metaphor for the tragic love between two cowboys.

'I felt they should have been put up for an academy award,' said Steve, 'but no one gives a shirt an Oscar.' To let me know that Rockmount shirts were great value for money, he told me how the two shirts later sold on e-Bay for just over $100,000.

The younger Mr Weil had loosened up a bit, and it had nothing to do with my saying I might want to buy a shirt. He told me a little about his grandfather, repeating an old gem from the man: 'He said to me when I first came to work here, "If you tell the truth, you never have to remember what you say."' That's how you run an all-American business.

It's kind of fitting that LoDo, near the confluence of Cherry Creek and the Platte River, is also where gold was first discovered in Colorado in 1869. This was before Jack Weil's time, and the mines are long gone. Weil's inventions, though, can be seen not just on the streets of Denver but in New York and Singapore. Why, they may even turn up suspiciously where they aren't shipped. Because 'the West is not a place, it is a state of mind.'

As for me, having initially decided to buy a shirt, I changed my mind.

✧ ✧ ✧

'All Aboooaard!'

Well, I knew I was. I had even found myself a window seat on the coach at the Denver Amtrak station, going further west. If there is one train ride I will recommend in the United States, it is this ride on Amtrak's California Zephyr from Denver to San Francisco. Yes, it takes close to two days, but the rewards are rich. Besides, you can stop at Provo or Salt Lake City to break the journey.

If you ever want to try and discover the meaning of life, you should take this train. I got a little help in this pursuit from Colorado's newspaper-sized four-page ballot paper, a sample of which I was carrying.

In a couple of weeks, as America decided on a new president, Colorado would vote on how to 'define a person' as well. The proposed Amendment 48 of the Colorado Constitution asked citizens whether they would want 'the terms person, or persons, to include any human being from the moment of fertilization.'

The US system allows voting on citizen-initiated laws on the presidential ballot, provided there are a certain number of signatures to support this. But the question wasn't a simple one. If the people answered yes, the implications were huge, said Curtis Miller, a 52-year-old pastor. He and his travelling companions were going through the *2008 State Ballot Information Booklet* as we approached Glenwood Springs through a surreal canyon landscape. It looked almost fragile. As if rocks might peel off the walls or minarets tip over if someone clapped too loud. A train had to be extra careful and roll gingerly along this narrow passage.

I could think of no better setting to ponder the kind of deep question the ballot paper posed, which was what the pastor and his companions were doing in the viewing car, as I took in the lingering rock faces.

They cut through the crap quickly. The question was a simple one: 'Do you want to ban abortion?' Pastor Curtis supported the amendment, of course. But he gave it a thought. There were practical considerations. Finally it boiled down to: 'Life is a gift. And you have to draw the line somewhere.' He was from Denver, but if you asked him, he'd say, 'I'm from the womb.'

If Colorado thought the same way as the pastor, abortions would be classified as murder, because the state guaranteed a 'person' the right to life. It would also mean a reversal of one of the most important judgements in the US Supreme Court's history. In 1973 (*Roe vs Wade*), the Supreme Court legalized abortion in the country partly on the somewhat technical ground that the 'unborn' were not included in the word 'person' as used in the US Constitution, and therefore didn't have rights.

A ban would limit private, personal choices and could even be employed to stop commonly used forms of contraception (the 'day after pill', for instance). Stem cell research would also become a criminal activity. But on the subject of criminal activity, Steven Levitt, economist and co-author of *Freakonomics*, wrote a jaw-dropping paper on the correlation between crime and unwanted births. Levitt's argument, based on hard data: if you force single-momhood on women who (1) do not want the child and (2) have no means to support it, you will get cascading waves of kids turning to crime.

One of Pastor Curtis' companions had filled out the voter 'cheat-sheet' for measures on the 2008 ballot. These were provided, along with plenty of background material on the issues, so voters could get a bit of practice for what was a fairly lengthy exercise on the big day. She handed me the booklet before hopping off at Glenwood Springs. I found that she'd ticked the 'yes' box for Amendment 48.

'I couldn't help listening to your conversation,' a lady in a seat nearby told me after the clergyman and his posse left. 'Please don't go away with the impression that everyone thinks that way.' I mumbled that I wouldn't, and then told her I was going to Utah next. She sighed helplessly.

The train pulled into Grand Junction Station. Once a very important hub for people and goods, the station was an elegant stone building from the early twentieth century, with decorative columns and clean lines. Now it was fenced off, its windows either boarded up or shattered. A sign on the fence read:

FOR SALE
Historic Train Depot
9,254 sq ft on .64 acres.
George Dunham Real Estate

A few hours ago, there was an announcement on the train that the town of Cisco, population three, was also for sale. That might have been a joke.

✦ ✦ ✦

Sometimes you really luck out while travelling. The night before, just as I was about to get off at Provo, one of the conductors on the train got talking with me. She had an adopted daughter in Delhi, a refugee from Tibet, and she'd been to the city. Cherie Hanks offered to show me around Provo and Salt Lake City the next day. She arrived in her 1985 Mercedes—a wonderful machine—and we were off to explore the neighbourhood.

Apart from the world summit of some skin care products company, there was nothing much going on in Provo. We headed off towards the Sundance Resort (founded by Robert Redford) and Park City with its ski slopes.

Utah in October has only one thing on its mind: the amount of precipitation expected in the coming months. The general belief is that good snowfall always beats any economic slowdown. Apart from the odd yard sign, I didn't find much excitement about the election, and to be honest,

I found the few people I spoke to somewhat dour and humourless.

Not Cherie, though. We drove to Park City, a quaint little hill station town, which plays host to the annual Sundance Film Festival. Thankfully, it wasn't that time of year, and we could head straight for one of the local breweries. There are strange rules about bars in Salt Lake (and I suspect in its surrounds). You can be served alcohol only if you pay to become a member, which isn't usually worth it for just a couple of drinks. Beer, however, is different. It flows freely, and backed by the tide of tradition, it can also take a few liberties.

At the Wasatch brewery I was offered a 'Polygamy Porter', a dark local speciality which carries the catchphrase 'Why have just one?' I could just as easily have gone for 'Evolution Amber Ale—created in 27 days, not seven' which was also 'Darwin Certified'.

The Mormon Church's hold over Utah is palpable (even if not in its breweries). But what is the source of this power? Unlike many of the religions it would like to compete with, the Church of the Latter Day Saints ('Mormons' started out as a pejorative) has a prophet who appeared quite recently.

Joseph Smith claimed that he was visited by a (levitating) messenger of God in 1823 by the name of Moroni. Moroni, the son of Mormon, a prophet–historian who had recorded God's dealings with ancient Americans, had been charged with handing over to Smith several gold plates with writings on them. He visited Smith frequently, and eventually told him that the plates and other divine items were to be found (quite conveniently) buried near a village in New York State, a few miles from where Smith lived. Smith retrieved the plates, apparently showed them to family members and friends who now became witnesses, and translated them into what is the *Book of Mormon*.

The plates were a problem. God's word was hard to protect in the original. According to Smith, as soon as people got to know he had the gold plates, 'the most strenuous exertions were used to get them from me... every stratagem that could be invented was resorted to.' So once the translation was done, God asked for the plates back. In 1838 Smith said, 'The messenger called for them, I delivered them up to him; and he has them in his charge until this day.'

The *Book of Mormon* is intended as a confirmation of Jesus' existence, but makes one special claim: that he had dealings with the ancestors of Native Americans who were from Jerusalem. (That's right, the First of the Mohicans, Jerusalem, 600 BC.) When it debuted in the publishing world, the book was to be sold as the special Bible for the Americas. Against very stiff competition, and with not a little enterprise and industry, this worked out in parts—a viable spin-off.

Once Smith died, Brigham Young (of the 54 wives) brought the Mormons to Utah, their version of the Promised Land, and here began the work of building a fortress of money. The secret of the church's power lies in institutionalizing tithing (the 10% religious tax/donation that every member must pay from his or her earnings).

The joke around Temple Square, whose centrepiece is the magnificent Mormon Temple in downtown Salt Lake City, is that the church's office building 'where all the money is counted' towers well above the spires of the actual church.

Evidence that the Mormon Church is very wealthy is not hard to find in Salt Lake City—or indeed anywhere in Utah. They own most of downtown. What is a little more difficult is finding out exactly how rich it is. I chanced upon the Faith section of the *Salt Lake Tribune*, which quoted a staggering figure of $5.3 billion as receipts from tithes in 1997. Returns on investments from properties or other assets came in over and above.

The Mormon Church also claims not to believe in debt. If they want to build something, they always have to have the money in hand, and this is seldom a problem. Look at it this way: if the Church of Latter Day Saints wanted to, it could, with less than 10% of its annual income, fund the richest presidential bid of all time. By October, Barack Obama had raised about $500 million—five dollars at a time.

In 2008 the Mormon Church did use some of its money for a spot of politics. Colorado wanted to ban abortions, but California wanted to allow gay marriage. The liberals scraped through in the election in Colorado, but were out-dollared convincingly in California by the millions that the Mormon Church spent to ensure men didn't get married to other men legally.

I wasn't to know this was going to happen as I headed for San Francisco from Salt Lake City that night. Otherwise, I might have passed the information on to relevant people there, which would be everybody.

In the morning, the train rolled along through the Nevada Desert, racing tumbleweed and mostly losing, and I fell asleep again. I was woken by a warning over the train's PA system that may not have been something as exciting as 'look for the mushroom cloud to your left', but it did have its merits:

> This is Reno, Nevada. This is sin city. But do not, I repeat do not, get off the train and start playing the slots.
>
> We know they're right here, at the station. But if this is not your final destination, and you do not want to make it your final destination, do not get off to play.
>
> We know you're thinking 'just a little won't hurt anybody' but the next train is 24 hours later. So.

Clearly, Amtrak had lost a few gamblers to Reno. I got off to smoke, expecting to see people sneaking off to the slots. But nothing of the sort happened. Instead, while we smokers puffed away, a fit, bald, middle-aged man in a T-shirt got off the train. He looked to his left, to his right, and then began doing push-ups on the platform for the duration of the stop. His lips moved, counting in silence, the full four-and-something minutes. Once it was time to go, he dusted his hands and bounced onto the train, pretending to be just another ordinary passenger.

Had I been smoking the right stuff, I might have come up with an explanation.

We reached San Francisco in the late afternoon and I headed straight for Pier 39 to watch the sea lions at sunset. They do not do push-ups because they are lazy. But they engage each other in animated conversation and negotiations. They do this incessantly, on subjects as varied as real estate and love. This much I understood. Had I been smoking the right stuff, I'd have got the details.

Alas, all that I was going to do that night was eat dumpling soup in China Town and get on the bus to Salinas.

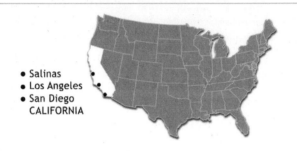

9

● Salinas
● Los Angeles
● San Diego
CALIFORNIA

The bin Ladens of Los Angeles

One day, up near Salinas, Lord, I let him slip away
He's looking for that home and I hope he finds it
But I'd trade all my tomorrows for a single yesterday
To be holding Bobby's body next to mine...
...Freedom's just another word for nothing left to lose...

Before I go into a pedantic diversion about *Bobby McGee*, let me just say that Bobby would have had a great chance of finding a real good home in Salinas at the end of 2008. Way better at today's prices, than in 1971 when Janis Joplin recorded the song on her album *Pearl*. Provided a 20% down payment was arranged, of course.

Salinas had the highest rate of foreclosures in California's otherwise upscale Monterey County. Banks were regularly taking over properties from defaulting homeowners here.

If yard signs were an index, 'For Sale' was clearly more popular than Obama or McCain and, with his running mate 'For Rent', made an unbeatable ticket.

Walk or drive, you could not miss the signs of the times. In hotel rooms, there were brochures advertising foreclosures and short sales (when the property is sold for less than what the owner owes the bank). So somewhere near Salinas, there was a five-bedroom house with a pool, guest quarters and caretaker's cottage that was a million dollars down, now available for just $2.65 million. One among scores.

But Bobby isn't rich (why else would he need to thumb a ride or have a dirty red bandana-sporting companion?), so let's look for something in his range. And here it is—a great little two-bedroom condo overlooking Sherwood Lake, at $122,300, provided you have loan pre-approval.

I doubt if Bobby could have got a pre-approval. A few months ago, before the credit crunch... maybe. Vagabonds, dangerous hitch-hikers, the terminally unemployed, people with long hair... everybody managed a home loan if they were willing to trade their tomorrows. But not now.

(Besides, who would offer a loan to somebody with a dubious identity? Here I take my promised diversion. Popular culture has given Bobby a sex change. She started out as a woman in Kris Kristofferson's original, but became a man for Joplin and almost everyone else, after *Pearl*. Also, Kris' Bobby was looking for 'love', not a 'home', an asset for which loan products do not yet exist, but would surely have been invented if Wall Street had just been given a little more time.)

✧ ✧ ✧

I had arrived in Salinas at around three in the morning. Having memorized two short streets from Google maps, I was able to make my way to the Traveler's Hotel quite easily, past what looked like a Jaguar showroom, with the cutout of a leaping animal announcing it. (By day, this turned out to be the front of the Greyhound station. The mascots look vaguely similar, which I think is a cruel joke.)

The hotel entrance was shut, though the light was on in the empty lobby. The usual glass cabin at the end of it was empty as well, but in disarray, like the counter of a bank that has just been robbed. I rang the bell and waited on the deserted street.

In a few minutes, a shrunken old man, wrapped in a muffler, emerged from a door that opened into the cabin. He could have been one of those caretakers of rural government guest houses in India, except that he pressed a button to release the door and waved me in, rather than trotting over to open it and ask whether I wanted chai.

This was Jagubhai Patel of Surat, 'Owner'. We quickly negotiated an 'Indian rate' through the reinforced glass and he slipped me a key saying, 'Any time, you call me if need anything. Morning, night.'

The next morning I found him sweeping the road in front of the motel, smiling. This, along with attending to guests 'morning, night' and other chores around his property was what took up his time.

I was very keen to talk to Jagubhai, but he had no English or Hindi, and I think he was somewhat embarrassed by this fact. With evident pride, he communicated to me that his son would answer any questions I had.

Son Cretin Patel's responsibilities around the hotel were purely managerial. He was in a 'meeting' when Jagubhai was sweeping the floor. This continued pretty much all day. What Cretin said at these meetings I would not know, because when I met with him eventually, he was the kind of fellow who would respond with 'I can't get into specifics' if you even said, 'Nice day huh.'

I thought of Jagubhai then, and I think of him now— doing his chores, waking up at strange hours, dealing with troublesome guests, at well over 70. And I always ask, 'Why?'

Well, I couldn't ask Jagubhai because I don't know Gujarati. I kind of asked Cretin, but he refused to 'get into specifics'.

✧ ✧ ✧

I left Jagubhai to his chores, walked past Salinas' premier breakfast place and a hair salon that warned 'There will be a $5 charge for whining', onto a side street, until I came to a glass door that had a poster with an election countdown: 13 days to go.

This was the Republican Party headquarters of Monterey County. Inside, apart from large banners that said John McCain was trustworthy, there was also a framed newspaper front page proclaiming, 'Shocking CIA leak reveals... CHENEY IS A ROBOT (when he went to the hospital, it was to get his circuit rewired).'

I liked the place—and Catherine Dolbec, the boss around the office. Turned out, Catherine was a born-again Republican. 'I used to work for (Democrat) Ted Kennedy.* And I loved Senator Kennedy more than anything. But, the older I got, I started to distance myself from some of those concepts and ideologies.'

I thought that the attractions of free market capitalism, low taxes and small government had probably dawned on her with maturity. But I was thinking too far ahead.

'I got married and figured out that I couldn't get pregnant.'

'Eh?'

'And I thought, oh gosh, 17-year-olds are having abortions as birth control. And here I'm 30 and I can't get pregnant. So I started to change socially on some of those issues, and the more I started developing those belief systems, it changed me personally. I was changing, but the Democratic Party wasn't keeping up with me.'

Once you fail to get pregnant, a lot of Republican ideology falls into place.

'We're taxed to death. We're taxed when we wake up till we go to bed. We're taxed for the sheets we sleep on. We're taxed when we turn the TV on, we're taxed when we buy a coffee, we're taxed when we fill gas in the car and then we're taxed on the car that we drive.

'We're taxed for the breakfast that we eat and we're taxed when we get to work on our pay cheques. We're taxed when we get home and go into our house—we're taxed on

* Ted Kennedy, JFK's youngest brother, died in August 2009. He spent nearly half a century in the US Senate. An orator of high calibre, he also drove a number of important legislations. His dream was universal health care.

that house. We have a death tax when we die. I mean, we're soo... taxed. It's exhausting...

'I'm afraid of national(ized) health care. I mean, I've gone to Canada and had to wait four months to get a basic appointment. I got the luxury now that I can get an appointment tomorrow, because I pay for it. I don't want to lose that right.

'You know, for example, we've got the government postal service and we've got FedEx. And if I'm going to send my wedding album to my mom, I'm going to send it through FedEx. Because I'm paying them so that it gets there. The postal service? They have no accountability. I don't trust the government with my photo album and I'm going to trust it with my healthcare? Forget it.'

People walk in and out of the office, selecting election-ware they want—buttons, posters, T-shirts, yard signs—displayed on tables at the entrance.

Up in Colorado, at the small skiing resort of Vail, hundreds of miles away, I had read about an epidemic of (exclusively Republican) yard sign thefts. I struck a chord the moment I mentioned this to Catherine.

'All of ours are getting stolen. And abused. We have four-by-eights of Senator McCain and 25 of them have been spray-painted or cut, and they're $55 a piece. So it's been a tremendous personal expense to me. But, there's nothing I can do about it, except to go out and repair them.

'People are trespassing into private homes and stealing them. We had a gentleman yesterday who had a letter to the editor, which said his yard sign was stolen 47 times—47 times! And the *Monterey Herald* said they weren't going to print it.'

There seemed to be a hint of conspiracy in that, so I asked Catherine if she thought the local Democrats, abetted by the socialist press, had done it. She wouldn't be drawn into that one. She just said that the only people with a motive were those who didn't like their candidate.

On that subject, I told Catherine about the button I saw in Tennessee: 'I'm voting for Sarah Palin—Oh yeah, and that old guy too.'

'Funny,' she said. 'Funny. A lot of people like her. And they don't care who she's running with. She could be running with Kermit the Frog and nobody would care. I think that's a shame... I think she's the governor of a state and deserves my respect...'

'Does she know anything, though?'

'Enough to run a state.'

'Alaska.'

'Still a state. There are people there who're working and paying their rent and raising their kids and they elected her to lead them through that.

'It's not like there's eight people and it's a small African country in the jungle. I mean, this is a US state. Has an economy, and you know.... I think people forget that. They think that somehow she's in a small village in Fiji, running 14 people and a cow.'

I cut to the chase. 'Are you embarrassed by her sometimes?'

'No.'

'Not even during the Katie Couric interview?'

'No, because it was cut. And edited.'

'But whichever way you cut that, she was still just babbling...'

'I've been in interviews where I've just blanked out and come across as a raving idiot. How can you judge someone when they've just had a bad day? I don't know what happened to her that day... if her kids were sick... I wasn't there. But I know that if she were a real idiot like people say, she wouldn't have gotten this far. Because nobody in any town is going to elect an idiot to city council or to school board when your kids' education is on the line.'

Then, she offered the best defence of Palin that I had heard since the strange Katie Couric interview.*

'And no way is a Democrat who's running as an incumbent in Alaska going to let an idiot beat them. I would like to know from the Democratic Party what she did to beat them. If she's an idiot, then how did she beat your Democrat? What does that say about your Democrat?'

'Or about Alaska...?'

'Or, maybe, she's smarter than we think she is.'

I got to ponder this improbability and was given a free 'I love McCain' T-shirt, as the honest, intelligent Republican waved me goodbye.

❖   ❖   ❖

* Palin's interviews with CBS' Katie Couric in late September 2008 started the slide in the McCain campaign. Palin, it was reported later, refused to prepare for the interview, perhaps hoping that charm would trump ignorance. But no matter how charming you are, you cannot get away by saying (approximately) that when Putin rears his head, Alaska is the first to see it; ergo, the Alaska governor has tremendous foreign policy credentials. The interview told the American public that their vice-presidential contestant would need serious help on 'Are you smarter than a fifth grader?' In addition, it was marked by the repeated use of the four-letter word 'also' (meaning, I've no clue). It is a must-watch, easily available on the CBS website.

The Traveler's Hotel is about a cricket ball throw—from long off to the wicketkeeper's end at Eden Gardens, Calcutta—to the Victorian home where Salinas' most famous son, John Steinbeck lived. It is now a restaurant, serving set meals with crunchy salads. The Salinas Valley is really a very large bowl of salad. The Salinas river, with timely rainfall, so slakes the earth that every year it gratefully sprouts a lush green carpet of lettuce and broccoli that stretches for miles. The produce finds its way to tables around the world.

I get my salad at Sang's Cafe. A spacious diner with standard red faux leather seating, which is impossible to enter without reading 'John Steinbeck ate at Sang's'. Diagonally across the street is the National Steinbeck Centre.

I had read a few of the great man's books. And while the outliers of *Tortilla Flat* or Lennie (the mentally challenged giant in *Of Mice and Men* who caresses the things he loves to death) are wonderful, I always liked Steinbeck most for his ear for authentic speech.

> 'Curtains? What in God's name do you want curtains for?'
>
> 'Only $1.98,' Mrs Malloy quavered, 'and you begrutch me $1.98...'
>
> 'I don't begrutch you,' said Mr Malloy. 'But darling—for Christ's sake, what are we going to do with curtains? We got no windows.'
>
> —From *Cannery Row*, in which the Malloys
> live in a boiler pipe.

The passage above was part of a cute little interactive exhibit at the Steinbeck Centre, whose centrepiece was

Rocinante, the vehicle Steinbeck drove on his 10,000-mile journey across America. In Steinbeck's words, it was 'a pick-up truck with a camper top, rather like the cabin of a small boat or the shell of a learned snail'.

Steinbeck undertook the journey with his poodle Charley when he was 58 and lived in Sag Harbour, near New York. He was not in the best of health. The lines of his route stood in front of me and looked suspiciously familiar—an imperfect, illuminated rectangle, sometimes rough and sometimes rounded at the edges, transplanted on the vast map of the United States. The little nodes where cities were gave the route the look of a major artery servicing all the parts of a massive body.

It was a crazy trip. But Steinbeck himself explained: 'I am trying to say clearly that if I don't stoke my fires soon, they will go out from leaving the damper closed and air cut off… what I am proposing is not a little trip or reporting, but a frantic last attempt to save my life and the integrity of my creative pulse.'

I stood in front of this quote at the museum and it got to me. I had not read *Travels with Charley*, so I bought a pocket edition at the museum store. It fit my pocket exactly.

I then took the bus to Monterey to spend the evening at the pier there and walk around Cannery Row. I watched the boats sway gently in the Pacific as the sea lions in the bay conversed and negotiated.

But the book was in my pocket, and that quote was in my head. At the pier, sharing a bench with some seagulls, I started reading. And I got stuck pretty near the beginning.

I have always lived violently, drunk hugely, eaten too much or not at all, slept around the clock or missed two nights of sleeping, worked too hard and too long in glory, or slobbed for a time in utter laziness. I've lifted, pulled, chopped, climbed, made love with joy and taken my hangovers as a consequence, not as a punishment...

I shut the book.

I was grateful for a light breeze of a thought that wafted to my rescue at this point. 'Great. Now all that's left to do is find the prose for a few classics (two would do), get an Oscar nomination and win the Nobel Prize,' I told myself.

A burden lifted. I was smiling like an idiot who had just got the joke, all the way back to Jagubhai's Traveler's Hotel. I had a little help. On the walk back from the bus stop, I crossed Steinbeck Plaza. 'Now Leasing', it said outside.

❖ ❖ ❖

Have you ever been ribbed by yourself? For allowing an embarrassing thought to cross your mind? Well, I still haven't heard the end of the Steinbeck thing. So much so, that as a defence mechanism, I told a couple of my friends. Result: now they too get on my case. Anyway, I 'drank hugely' that night and did not sleep at all. At about two in the morning, I think, I was able to stagger into the bus to Los Angeles. I didn't wake Jagubhai.

❖ ❖ ❖

Having accepted my hangover as a consequence of the previous evening's excesses, I was now being punished by a loud and baffling conversation going on in the seats behind me. It was eightish in the morning and we were in Santa Barbara.

The parties conversing were a woman in her late twenties, perhaps, and a slightly younger man. The woman had a cough that could hack a man to death. Each time she let go, I thought her tonsils would fly out and cause me a head injury. It was the kind of sound that only she, or a large grating cello, could make. I thought she must be extremely ill. Her companion, who had softened her up by saying she looked no more than 25 (she did), was trying to impress her in the following manner:

She: What time is it?

He: It's 7:45.

'Still a while to go…' (cough)

'It's 7.45.'

'Wonder what my kids are doing.'

'It's 7.45.'

'I'm really looking forward…'

'It's 7.45.'

'I think I'm going to give up smoking…' (cough)

'It's 7.45.'

'Aren't you getting tired of this?'

(heh, heh) 'It's 7.45.'

'Weird.'

'It's 7.45.'

'Love LA.'

'What's your phone number?'

'What do you want my phone number for? I don't even know you. I just met you.'

'What's your phone number?'

'I don't know about you… you know. I think you're kind

of creepy. You know, like, there are some guys who give you the creeps... like you give me the creeps.'

I had expected silence after this. But I was wrong.

'It's 7.45.'

Take two had begun. There was no hint of hostility in the conversation. She spoke normally, without irritation even, about other creepy men, a failed marriage, a former boyfriend, a kicked drug habit and how much she loved her children—and LA. She also coughed incessantly.

He said it was 7.45 till about a quarter past nine and asked her for her phone number at five-minute intervals. When I finally saw HOLLYWOOD written on the side of the hill, I was tempted to squeal like an American Idol contestant.

But I was not going to Hollywood.

❖ ❖ ❖

If you go there now, it is impossible to tell that 15260 Ventura Boulevard in Sherman Oaks near Los Angeles is an important building. Its 21 glass-covered floors shine blindingly in the California sun, but so do many others. It houses a branch of the bankrupt Washington Mutual Bank. Although it retains its name, a purple A4 notice at the entrance says it is now a branch of J.P. Morgan Chase, the guys who took it over. But that doesn't make it different from the Citibank building across, or the mall selling home products diagonally opposite.

What makes Valley Executive Tower, 15260 Ventura Boulevard different is a former occupant. Khalil bin Laden, Osama bin Laden's half-brother, who some say has a striking resemblance to Osama, ran a business out of one of the suites in the building. His company was called America In Motion.

The building's history has faded in collective memory. To be fair, there is little or nothing to suggest that it had any direct role in 9/11, or the crippling war in Iraq thereafter. At the end of October 2008, with a depression looming, two wars running, a new president on his way, perhaps even a new world order, Khalil bin Laden's former office is, nevertheless, rich with unintended metaphors on post-9/11 America.

Valley Executive Tower's most prominent current tenant was Washington Mutual. It also housed the brokerage firm Smith Barney, Citi group's (now sold) 'jewel'. And the troubled real estate major, Grubb & Ellis. All three were embroiled in the economic war within.

And the war without? Next door was a school that offered training in Krav Maga (the 'there-are-no-rules' Israeli martial art) which would never be proved to have anything to do with anything.

Finally, at the vacant lot a few buildings down, there was a poster of Oliver Stone's film, *W*. Josh Brolin (as Bush) holds his head in his hands. In frustration? Surrender? An attempt to avoid talking to Dick Cheney? Or is it just a hangover?

America In Motion was an interesting enterprise and Khalil bin Laden was an interesting businessman. According to Steve Coll's *The bin Ladens,* the company's investments were eclectic, such as leasing a jet to a company in which actor Clint Eastwood had a stake. But the company didn't have any apparent reason for leasing a jet—and promptly stopped paying America in Motion. This ended in a lawsuit, at the end of which all Khalil got was the old airplane.

Incidentally, there were also movie company offices in Valley Executive Tower, along with real estate and financial services businesses. Paramount Pictures occupied offices on the 11th floor.

Khalil bin Laden had an affinity for showbiz people. He earlier had a role in financing a $10-million-plus horse for singer Kenny Rogers. That deal, though, was profitable.

But there were other unusual investments. Even as Osama was setting up Al Qaeda in 1988, his half-brother was buying stakes in private prisons. A large number of prison facilities in the US are privately owned and/or managed. The government pays rent or a fee. Khalil's company bought into such facilities in Massachusetts.

That the bin Laden family had owned prisons in the United States may seem odd, but the tentacles of their multi-billion-dollar business were to be found in plenty of unexpected places. They had even considered owning a McDonald's franchise. This didn't materialize, says Coll, because it is apparently necessary for franchise proprietors to fry burgers in the kitchen—a job no bin Laden particularly wanted.

However, America in Motion ran into legal trouble in the early 1990s. There were allegations of kickbacks on deals and court cases. Khalil led a quieter life through the 1990s. On 19 September 2001, eight days after 9/11, he boarded a plane out of Orlando that hopped around the States to pick up different members of the bin Laden family and take them out of America for good. The flight was cleared by American security agencies even though some investigators might have wanted to talk to the passengers. They never got the chance—the Saudi ambassador Prince

Bandar was able to convince President Bush to allow them to leave.

A lot has happened since then. Valley Executive Tower, for instance, is now owned by a company called Douglas Emmett. They have records of previous tenants dating back only to 2003.

'America In Motion? Never heard of them,' says the security guard, directing me to the 11th floor administrative office. Nothing there either. Los Angeles seemed to have forgotten that so many bin Ladens once made their homes in the area—driving their Rolls Royces around Bel Air, visiting clubs and eating at fancy restaurants, as their kids acquired American accents in prep schools.

Wisely, I think, I didn't poke around too much about all the 9/11 and bin Laden stuff at the Tower. I say wisely because it could have got me into a lot more trouble a few days later, had I done so.

✧ ✧ ✧

These were turbulent times in California. The proposal to make gay marriage illegal had got the population excited, polarizing a state that prided itself on its liberalism. There was a hell of a lot of (televised) shouting and screaming and marching and pamphleteering going on.

Meanwhile, pragmatic gay couples took a little time off from all this and rushed to say 'I do' before election day on 4 November. Same-sex marriages were legal till then, at least in the state of California. As things turned out, that's all the time they had.

My next stop, at the southern tip of the state, had something to do with placing gay marriage back in the same category as pot. (Which, despite the best efforts of a legion of liberal users, remains illegal.)

But this was only part of the mandate of the Institute of Creation Research and the Museum of Creation and Earth History, in Santee, on the outskirts of San Diego. The museum stood in the middle of nowhere, a solitary, modern white building baking in the sun, surrounded by hillocks. It was a defiant, multi-million-dollar bastion of the moral majority, dedicated to better understanding life, the universe, and any restaurants at the end of it.

The institute was also the fount of reams of scientific papers on a variety of subjects, with titles such as: 'The Sky Has Fallen' or 'The Christian and the Greenhouse Effect'. Papers that calculated the earth's age at no more than 20,000 years, asserted that men and apes had separate ancestry, and concluded that 'Because of the Fall, and because most men are either ignorant or choose to be disobedient to the revelation God gave in the Bible, *fallen* men inevitably arrive at divergent views of the origin and operation of the universe.'

The Noah's Ark exhibit has been described in an earlier chapter, but I cannot help quoting from some other gems:

Acts of God on Day 6...
Formation of all land animals (except for flying animals on day five).

Sin...
The billions of fossils of both men or animals... speak of sin and death, not evolution of life. They all must be dated *after* Adam's fall.

Dinosaurs...

Dinosaur-like beasts are mentioned in the Book of Job, who lived about the time of Abraham, soon after the Flood and Babel episodes. God, in stating His Sovereign control over all Creation, describes these beasts to Job.

Darwin...

(His) only college degree was in theology. He came in at just the right time to be the catalyst for a renewal of paganism.

Pagans...

According to God... pretending themselves to be wise, they became fools. And changed the Glory of the uncorruptible (sic) God into an image made like to corruptible man, and to birds, and four-footed beasts, and creeping things. Wherefore God also gave them up to uncleanness through the lusts of their own hearts.

I saw the exhibits with enthusiasm, interest and a little amusement. But there are people who view the movement to source science from scripture as dangerous.

A week ago in Boulder, Colorado, the hotbed for climate change studies, I had visited the National Center for Atmospheric Research and the National Snow and Ice Data Center. At the latter, I met Mark Serreze, one of its best-known scientists.

Mark was a middle-aged pony-tailed gent who liked to wander off and drill holes in the Arctic ice whenever he could. At other times he studied satellite images of ice caps, with his feet on his desk. He had been getting hate mail and all manner of literature from the so-called 'climate sceptics' in growing numbers; from people (like the scientists at

Santee) who didn't accept that humans were causing climate change, and credited God with the phenomenon.

Said Mark, 'There was one from somebody who called himself Dr Detail—I have no idea why—which bordered on threatening. But he was so clearly ignorant of the issue that it was almost comical. Most of what we get from the sceptics, though, comes with a veneer of science attached to them. The sceptics aren't dumb. They're very, very smart.'

Waving a sheet of paper, he continued, 'Here's an example. I just got this thing today, someone sent it to me. It goes: "The myth of dangerous human-caused climate change." Put together by some group, I can't quite figure out yet. But you look at the paper and it looks so professional. So slick and professional. Nice coloured figures... it looks almost like a paper you'd see in a peer review journal. It's got an abstract, footnotes, everything.

'It's the sort of thing that someone who's not really familiar with the science would look at and say, "Oh my, this is really disturbing. The climate scientists have it all wrong, it's all natural variability." But I was just looking through it this morning... nonsense. Outright misinformation, distortions. Yet, this is the sort of thing that people read.'

Mark said he wished he knew why people didn't understand our role in climate change. 'Something has to force climate change... It doesn't happen all by itself, say by Voldemort being in a bad mood or something. If more solar energy comes in than there is emitted energy going out, the system must warm as a result. Wishful thinking won't get you away from it. This is a fundamental physical law.

'We know that the rise in CO_2 is because of human activity, because our fingerprints are all over it. The basic physics behind it is quite simple. But when Governor Palin was talking about "well, this is natural climate cycle" she was talking from a simple viewpoint of ignorance. Because she doesn't understand science.'*

On the other hand, she could have read the papers put out by scientists at Santee. 'The Christian and the Greenhouse Effect', for instance, says we don't know for certain whether CO_2 can be linked to rising temperatures.

What we do know, it concludes, is that 'We should not adopt the secular view that Mother Earth must be protected at all costs... We need to understand the mandate to have dominion... over all of the earth that God gives us in Genesis 1:26... Man is responsible to use the earth to sustain himself and to occupy (it) until the owner returns.'

And what if the landlord came back and complained that the place had become hot as hell? He might. Mark Serreze said we were looking at the loss of the summer ice cover over the Arctic by 2030.

Better get in and out of Florida before the flood comes.

* There is a small group of serious scientists, some of whom were previously proponents of man-made global warming, who have a different view now. They feel that CO_2 emissions are not enough cause for the effects we have been experiencing. These scientists do not mention God, but unfortunately find themselves on the same side as right-wing nuts on this issue, making their science suspect by unintended association. A documentary *The Great Global Warming Swindle* makes their case.

10

● Sarasota
● Venice
FLORIDA

'Listen Me!'

Why do people chase the American Dream? And what price do they pay? In my travels I found that people have different persuasions—and this is obvious. But I also found that there was no retirement age for dreaming—and there was no measuring the cost. The dreamer always convinces himself that it is worth it.

I met Shailesh Vyas for the first time where I also met him for the last—in a secure glass room at the Sunshine Motel in Sarasota, Florida. He looked older than he was—his grey sweater resting on the protruding bones of his shoulders, as if from a coat hanger a few sizes too small. He wore a woollen cap and shorts. A grey stubble hung from the folds of skin on his sunken cheeks.

'For you, $35,' he said from the window to his world. 'Plus $10 key deposit,' he added quickly. I was grateful for both the room and the 'Indian price'. And I was intrigued by Vyas. His son, a thin boy of about 19, stepped out of their one-room living quarters behind the glass prison. He was a bright young fellow. His favourite phrase was 'no problem'. He may have breathed the stale, depressing air that seems to surround working-class immigrants wherever they are, but with a 'no problem' he exhaled optimism with unfailing regularity.

I took an instinctive liking to him. One by one, more Vyases emerged. A daughter a couple of years younger than the son, and a track-bottomed, sweat-shirted matriarch. There was a red neon sign on one of the windows where I could read the word 'Open' backwards every few seconds, as it kept winking at the darkness of the town. But Shailesh Vyas and his family had opened their door to me in a different way. It was about nine at night.

My room held nothing but the damp smell of disuse and the promise of fauna. 'American cockroach very tough,' Vyas would later tell me. He had tried insecticides shipped all the way from India. 'But again, same problem. Again they come.'

The next day I would find out more about the cockroaches, Vyas, and his prison. But first I had to get to the school where the president was on 9/11, and have the shadow of that day fall on me.

✧ ✧ ✧

'We are what is called a school in need of improvement,' said Ms Marya Fairchild, assistant principal of Emma E.

Booker Elementary in Sarasota, scene of a still famous video featuring George W. Bush.

This is where, on 11 September 2001, the president got the news that commercial planes had been flown into the Twin Towers. He was, as some people might recall, listening to second graders reading 'My Pet Goat' at the time. (There is a controversy over whether he had his own copy of the book upside down, but let's not digress.)

In the minutes before he heard the attacks had taken place, President Bush heard the words 'get ready' repeated over a dozen times. But it wasn't Dick Cheney speaking into his earpiece—it was the teacher orchestrating a reading performance by the kids as the president promoted his recent 'No Child Left Behind' (NCLB) legislation.

Seven years on, it turned out that not just one child, but the whole school had been 'left behind'. Booker Elementary remained a 'C' school, whereas every other school in the county is rated 'A'. 'Think of it like a trajectory,' said Ms Fairchild, 'we're not on the path to meet requirements.'

How could Booker Elementary meet requirements? It was a 'neighbourhood' school in the town's roughest neighbourhood. 'If you were to pull out a demographic report by this zip code, my guess is that this area would have the highest crime rate in Sarasota,' said the prim assistant principal.

The school had 537 kids, 94% of them were from the (mostly black) minorities and 91% lived below the poverty line. To get to it, you passed places that sold 'soul food' on the outside and drugs on the inside. You crossed shacks and shanties and bums and cats. And, of course, a railway line. This was where most of Booker Elementary kids lived.

Here, you could find every reason why the Republicans flunked Florida. People were wary of four more years of the same. A lot of them blamed the war for everything. For instance, couldn't the poorly funded NCLB programme have benefited greatly from a fraction of the $10–12 billion monthly war bill?

Ms Fairchild had taught history at the Booker Middle School, to which a number of kids from the elementary school ended up going. I asked her whether she taught any of the kids who were there in the classroom when President Bush visited on 11 September 2001. She said she didn't recall the event having come up with any of her students. And then, quite suddenly, she refused to take any more questions. The interview was over. She told me to get in touch with the school board for more information.

I stepped outside into the parking lot and was in the middle of a call to Gary Leatherman at the board's communications desk, when a police car pulled up next to me. It had been less than five minutes since I left the school building.

Deputy Perrin from the sheriff's department asked me how I was doing—and what I was doing. He then told me the reason why he asked this: 'Someone called saying a guy was roaming around the campus—with a bag.'

This was true. I was carrying a (rather cool, if I may say so) blue laptop bag. I told him I had just been inside and spoken to the assistant principal. He said he'd better go and check.

A few minutes later, he found me again at the head of the road. As he pulled up, another cop car arrived. Deputy Scott had been sent over as well. Perrin asked for my passport and diligently began entering its details into the computer in his car. He told Scott that I was asking about 9/11.

For a brief moment I didn't hear that right and was about to say that I didn't call 911 (the emergency number) when I realized that someone from the school had. Fantastic.

The conversation went as follows.

Scott to me: You don't have any weapons or anything, do you?

Me laughing somewhat nervously: Certainly not.

Scott to Perrin: You patted him down yet?

As Perrin kept working with my passport, Scott started another round of questioning. Knowing that anything I said might be held against me, I told him the whole truth and nothing but the truth. I was there because George W. Bush was in one of the classrooms on the campus on 11 September 2001.

Scott's badge said he'd served the department since 1994. He went on, 'Oh, I was there that day. Spent anxious hours, traffic blocked all over the city. The president could have been a target. We had to get him out of here.'

I was thinking, well, the president was probably safest around here. The guys who executed 9/11 had been based close by, a few months previous to that day, training at flight schools in Venice, Florida, but they'd reportedly left by August. On 9/11, President Bush was safer at Booker Elementary than he would have been at the White House, which was a definite target.

Meanwhile, in Venice, where Ziad Al Jarrah trained in order to hijack Flight 93, which crashed in Pennsylvania, Arne Kruithof was still in business. When I went to Venice and called Kruithof's school, Florida Flight International, he was unavailable. But a well-spoken lady said he would call back.

Fat chance. The man had been at the centre of conspiracy theories ever since the 'smiling' and 'helpful' Al Jarrah trained under him in 2000. But he still ran his school and, according to reports, still trained people hostile to America for a perfectly sensible reason—these countries also bought aircraft and needed to transport people. Not every Iranian or Saudi was a terrorist.

But if you were from the sheriff's department, it was worth checking. After all, Iran and India would both be in the 'I' folder on the database. Deputy Perrin finally completed the data entry and said that his colleague required a photograph of me. I was, of course, the picture of cooperation. So, right below the sign that said Booker Elementary, I posed for the snap.

I called a cab after the shoot was over and my passport was safely in my bag. Deputy Scott asked me where I was headed next. I told him that I was bound for Orlando, then on to Alexandria, Virginia; Toledo, Ohio; Chicago, Illinois; Madison, Wisconsin; and parts of North Dakota.

'Man,' he said, 'I wish I could travel like that. But I'm stuck here.' He was. On a patch across the street, till the time my cab arrived. Protecting the kids at Booker Elementary. And I, with depressing visions of now being on a suspects' database which said 'must strip-search' at every airport, headed back to the familial warmth of the Sunshine Motel.

✧ ✧ ✧

Back in the motel, I told a mildly perturbed Vyas the story. 'When we dial 911, we say "known emergency",' he said.

'It means somebody coming to the hotel on the bicycle and distributing drugs. That time the county police come.'

It took me a while to figure that what he meant was 'non' emergency. Vyas had retained most of his Ahmedabad roots, so 'known' was non, just as 'hole' was hall. (I suppressed a smile when I realized this, because I was reminded of the old joke where the rich Gujarati said, 'Come to my house, I have a very big hole.')

But Vyas, he was in a hole articulated the correct way. He and his wife left the building once a week to go to the grocery store down the road. Yes, his kids went to school— the boy was studying computers at the local college; the girl had ambitions of getting there. They took the bus to and fro, spent the evenings in their glass cabin looking out, almost never stepping out.

It was Diwali that night. But on this street in Sarasota, the only bright light they saw was their own winking 'Open' sign and the Subway neon across the street.

My laptop proved a welcome distraction—a Macbook Air, the sleekest they (or I) had ever seen, enhanced with the boon of Skype that allowed you to speak to a familiar voice in the machine. The family loved it, and readily accepted my offer to use it to call Ahmedabad.

Relatives spoke one after the other. The 86-year-old father, hard of hearing, was asked about his health and told 'maje me chhe' (we're fine, happy) over and over. It was a lie.

Mrs Vyas retreated into her room to wipe her tears. The daughter was asked when she would come home to India and she said not in the next five years. It was the truth.

And I wondered, why? Why should people subject

themselves to this when there was a modest life to be led back home?

They came to the States in 2006. Vyas told me his story, starting at the very beginning. 'At the time of when we are in school I am passing through very critical position. I am five brothers, including myself, and two sisters. And earning is only father. Nobody in this family can earn. Even I have no money to give the fee in the school—at that time.

'At the standard of 11, I am going to the factory and working hard. I go to school, and after, we go to part-time job in the factory at the night time. Then I am studying in standard 11.'

'I *was* studying...' says his son, somewhat embarrassed, trying to correct his father's English.

Vyas continued, unperturbed. 'At that time it's SSC,' he says, emphasizing the acronym. 'Secondary School Examination Board, that time called SSC. After my passing all these things... standard 10, 11, 12. And during my college, four years, I have completed my LLB.'

'So you're a lawyer?'

'No, we can take some information from the lawyer. And we attend the court...'

Finding that he was struggling to explain this, I asked whether he was an advocate.

'Yes, advocate. Advocate.'

But he gave that up for a job in Calico Mills, the cloth manufacturers. 'I am serving there for 22 years. I am in share department... there are different type of department in Calico Mills, just like weaving, thread and chemical division. I am in the share department. There are 32 people serving in share department.

'Clerical works only. Some shareholders are come, he made the transfers of shares, we made the receipt and give it to him. And after the process, after we process on computer—IBM—after we made and prepared the process of computer and we put on the IBM and they take the print-out.

'Once in a year we give the dividend. At that time, the work is very busy. Because we took cheques in the envelope and tied the ribbon and we put into the mail. At that time there are lots of works. And the bonus share issue, Calico Mills, at that time also lots of work. We call other persons from outside. We call this daily wages person and Calico Mill is giving this person Rs 7 per hour. At the time of 1976.'

At today's prices, such a daily-wager would be way better off than Vyas—he got $2.5 for each room he cleaned when he got to the US (his family helped, so in effect that wage was divided by four and often there were just 10 rooms to do).

'At the time I joined Calico, you can guess what my salary.' Before I could say anything, Vyas told me the figure: Rs 125. This was uncanny. It was exactly the sum of money that my father got in his first pay cheque. I was about to make a point, but Vyas continued and made it for me.

'And in Rs 125, I lived satisfactorily. I also saved. In this amount I also saved Rs 50. But today, you earn Rs 7,000– 10,000, you can't save anything. In India. Not here. In India. I talk of India.'

I wasn't too sure whether the US was less expensive to live in, but I let that pass. I asked instead about the rest of Vyas' stint in Calico Mills. What happened? Did he retire?

'No, the Calico Mill are slowly, slowly... the textile industries are down at that time. Then at the time of 1992 all the mills are down, so many mills are closed at that time of 1992. And at that time, the Calico Mills are giving me a layoff.' (It strikes me that he would have had two infants and a wife to take care of, 'at that time of 1992'.)

'After we go into the mill and "present marking" and after that you can go at home. I also remember the mill is not good now. I am searching the job now. And you know the name of Siddharth Chimanbhai Patel? The chief minister of Gujarat, Chimanbhai Patel, you know this person? His son—I joined this person—his firm in Ahmedabad. Because I have a 22 years experience in the share department. And now, the Siddharth Chimanbhai is president in Gujarat Congress party. And I am the PA (personal assistant) of this Siddharthbhai Patel.

'And his little brother Surut... You have heard the name Latif?' I had. (The late) Latif was one of India's biggest gangsters, a crony of India's top gangster Dawood Ibrahim, who got several mentions in the American media after the November 2008 siege in Mumbai.

At the time when Vyas' job at the textile mill was in jeopardy, Latif was busy arranging the landing of arms and explosives in Dighi, Gujarat, in preparation for the Bombay bomb blasts of 1993 masterminded by Dawood. Latif was eventually caught by the CBI's Special Task Force in the old Delhi area. (Neeraj Kumar, then an officer at the Special Task Force, had told me that Latif was caught because investigators who eavesdropped on his phone conversations knew his habit of saying '*aaisa?*' or 'is it?' in a particular way. Years later, he was shot dead while in custody.)

'The Latif kidnapped this little brother,' said Vyas, trying to give me another pointer to the importance of his employer. He spent 10 years in Siddharthbhai's employment. From what he said, Vyas had a good thing going.

'He also confident on me. And give the charge of the primary and secondary market and I look after everything. The three computers and the three persons under me. And I also look at everything. He trusts on me. Nice and good. But after do this job, the visa call are coming.'

And that would prove to be a turning point. His brother, who had been in the States for more than two decades, had put in the application 10 years before—as a favour.

'I am not interested in coming here. My visa call is cancelled at the date of 8 August 2006. Cancel. Okay? And which date we came here? 6 August 2006. Two days before, we came over here. At the last time, we take decision we are going in US. My brother, each and everyday call me. You take decision, you take decision, because there is nothing in India. Here there is lot of opportunity for you. Come over here! And 6 August, we came on US.

'First time we go in Maryland, near Washington to my brother. He is searching a job for me, in Quality Inn—it is a motel also. And there we work as a housekeeping, but they cannot give me too much rooms (to clean at $2.5, a room) only 10, 12, 15 like that per day. If he give me 30 room per day then I will stay there more, but they cannot give me this type of room.

'I told my brother it is not good for me, why you call me here? After my brother is calling his friend, he is owner of Days Inn. And tell to send your brother and his family I will give good job over here. So I come here.

'The owner of this motel saying me, you come over here and you are in the charge of this motel. I say I am agreeing with him. I say how much you can give me?'

Vyas let me know that he had asked for $2,000 a month, but that he had settled for $1,800.

'He tell me this type of amount we will give you. I am agree. Okay. This is done. After two or three months, the motel business are slow and he telling me... he not directly telling me. He telling to my brother at Maryland. And my brother tell me that business are slow so that is why the amount will reduce.'

Result: a $300 pay cut for Vyas.

'Why he didn't tell me like this? If you are in the business for a long time, you know each and everything...'

Talking about this betrayal of trust—and its direct consequences for his family—Vyas was on the verge of breaking down. I could see it on his face, his voice began to quaver. I could barely look at him.

'I tolerate this thing. Because nobody can hear to my voice. Here. Only for benefit to these kids. Because I think the future of these kids. Otherwise, I left immediately...'

He was choking now, and asked for water. Even so, he noticed my discomfort. 'No, no, no, tell me anything... But the owner attitude is not good now. It is not good. Not fair.'

He could not hold back the tears. I tried to change the subject, but what aspect of this life was less painful? After a few hollow assurances that things would get better, and that the children were growing up really well equipped to handle any circumstances, I went quiet.

I had no idea what circumstances they had dealt with already. Young 'No Problem' started work at a liquor store in Washington, having just landed in the States. His English, even now, was only slightly better than his dad's and I wondered how he managed.

'We got lot of experience,' he began.

'Listen me,' his dad cut him off. 'Every Indian people are interested to come over here. Right? But those people who are well graduates, they are speaking English well, he do good business or good job here. But those people who didn't know English, no writing, no nothing, they do here *hard* work. Job.' The last words were full of conviction, and had a terrifying finality about them.

No Problem piped up, 'Here the doctor is doing housekeeping.' They had relatives who had come down. A cousin armed with a completely useless master of computer applications degree from Bangalore who worked as a salesman in a store before finding his feet.

Then there was the (Bengali) brother-in-law who had a government job in Ahmedabad and tried giving America a shot. He went back to his benign previous employer and the comfort of being the secretary of the local Durga Puja organizing committee after two months at a Dunkin' Donuts.

But Vyas stuck on. 'For the better future of both of them,' he said, pointing to his children. It was a chance that he was willing to take, despite what he had seen of America through his glass prison and on his occasional forays out.

'At the night time you cannot go walking. Some people are the drugs person... Or some people are the threat to you. They hide in the tree and they catch and take your everything.'

There were parts of Sarasota where this might well

happen, so I asked if it had ever happened to any of them. It hadn't.

But young No Problem had a story. 'When I was working in the liquor shop in Washington, that is a happened. But I was not there.' Luckily, it was someone else who had a gun to his head at the store that day. No Problem, who used to reach the shop at 10 in the morning and lock up at 10 at night, taking two buses and a train to get home, fortunately had the day off.

'Very risky, very risky,' said Vyas. 'And the owner of the store, he tell my son, when this type of person come, give it to everything. Money also, liquor also. Don't against him. Don't against him because sometime they kill immediately. They have a gun.'

No Problem said, 'Lot of black people they have gun.'

'So white people don't have guns…?' I asked.

'No, no, sometimes they are also having,' said Vyas. And then in a tone, which to my ears was innocent of racism, said, 'But they are very nice.'

He went on, 'But the black people are doing some bad business. In US the black people are doing the drugs business. They knock at each and every room and if the drug person is inside, he give money and buy the drugs.'

This was happening on a night when every respectable media outlet (and some not so respectable ones) was saying that America would have its first black president, while I had just been sent yet another mail asking for five dollars, to make it about $640 million and five for the campaign. I visualized Barack Obama as a 'drugs person' hopping off his bike and knocking at doors in the middle of the night and started laughing.

But then again, this was pretty much in line with what the McCain campaign had been trying to do through the previous weeks. One of the suggested answers to the question 'Who is Barack Obama?' was 'A cocaine-using guy of the street.'

At a McCain rally, when a woman shouted that Obama was an Arab, the candidate babbled a startling clarification to distance himself from her bigotry, 'No, ma'am. He's a decent family man.' (Arab and decent family man are two mutually exclusive sets—Venn diagrams that do not intersect.)

Looking back, my laughter was a way to avoid judging Vyas for what he'd just said. I judge people all the time. I will admit this. In Salinas, at the Traveler's Hotel, I had met Jagubhai Patel. A man who was also held in a glass prison—except when he had to come out to sweep the entrance of the motel.

I wanted to speak with him, but he had even less English than Vyas, and had directed me instead to his son Cretin Patel. I judged Cretin. Judged him because he didn't seem to care what Jagubhai's dream was. Because, surely, it couldn't have been answering the door at 3 a.m. And surely, it couldn't be sweeping floors at age 70, living in a room that seemed to lead only to a wall of reinforced glass, reaching out for small dollar bills slipped underneath.

This could not have been Jagubhai's dream. And I blamed Cretin for this. I will not apologize.

11

Washington DC

Winston Salem Spits It Out

A certain kind of person will orchestrate his own send-up better than anyone else. I love meeting such people, it spares me lots of effort. That's why the short, black, self-important (no, not everybody who fits that description looks like Spike Lee) coach attendant on Amtrak's Capitol line to Chicago fascinated me.

I saw him scuttling around the train, counting—and recounting—seats and passengers with an urgency and concentration that would have brought gravitas to the task had it not been for the fact that it was done at Pentium 1 speeds, with lots of start-overs, accompanied by the kind of head-shaking you associate with fourth graders who have just realized they've made an addition mistake.

His job done (or not), he headed for the cafe downstairs,

where I was seated already, sipping a six-dollar Jack and Pepsi. I found a partial explanation for why his arithmetic was so error-filled and slow: two young ladies.

The man was laying it on thick for them. Playing Lothario in his Amtrak uniform (blue slacks, white shirt—you earn a cap later, I believe, when you make assistant conductor, and I could be wrong), he was at the first stage of his little mating dance, telling the ladies how 'faane' they were, when he was interrupted.

'Are we running late?' a passenger asked.

The question had the effect of a blow dart on the posterior of, say, Tiger Woods, as he lined up his championship putt at the Augusta Masters. It was too much to expect our man to hide his irritation. 'I don't know. The only thang I know is we're going to Chicago.' And he quickly went back to the ladies to pick up where he'd left off. He was in the middle of trying to use the source of his power, a bunch of keys around his waist that opened the carriage doors, as a sexual signal (I am not making this up) when he was interrupted again.

Another passenger asked, 'What time is the cafeteria open till?'

This time, little Lancelot was downright rude. 'I told you the only thang I know is we're going to Chi-ca-go. Don't ask me no other questions.' The slightly stunned passenger, an old man, retreated quietly.

Left with no choice, I asked, deadpan, 'Are we going to Chicago?'

This started a flurry of questions from almost everyone else in the car.

'Are we really going to Chicago?'

'Are you sure we're going to Chicago?'

People who would otherwise have asked whether the spicy wings had run out, asked instead, 'We are going to Chicago, right?'

Winston Salem, whom I hadn't met till then, joined in: 'You mean, we aren't going to Pittsburgh or Cleveland. Like, we're only going to Chicago? Are you from Chicago? Why are we going to Chicago?'

The objects of Lancelot's affection were giggling now. And he was doing his best to play along. Smiling weakly, but valiantly holding his position, he said, 'Iss all I know, man. Iss all I know...'

But it was futile. The mating dance would have to be resumed some other time. He pretended something was the matter with his keys and hurried up the stairs to resume counting, I think.

The people in the cafeteria bid him farewell. 'Hey, are we going to Chicago...?'

That's not the last we heard from Lancelot. A smoking stop was coming up when he launched into a second routine.

'Mind your head, people... Don't try to open the window and stick it out. It'll come right off...'

He repeated this ad nauseum and, frankly, it got to me. Who would be daft enough to try and open one of those windows just to stick their heads out? On the other hand, if people could just get off at random stations and wander off to play the slots...

At any rate, I felt that the message was well understood the first time by those of us waiting for our nicotine fix. Besides, the man was blocking the window anyway. You would have to fight him to get to it.

But now that I knew there was more to him than the knowledge that we were going to Chicago, I felt it was appropriate to ask a second question.

'Why shouldn't we open the window?'

'I told you, your head will come right off.'

'How?'

'It'll come right off, that's how. From the neck.'

The conversation had now begun to interest everyone in the narrow passage that led from the stairs to the door of the carriage. Salem was there, as was an old lady with a rather mischievous smile, travelling with her relatively dour husband.

'From the neck,' she repeated, nodding seriously, giving me a nudge.

'Why will it come off?' I asked as a follow-up.

"Coz the other train come,' said Lancelot. And then, putting (at most) 18 inches between his palms, he said, 'That's how far the other train is...'

There was a dispute about this. Some people suggested six more inches with their hands. Then a train actually passed, so everyone was making their own estimates based on empirical evidence. To a man, everyone agreed that the distance had to be more than the 18 inches between Lancelot's palms. This was communicated to him in a matter-of-fact chorus.

In a spot now, Lancelot parried with a real gem.

'The main thang's the *suction*. Iss the *suction*.'

'The suction?'

'Iss the suction... will take your head off.'

At this point, something unfortunate happened to Lancelot. Since we were approaching Pittsburgh, as part of his duties, it appeared, he had to open the window and stick his head out. There were wild cries from the passengers.

'Hey, stop!'

'The suction! The suction!'

The mischievous old lady said, 'We don't want your head in Pittsburgh, Pennsylvania, and your body in Alliance, Ohio...'

'Alliance is a handicapped-friendly station,' said Salem, who was always on the ball with his facts, adding, 'any case, the body goes to Chicago.'

'Aren't we going to Chicago?'

Lancelot would not dignify any of this with a response.

Salem wasn't giving up that easily. 'What, now we aren't going to Chicago?

But Lancelot stood firm. His head was stuck nobly outside the window, his brow fiercely wrinkled, ready for an oncoming train or the onset of suction.

Amid the mirth in the passage, I turned around to see the two women Lancelot had been hitting on. They were giggling, 'Suction!'*

Poor fellow, he'd have to make love to his keys tonight, I thought.

✧   ✧   ✧

* I have checked with an authoritative source on 'suction', Mrs Gopa Sen, the best high school physics teacher in the world. She said that the trains needed to be travelling at ten times the speed (conservatively, 1,000 km/h) for any harm to come to a moderately built individual sticking his or her head out. (But why would anyone want to do this from a vehicle that was about to break the sound barrier?)

Winston Salem spat a lot. This was not an uncommon trait among travellers on Greyhound and Amtrak. But he spat so close to you that you always imagined a few splattered globules must have hit your shoes. It was too risky to bend down and check—because he might spit again. And it was pointless to take a step away—Salem followed you with his spittle.

I looked up, rather than down, therefore. He was a man-boy under 25, I'd say, but with a baby face corrupted by acne. He wore a T-shirt and a formal jacket, jeans and slippers, even though it was freezing cold in Pittsburgh.

We were smoking, and inevitably, someone came up to ask whether they could 'buy' a cigarette off me. This, or the straightforward bumming, was very common once you got off trains or buses. The first time a 'buyer' came along was in Gary, Indiana, where I instinctively said, 'Sorry, I don't sell cigarettes.'

This was now my default response. Salem was mighty chuffed by it, and he launched into a passionate lecture on bumming.

'Why the fuck can't they just ask? I mean, why show us like a few quarters? And the worst is the other type, the guy's like perfectly healthy, got some clothes, sneakers and he'll say like, "Got fifty cents?" Or like, "Got a dollar spare?"'

'I've thought like, fuck, I must do something one day that I've been thinking about. Like you know, wipe my ass with a dollar bill and roll it up and keep it. And the next dude comes and asks me for a fifty cents, I'll say, "Sure thing, dude, why just change, here, take a dollar."'

He found this incredibly funny, as did the rest of the smokers' club. I did too, but primarily because it somehow reminded me of my favourite scatological story. I was about nine, I think, when there was a big weekend carnival in my boarding school. On Saturday night, all of us boarders had gone around the grounds, looking longingly at the food and cold drinks. The cold drinks. If there was anything we craved in this world, it was sweetened aerated water. Having no money, we all went back to the dorm thirsty.

But Sunday brought answered prayers. The stallholders wouldn't arrive till the afternoon, so we pretty much had the grounds to ourselves. Getting into the stalls was easy— tarpaulin is hardly an obstacle for seasoned stealers. (Back in those days, boarding school boys were accomplished thieves. I hope this has not changed.)

The cold drink stall was the obvious one to raid. So a bunch of us got in and guzzled all we could, burping and belching our way through bottle after bottle of warm Gold Spot and Thums Up (Coke, the imperialist force, had been banished from India at the time).

We threw up and then came back for more. After about half an hour of this, one of the boys had a great idea—one that would rid anyone who followed the instructions of this horrible, frustrating thirst for good.

'I'm going to wash my ass with Gold Spot,' he said, then took a couple of bottles and headed for the bogs. When he returned, he had a smile on his face and was, to the best of my knowledge, cured.

He had anticipated that some of us would be sceptical about whether he had actually done as he said. He therefore told us that he hadn't flushed the toilet, so we could find the evidence, floating amid dying orange bubbles in the third stall on the second floor. He also said he had used no water, so the sticky remnants of Gold Spot on his ass were very much there for us to feel, in case we required further confirmation. As I recall, some of us went up to the toilet to check and were satisfied that further investigation wasn't necessary.

Salem was laughing continuously—and spitting at my feet—while I told myself this story. But his eyes were on someone else. Among us was a black girl who had her hair stretched back flat over her scalp, as tight as high-tension wires. She had piercings, with plastic beads, over her left eyebrow and on her tongue. When her brow creased, which was often, you could read 'I'm tense and troubled' written across her forehead. Her name was Lattrice and she was stunning.

I could tell that Salem was making a little play for her. He saw her allow herself a short laugh at his dollar bill story, so he decided to take it a little further.

'I mean like, fuck, I'd spend 20 bucks on something like that. Wipe my ass with a 20 buck bill and then give it to a dude who asks for a dollar. The bastard'd be so thrilled…'

He was now doubling up with laughter.

'…And then like, when he unfolds his fucking 20 bucks, there's my dried shit, right on President Jackson's face…' Winston Salem was in the midst of a fit.

I had to ask, 'So you'd spend 20 bucks and then you'd carry the shit-covered bill in your pocket till you found someone to give it to?'

'Totally fucking worth it, dude. Totally fucking worth it… So like he takes the bill to buy some food or whatever and he hands it to the waitress… and there's my shit on it…' He was laughing uncontrollably—stopping only to spit—when we heard the conductor call out: 'All *abooaard*!'

Back in the train, we decided to take the cafeteria over—the guy manning it had locked up and left, and Lancelot was probably looking for a friendlier coach. There was only one problem—we were running out of alcohol.

Then a fat guy joined us. He wore low-rise jeans which showed the crack of his broad, hairy butt (the latest fashions seldom suit the fat, I'm sorry to say). He also wore a studious, intelligent look, emphasized by a pair of glasses. He sat with his butt facing me, which is why I provide the gratuitous details about his backside.

Salem, meanwhile, had his eye on something far more useful—the guy was carrying a bottle of red wine. We soon realized, however, that he was a stingy socialist who would not contribute to the community. He would take part in our conversation, but not let us partake of his drink.

Salem did his best to get a bit of that wine. He produced a packet of Skittles from his pocket and made an initial offer. The fat guy really liked Skittles, but when it became clear that the Skittles–wine trade was not on, Salem worked out some entertainment instead.

'I'll give you Skittles, one at a time, and you've got to sit where you are and keep your mouth open. I'll throw, you catch.'

I happened to be in the middle. So I watched little red, blue and orange candies loop across me, as in some surreal free throw shooting contest, with a scaled-down hoop and teeth for a rim. Winston Salem shot, sometimes with feints thrown in, as Hairy Butt tried to catch and swallow. Some Skittles hit his glasses, others bounced off his teeth with frustrating little clinks.

Salem was saying, 'Yeah, you're my Skittles whore.

Open your mouth, Skittles whore, here comes another one…'

Hairy Butt's head was bobbing up and down obscenely, as he tried to catch as many as possible while still hanging on to his wine. He was saying, 'Yeah, give it to me, I'm your Skittles whore…'

It's not particularly important, but I learned that Hairy Butt was the 'marketing guy' for a leading 'motorcycle hearse company'. That was, he explained later, a company that dealt literally in hearses pulled by motorcycles. I tried to reconcile this with his other life as a Skittles whore, but it was futile.

If you are ever in a situation like this in the US, you can trust good old American entrepreneurship to rescue you. And this was exactly what happened in a matter of minutes.

A long-haired guy walked in with a bottle of (foul) Jim Beam. Salem, with his unshakable faith in market forces, went to work right away.

'I'll pay you a dollar for a shot,' he said.

'Oh yeah? Okay.'

A dollar was put down. A small paper cup (they had these 50 ml things next to the train's water dispensers) was brought. Long Hair filled half and then, noticing Salem hadn't removed the cup, added a little more. The buyer, satisfied, quaffed it down.

Two things had been established: the price and the quantity.

'I'll get another one. And I'll buy him one too,' Salem said, pointing to me. I protested mildly because I *hate* the taste of Jim Beam, no matter how well it is disguised by mixers or by my level of drunkenness. But no, Salem was going to buy me a shot, which I was to down. 'Be a man,' he said. It was a test I had to pass.

I got my shot, downed it, and it wasn't that bad. I noticed now that there was a small queue—others, including Hairy Butt, had also brought their paper cups. I went and got me one as well.

This was a wise move. With all the shots being sold, the bottle was fast depleting. In fact, I was the last to get a shot for a dollar. Long Hair doubled the price once the bottle went down to half. And then, at a quarter, he announced that there would be no more sales—the rest was for personal consumption.

I said that this was pretty much how Saudi Arabia would behave when it found that its oil was running out, and found that I had unwittingly started a drunken conversation on geopolitics. After a few seconds, Osama bin Laden inevitably came up...

Long Hair: This guy Osama was a friend of ours... you know that. And he had an oil company with the Bush family...

Hairy Butt: That is a fucking conspiracy theory... And yeah, you know what, he financed Barack Obama and Bill Ayers...*

* Bill Ayers was one of the 'characters' of the 2008 election. A former radical leftist/terrorist, depending on your point of view, Ayers' organization, Weather Underground, mounted a series of bomb attacks on government buildings in the 1970s. Ayers was let off, and is now a college professor. He and Obama lived in the same neighbourhood and sat on a couple of boards together. Though their relationship was established as 'not' close, Sarah Palin accused Obama of 'palling around with terrorists'.

Long Hair (with an air of finality): My grandfather was in Desert Storm and Vietnam, my father was in Afghanistan and Eyeraq... and my great-grandfather was in World War I and World War II... so I know my history. Osama was in the States. Kept safe by Bush. He was brought to a hospital by the FBI and CIAs and it was only when the hospital staff leaked the story that he was removed. And then Bush kept him safe, instead of killing him... which we'd have done in a heartbeat—as Americans.

Salem: You know why? Why they didn't kill him?

Long Hair: Why?

Salem (raising anticipation levels): You really want to know why?

Long Hair: Tell me why.

Salem: It was money.

Long Hair: Screw fucking money. We spend over 200 billion dollars a year on Afghanistan and Eyeraq...

Salem: No, we spend nine billion a month. That's it. Seriously, think about it, nine billion dollars a month ain't shit.

Long Hair: So why are we spending money on shit we don't need?

Salem: Because war makes money.

Long Hair: A war in two, and trying to go to three, countries—*loses* money. If we had just been in Afghanistan like we'd planned, it would have been good for the economy and brought peace there.

Salem: I've lost several friends in Afghanistan...

Long Hair: I have too. I've lost my dad, and several friends...

The way he slipped that in, about losing his dad, jarred a little in my ears. I turned to see what Lattrice was doing. She was looking outside the window into the darkness, her fine jawline given more definition by clenched teeth, her nostrils slightly flared, her brow creased. She was thinking of something I wanted to know about.

Long Hair continued, 'Now, if you were trying to make money as an American citizen, you think you'd make more money by making less war in different countries, or more war in all three countries?'

I let out a chuckle.

Salem had no doubts about where he stood. He opined, 'More war. I'd go for more war.'

Long Hair said, 'For each war we start, we start at least five American programmes to get them to go our way, which cost billions and billions of dollars. That's why we're going down now. That's why the dollar's down...'

This would have meant devalued wipes (in global terms) for Salem's backside, but he disagreed with the facts by saying, 'We've raised, actually. When oil goes down (it had), our dollar is worth more.'

I was only thinking of the rupee and I tended, therefore, to agree with Salem. In March 2008, it was 40 to a dollar. At the end of October, it was closer to 50.

The conversation meandered to the possibility of a revolution over the next four years. Hairy Butt felt that Russia and China would 'jump in' and there would be a Bolshevik-type thing that would eventually result, according to Long Hair, in microchips being embedded in everyone's head.

The part of the world they were not worried about was South America. 'Our biggest allies are there,' said Hairy Butt, 'like Colombia.'

'Yeah, because of cocaine,' said Long Hair sardonically.

Hairy Butt said, 'Bullshit. The problem in Colombia about cocaine is because there's fuckin' Americans that want cocaine.'

Salem offered a tangential insight: 'All Americans fuck.'

Lattrice, meanwhile, seemed to have her ears perked up, her face showing even more tension than usual. To begin a conversation, I lamely asked, 'So what do you think is going to happen in the election?'

'Nothin'.'

'Nothing? Well something will happen, surely...'

'Dunn matter. To me...'

'So what do you do? You a student?'

'No. I do nothin',' she said, looking away.

'You mean you're unemployed? That makes two of us.'

'No. I can't find a job.'

'Why?'

'Because of stuff.'

'Like...?'

'Stuff that I've done...' She was trailing off, and yet she somehow wanted to tell me more.

'Got involved in situations... with drugs. Did some really bad things... I've done my time, though... two years. But I'm still paying for it. Can't find a job, can't vote... got to see the probation officer...'

It happened, I gathered, when she was 21. An armed, drug-related robbery or assault, apparently, but she wouldn't tell me exactly what. It took place in Salem, Illinois, a town of about 8,000, dependent on the transportation industry and small manufacturing, in decay ever since she could remember.

Her eyes were filling up with tears that stopped right at the brim. She looked even more beautiful now.

Salem, noticing that Lattrice seemed to be involved in what might have appeared to be an intimate conversation with another man, jumped right on her seat from across the aisle, his head coming to rest on Lattrice's right breast.

'Your head's on my boob.'

'Do you like it?'

Lattrice made a face, but didn't make any effort to move him.

'Did you say you're from Salem, Illinois?'

'Yep.'

'Well, I'm from there too.'

'No shit. When you going to be home next?'

'Umm... next week. It's my birthday. I'll be at The Industrial.'

'No wayyy!'

She knew the joint. And it turned out that they had a number of common acquaintances—most of whom had problems with the law. But just talking about it seemed to lift Lattrice's mood. That was when I mentally coined the name Winston Salem.

I would always remember the name, because by a set of coincidences, Salem seemed to follow me around. Almost as if he was taking the same trip that I was. All I got to know about him at a material level was that he had a 'good job' that required him to 'wear jackets'; an apartment in Chicago where he partied a lot; and enough money to wipe his ass with $20, though he did say that the six-dollar drinks on the train were expensive.

Meanwhile, in the carriage, Long Hair needed some attention, but he chose a poor way to get it. 'What you talking about, bitch?' His question was directed at Salem, but Lattrice answered, 'What?'

Long Hair just made it worse. 'I wasn't talking to you, dude.'

I had a bad feeling about this gender swap.

'Did you just call me a man?'

'Why the fuck did you call her a man?' Salem was in battle mode, having lifted himself off Lattrice. He made a slight advance towards Long Hair.

Long Hair hadn't come into the cafeteria with just a bottle of Jim Beam. Around his neck hung a small knife, which he slid out, if a little hesitantly. Everyone went quiet. I was thinking 'not again', remembering a parking lot in Birmingham, Alabama. The only difference was that it was beer rather than whiskey.

But Jim Beam, which was at the root of the problem, also provided the solution. Jim Beam had just run out. Long Hair used this as an exit clause. 'Well, it looks like I'm done,' he said, staring at the empty bottle, toying idly with the cord around his neck and unobtrusively slipping the knife back into its little sheath. He then headed off to his seat upstairs. Hairy Butt was fairly drunk by now and staggered upstairs almost immediately after.

Salem dusted his jacket with the earned dignity of someone who's just won a fight for a noble cause. He sat down with a swagger to resume a budding romance.

I left as well. But I would meet Winston Salem again—in situations where his bravado would be more thoroughly tested and his candour would find even fuller expression. Right now I was headed to my seat, to pull the thigh rest out and try and sleep at the angle designated by Amtrak. Before daybreak I would be in Toledo, where I'd have to find Joe the Plumber's house—in order to avoid meeting him.

12

• Toledo
OHIO

Say, Where's Joe the Plumber's House?

I was brushing my teeth at the Toledo Amtrak station just after five in the morning when Winston Salem entered my thoughts again. This was because a man with a plastic bag had just entered the restroom and asked me for 50 cents. He had scoured the station for people and found two: one asleep on a bench and the other brushing his teeth. You had to hand it to him for his sense of timing.

Before the agent at the counter had retreated somewhere into the unseen intestines of the station, I had asked her how I could get into town. It was dark, but I could see the outline of the historic 1931 Anthony Wayne suspension bridge across the Maumee River that washes into Lake Erie a few miles down. To the north was the city's deep grey, predawn silhouette. The agent told me not to venture out before sunlight, since the station wasn't in the best neighbourhood.

An Indian lady who claimed to know the town gave me different advice. She asked if I had an airline ticket and said I should take a cab to the airport, go through security, and wait there until daybreak. That's the only way I'd be safe.

I thought the second plan was too complicated, so I waited at the station. At about seven, when I could see across the river clearly, I headed out to the road and caught a bus to get to downtown where the pigeons were just about completing their morning flights around the city's (relatively short) high-rises.

I passed two strip clubs that said 'Open'. And a big billboard that had a bald man with a T-shirt saying 'Army'. His message: 'John McCain *opposed* the new GI Bill. That's why I *oppose* John McCain.'

There were lots of people at the bus station, almost all of them black. But it was difficult to tell who was waiting for a bus and who was waiting for life to turn around. I looked about me and saw on faces young and old, a strange expression of anticipation that something would happen right there, which would change their lives. If it didn't, in a few hours, they would pay a dollar to get on a bus—just to give fate an hour's grace. They had no reason to believe that a life-changing election was days away—they had more faith in the bus stop.

In New Orleans, more than three years after Katrina, I saw glimpses of the same glazed expression. But the eyes were not as disturbing as at this bus stop in Toledo.

A young, round girl in a dirty T-shirt and frayed jacket, with several teeth missing, was swinging her plastic bag around with that same demented mixture of despair and aimless hope—like bubbling alka-seltzer in sour milk—when an older woman who looked much more sorted said, 'Heyy girl! Haven't seen you around…'

I thought she looked more sorted because she was older, dressed neater, in black tights and sweatshirt, and carried a faux leather handbag. But one of her earlobes was split—the kind of disfigurement that happens when an earring is ripped off.

She asked the girl how her boyfriend was, and the girl said she was done with him.

'So you don't have a boyfriend now?'

The girl giggled and said, 'No.'

The older woman was genuinely concerned. There were questions about the girl's health and home (nothing was particularly good). And then, with an expression that said 'your life's going to change right now, at this very bus stop,' the woman said, 'Come here girl, lemme tell you something.'

The girl took a step forward in optimism, and I must admit I hoped with her. Maybe, just maybe, something really good was about to happen. The sorted woman said, 'Give me ten dollars. I really need it.'

❖ ❖ ❖

This was the town in which Samuel Joseph Wurzelbacher, or Joe the Plumber, plied his trade. But he didn't really live here, choosing instead a sunny suburb where things seemed a lot more 'normal'. For a dollar, I could get pretty near Joe's house in the suburb of Holland, west of downtown, in about 45 minutes. I thought I'd walk the rest of the way to his street, but this was a bad idea.

It is a bad idea to try and walk around *any* suburb in the States—they stretch on and on. So there I was, off Airport Road, then off Angola, past Patterson's Tax Services (Their advice: 'When all else fails, read the instructions.'), past pretty condo complexes with names like 'Walnut Woods', with ducks in an artificial pond across the street, fed by the waste of a flat shopping complex. By the time I reached Strachn's Bakery, I was kind of lost.

So I did what I had to do. Walked in, bought a doughnut and asked, 'Say, do you know how far Joe the Plumber's house is from here?' There was laughter all around. Joe lived not more than a few miles from Strachn's, but not everyone had heard of him. They called me a cab.

Within a few minutes I was on Shrewsbury Street, home at the end of October 2008 to the seventh most famous person in the United States. Until the day John McCain invoked Joe (13 times, I've been told) in a presidential debate on 15 October, Joe was an average guy. Since then, he had become one of the characters of this election and his every move was watched.

And judged. Joe had joined people like Bill Ayers (former terrorist and Obama associate, innocent according to the US judicial system); Jeremiah Wright (Obama's former pastor, guilty of being a Christian isotope of Louis Farrakhan, though with different views on Obama); and Sarah Palin (vice-presidential candidate, guilty of opening her mouth).

His claim to fame was an encounter that lasted under 15 minutes, but took up several hundred times more airtime thereafter. Obama had come campaigning in the neighbourhood, and intrepid Joe had confronted the candidate with questions on his tax plan.

To summarize, Joe had said he was afraid that Obama's plan to tax families and businesses that earned over $250,000 a year would hurt him. He had ambitions of owning his own business. While it was true that anyone earning more than that sum would pay an extra 3% on the difference ($300,000 would mean they'd pay 3% above the current rate on $50,000), this was no real danger to Joe (he made approximately $40,000 a year). He had not taken neighbourhood tax consultant Patterson's sage advice: 'read the instructions'. Nevertheless, he was dismissive of Obama's patient, personal explanation.

There was a conspiracy theory that Joe was actually planted. (The theory gained credence when it was alleged, after a few public appearances, that Joe's shaved head was in fact a pale beetroot.)

In the last days of a floundering campaign, team McCain felt they were onto something with Joe. He was projected as the brave, patriotic American who had signed up to fight the fast-advancing forces of socialism. In a matter of days, this changed both him and his street.

To begin with, there was the media attention. On this day, Joe was out on the campaign trail in Utah (the precise reason that I came to his house), but in spite of that I found another journalist, a radio man from Holland (not the suburb, the country).

No one on the street would tell us exactly where Joe lived, but the man from Amsterdam wasn't short of initiative. So I just followed him to No. 355, Joe's house. There was an SUV parked there. No yard sign. (Come to think of it, would there be a yard sign in the Palin home in Wasilla?) Joe was busy, being the showpiece at Republican rallies, and the doorbell was answered by a tall, fit, middle-aged man and two dogs. This was Tom, Joe's 'business manager'. We couldn't get a second name out of him. But if you added Dick and Harry, you'd get your average plumbing firm, complete with business manager.

This business manager thing freaked me out a bit. Two weeks ago, Joe worked in a firm that had three employees, making a modest living. Now he had a 'Tom', whose additional responsibilities included taking care of dogs and journalists.

Joe's house was fairly typical of the neighbourhood: a garage, a little drive, a nondescript screen door with a wire mesh—so we saw the business manager divided up into tiny squares. He wouldn't open the door. He told us that we needed to have given notice. When the Dutchman persisted, he put another latch on the screen door and said, 'Look, Joe's holding a press conference Monday, give me your emails if you guys want to be on the list.'

The Dutchman, undeterred, stuck his mike at the face behind the mesh: 'But vat has life been like... tell us...'

'Do you guys want to be on the list or not? Yes or no?'

The enterprising reporter gave up. We dutifully wrote down our emails and handed the paper to Tom who held the door ajar just enough to allow this.

Thwarted, the Dutchman resorted to a journalistic technique I had initially thought was invented (or at the very least, perfected) in India. When we can't get anyone to interview, we interview each other. No sooner had we turned our backs on No. 355 than I found a microphone in my face.

'So vhy have you come to Joe dze Plumber's house?'

'To see where he comes from, find out what the neighbours think of all this...' I actually found myself answering!

'Is it true that Joe was set up by dze McCain people?'

'I wouldn't know...'

'Come on, you can tell me...'

After about a minute of this, I said to him that it was pointless—from both our perspectives. Why didn't we instead fall back on another journalistic technique tested in India and tried *all* the time during any Indian election—the taxi driver interview. In this one instance, I thought the technique was valid.

Tim Antoine, the helpful man whose taxi I had taken to Joe's house, had plumbing in his DNA. Tim's grandfather was a plumbing inspector, his father was a plumber, his son was a plumber, a certified one—unlike Joe—and was a partner in a business. Tim's son earned $85,000 a year, tops. Tim knew his plumbing history, his plumbing economics and his plumbing current affairs.

Although Tom from behind the screen door had let us know that Joe wasn't average any more, I asked Tim if the alleged plumber represented the average guy. Tim said he didn't. 'That guy (the average guy) wants a job, thinks of keeping his job, in these times, before thinking about owning a business.'

'Many years I've been driving a taxi here in Toledo... I've seen a glass plant on the other side of the city, where I grew up in East Toledo, and that glass is now in China. It used to have 5,000 employees, there's nobody working there right now.'

There were also clear signs by now that the much larger automobile industry was in deep trouble. Detroit, a few hours to the north, was going down (a sinking that had started decades ago) and Toledo, where about a tenth of the workforce depended on work handed down by GM, Ford and Chrysler in auto parts manufacturing, was being dragged under with it.

But Toledo had a history of its own with regard to automobiles. One of the most iconic vehicles of all time, the jeep, had its home here. Willys-Overland, which manufactured the vehicles in Toledo from the late 1930s, was sold in the 1950s, but the jeep lived on. After several changes of hands, Daimler Chrysler came to own the company in the late 1980s. Till 2001, they were rolling out the Cherokee, the last successful model, from a brand new assembly line in Toledo.

And what of the company that built the first jeeps? Willys-Overland exists as a niche business for jeep freaks, supplying parts for vehicles dating back to 1941. They're still in Toledo. Hanging on. But for how long?

It was in this environment that Joe was opposing tax raises for rich people and *future* business owners. Not a very popular theme in Ohio, from not a very popular man in his neighbourhood.

'Hadn't heard of him till last week,' said the lady at No. 457 Shrewsbury Street, down a few houses from Joe's. 'Worked for the postal service till five years ago, and I don't remember him,' she said implying, of course, that this old(ish) community was mildly under threat by recent infiltrators.

The McCain people can hope all they want, but Joe wouldn't make any difference at all, she added. With the cameras and the constant stream of reporters, and the continuous coverage on national television, it had all become a bit of a joke in the neighbourhood. Seeing us walk up and down, a few jobless young adults shouted, 'Joe! Joe!' and ran into a house.

But that was fine with Joe and his business manager. There were book deals on offer; a possible country music recording contract; and the chance of holding elected office. Joe was considering the Congress, even though it was doubtful that he could win the neighbourhood homeowners' association election.

That such a character became the McCain campaign centrepiece as the election marathon entered its 'kick' phase baffled many people and amused me. When I thought about it later, the only explanation I found was the profound dumbing down of Republican politics. To the extent, almost, that it became the politics of dumb people. Venerated conservative commentators and journals like the *National Review* had expressed variations of the same thought, if a little more delicately.

In the context of this election, the dumbing down process seemed to have begun with the nomination of Sarah Palin as vice-president and ended with the choice of Joe the Plumber as mascot, but there was more history to it. That the Republican Party had run out of ideas had become clear much earlier. In 2004, Karl Rove* cynically flogged the hard base of the party to engineer a narrow win—but a win, nevertheless. The hope at the time was that just a little

---

* Bush adviser Karl Rove has widely been credited with heading by far the best-run department under Dubya: the dirty tricks department. Particularly nasty political moves are routinely described as 'right out of the Karl Rove playbook'.

over half of America was a petrified forest of conservatives, and would remain that way.

What wasn't taken into account in 2008 was that it had been simpler to win in 2004. There was a war being waged (that hadn't yet been lost), which always makes it easier to polarize people into two solid groups (patriotic and anti-American).

What was also ignored was that poor governance—the low point of which came with Hurricane Katrina—can make even petrified trees walk away. What remained, as John McCain made his run for office, was the debris of bad governance that Bush had left (hardly a platform for winning an election); and buried just underneath, fossilized conservative ideas from Richard Nixon's time.

Nixon won in 1968 by making his own anger against the liberal elite the collective anger of a people who were witnessing anti-war protests from 'the educated classes'— college students and an increasingly confident civil rights movement. The message he transmitted to the non-demonstrative majority was that he too was a victim of rejection. This found great resonance in the South, which to this day remains the steadfast core of the Grand Old Party.

Nixon moved on to level two in preparation for re-election. His re-election formulas were brilliant for the purpose of winning, for the time in which they were invented. George Packer wrote in the *New Yorker* (26 May 2008) how 'Nixon was coldly mixing and pouring volatile passions' to get that second term.

He was helped, in no small measure, by the then fresh intellect of Pat Buchanan, who wrote a note quoted by

Packer in the article. This was both a road map for a Nixon re-election and a trail that would lead into the Democratic constituency and divide it for the next three decades. Not all of Buchanan's recommendations were acted upon, says Packer, but they included, among other things:

- Highlighting the Democrats' elitism and apparent anti-Americanism.
- Appointing a strict southern constructionist to the Supreme Court to divide Democrats regionally (southern Democrats would lean towards the Republicans).
- Using issues like abortion to sharpen the division between Catholics and social liberals.
- Getting white working class support by supporting tax relief and opposing welfare.
- Using racial tension within the Democratic fold to force a wedge in it. 'Bumper stickers calling for black presidential and especially vice-presidential candidates should be spread out in the ghettos of the country... We should do what is within our power to have a black nominated for Number Two...'

According to Buchanan, this, and a complement of other tactics, could 'cut the Democratic Party and country in half'. He said, 'My view is that we would have far the larger half.'

I have a pedantic point to make, which is that you cannot have a 'larger half', but apart from that, these were real ideas for their time. Whether you liked them or not, the evidence of a brain/brains at work is overwhelming.

If you cut to 2008, that factor was completely missing. Yes, there was some cleverness—like Rush Limbaugh's call to Republicans to infiltrate Democratic ranks* and vote Hillary during the primaries, in order to skew the nomination calculations. Limbaugh, to give him credit, probably saw that Obama was unstoppable, if nominated. (Some Republicans think this idea backfired. The Democrats apparently stole it to get the 'pushover' McCain nominated!)

But really, there was no new idea, just a defence of the war, excuses for the economy and the loss of jobs, and a dependence on the core 'values': fear God (oppose abortion/gay marriage), love your country (support the war, delude yourself about winning), and so on.

So what were the heavyweight conservative thinkers doing while Bush played the lyre? Actually, they were just listening to him—and Donald Rumsfeld. But they had done something fatally damaging in the process—they had surrendered the thinking jobs to a bunch of radio and television talk show hosts. Thus Limbaugh, Sean Hannity and Bill O'Reilly were what the constituency saw or heard as the faces/voices of the party. (And then they saw Sarah Palin and Joe the Plumber.)

Each of these media stars was innocent of the idea of intelligent debate. (For instance, they blamed Obama for the recession—which began a year before he was elected.) Arguments were 'won', according to them, by shouting, bullying and babbling, often simultaneously. The hosts were megalomaniacal to the point of being caricatures. O'Reilly asked, without a trace of irony, why a person as qualified

* Undecided voters can vote in both Democratic and Republican primaries. Limbaugh was encouraging committed Republicans to pass themselves off as undecided in order to prevent Obama from winning the Democratic nomination.

as himself wasn't nominated to chair one of the presidential debates. When a guest came on his show to say that America wasn't there for its war heroes, he said without missing a beat: 'I was.' And he raved for weeks about how good his book was and ranted for days that it wasn't making the best-seller list due to a conspiracy at the *New York Times*.

Cowering obeisance was paid to the Gods by senior politicians. At the end of an (job?) interview with Hannity, Michael Steele,* who hoped to become chairman of the Republican Party, could not hide how much the interviewer's final words meant to him. As Hannity said, 'I think you're the right guy for the job. You have my support,' before waving him off the show, an expression of canine gratefulness came over the next chief of the Republican Party, leaving the viewer in no doubt as to who the master was.

All of this made for great television for a certain set of subscribers, many of whom liked endorsements of their dogmas repeated to them on a daily basis by such intellectuals as O'Reilly. This was precisely the point the 'thinkers' in the Conservative Party seemed to have missed—each of these hosts had a completely selfish motive. They had to keep the ratings of their shows at least where they were. It was in their interest to retain viewers; and if that meant losing a few voters, they would make the trade ten times out of ten.

If it meant they needed to shriek, they would. And if the party sounded shriller as a result, that was too bad. This was a necessary by-product, a consequence of allowing them to commandeer the ship. The tragedy for the party was that

---

* In January 2009, Steele got the job he was applying to Hannity for—chairman of the Republican National Committee.

it wasn't lacking so desperately in coherent voices. Just that America didn't hear them. Were they deliberately kept on mute?

Something in George Packer's *New Yorker* article got me thinking. The now disillusioned David Brooks was one of the brightest stars among conservative writers when the legendary William F. Buckley handpicked him for the *National Review*, the magazine he founded. But when the time came for Buckley to choose a successor, Brooks was passed over. A note from Buckley published in the *New Republic* in 1997 gave the reason: Brooks was 'not a believing Christian'. Brooks is a Jew.

Today's talk show hosts could claim that they were merely being faithful to the spirit of the Buckley doctrine. But what about the politicians? That it is not enough to have only the viewers of Fox News come out and vote for you to win an election should be obvious to anyone who knows basic arithmetic. If the number of votes required to become president equalled the viewership of the O'Reilly Factor, would anybody but O'Reilly get the job? Or even be allowed to apply?

13

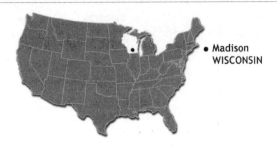

• Madison
WISCONSIN

No I Didn't...Yes We Did

'Says he's an Indian journalist. *Economist's Times*.'

'Paper like that?'

'Seems so. Has an ID. Signed by... can't read it.'

I'm at a police precinct, for reasons I can fully explain, but this is not the time. The guy who asks whether the '*Economist's Times*' exists happens to be the captain/boss/chief, whatever you call him, and he steps out of his den to refill his coffee exactly when I am brought in.

'Run him by our friend.'

'Sir.'

Valdez goes to the IBM.

'What's it say?'

'Authorizing sir.'

'Kay.'

'Sir...'

'What is it, Valdez?'

'It's, ummm...'

'Shift, enter, Valdez. Shift, enter. Should I say that in Spanish?'

'Sir... I'm in, sir.'

'Say somethin'.'

'Somethin'... I mean nothin' sir. Mean nothin'... mean nothin' shows up.'

The captain hauls his behind off the subordinate's desk it had been occupying, and takes a sip of his freshly poured coffee.

'Indian jour-na-aa-list. Travelling around the U-nited States. Readin'... *The Onion*...??'

'Sir.'

'And you innerviewed him, Valdez.'

'Sir.'

Referring to Valdez's notes, 'Hmmm. Knows Ned Flanders is left-handed... Fantasia is a person for him... 'Merican Idol... not a country...'

I glow inwardly. It isn't everyday that someone accuses you of being the Man Who Knew Too Much.

'And you say nothin' shows up? Valdez, may I ask you a question?'

'Sir.'

'If someone says to you. You, that is, you. Take this personally, Valdez. If someone says, to *you*: "Hit me!" Would you, Valdez, expose that fine set of teeth and run real hard into his fist, *face first*?'

'Sir?'

'Valdez, do you really want Smelley and Coulder to waltz

in here from Washington and tell us we need to hit "*control, shift, enter*" in cases like this? Do you really want that?'

'No sir.'

'Good answer. Hit it.'

✧ ✧ ✧

Fine. Fine. This did not happen. But who can ever know what happens in Madison? Could I have, for instance, ever found out, except in Madison, that some Americans want a green card real bad? (The green card is actually pink, this I know. But the Bell Labs employee of two years who finds a 'pink' card in his mail, instead of a green one, does not: 'Shalini, looks like it hasn't worked out. We're going back to Kanpur.')

It is a common misconception that techies and truck-drivers from the poorer parts of the world are the only aspirants for a green card. Some Americans desperately want a green card too. It is their passport to wealth and happiness. This I was told by a drug dealer who had recently debuted in the business. He arrived in a small car—with a friend, whose vehicle it probably was. He carried his stuff in small packets on different parts of his person. Amateur. And as if this wasn't enough, his hands trembled. To make him feel at ease, I asked him where he lived.

'I have friends who live close by... I live on the west side of Madison... There's like three different kinds of weed in here...'

'That's sweet, man,' said my friend, at whose home this was taking place.

The debutant laid out the packets, which were filled with little balls in various shades of green, some packed tight, others more powdery. He pointed a trembling finger at one, then the next.

'This is obviously something different. Now this, this is like my favourite of all of them. But... then there's stuff like this. There's like three different kinds of weed in here. But that (pointing back to his favourite), that's the good stuff right there. It's $325... if that's okay with you.'

Once he was given the money, he inexplicably broke into a nervous babble: 'I can get some other stuff that's cheaper, but I rather... I buy the expensive stuff because all my friends want the good stuff, man. That stuff doesn't have seeds in it. The cheaper stuff doesn't have seeds in it either... But I...'

'So where is this stuff from? Grown, cured locally?'

'I don't... this is actually all from one of my friends. He grows about a half-an-hour outside of Madison. He grows hydroponically, so after he cures it, there's like a lot of weed, but it weighs so little.* And it's like expensive. So I'll get that for like personal. And I'll give it to my friends. When the harvest comes, I get quarter pound of that maybe—if I'm lucky.

'I know like two growers in Madison. But otherwise, this stuff, it comes from British Columbia or California. (Humboldt County, north of San Francisco.)

'I've actually taken a few trips. My friend Keith, he lives there. And there, everybody's got a green card. And they smoke marijuana legally. I bring some of that back every time I return.' Our debutant dealer was reflecting a

---

* Hydroponic farming is soilless. Roots of plants are placed in liquid nutrients, instead, and grown in controlled conditions.

widespread feeling of envy about the grass being greener in California. Few Americans have the privilege of being issued this, the most wonderful green card.*

('But I filled the forms correctly Shalini! Looks like we have competition from people in northern California, for some reason.' It was at this point that Valdez accosted me, read out my rights, and dragged me to the station.)

❖ ❖ ❖

I had arrived in Madison, Wisconsin, for Halloween. Me and about 57,000 other people, to spend the weekend with my friends Ankur and Ashwini and make it to State Street for the party if possible. About the only thing Madison takes seriously is Halloween. People spend hundreds of dollars on elaborate costumes and accessories and are admirably fastidious about how they turn out. No witch can have a wart out of place, no Satan asymmetrical horns. Exceptions are made only if the flaws are part of the character. Everyone is a method actor for a day.

Ankur, who is a brilliant photographer, took on a persona that was very 'him': paparazzi. I scratched my head for a bit, then found a black shawl, covered my face and went as a terrorist. This was sloppy by Madison standards, but I justified it by reasoning that I had been something of a terror suspect even without any accessories—if you discount the dangerous blue laptop bag.

* The pot fraternity refers to the 'green card' which Californians can get to grow marijuana for medicinal purposes, with a justifiable degree of jealousy. A lot of the produce obviously doesn't make it to legal drug stores. At last count, 14 states in America had some form of legal marijuana, Alaska being one of them.

We waited for Satan and Boy Scout to arrive and then drove off in the direction of State Street. Boy Scout apprised us of a future problem—there was absolutely no parking within a three-mile radius of the action.

None of us was particularly keen on walking, and we tried to figure out what to do, but Boy Scout didn't seem interested in helping out with ideas.

'Can we stop for a bag of chips?' he asked.

This was odd, and we told him that there would be plenty of time for chips. Let's first figure where we would park.

'Okay, can we just stop, please?'

We ignored him some more. But finally, he just said, 'I *need* a bag of chips.'

This was getting slightly out of hand, but we decided that if the man wanted a bag of chips so bad, we'd let him have it. It would clear his mind. We stopped the car at a convenience store. Boy Scout returned with a large bag of chips and said, 'Now we're set.'

The vicinity of State Street was crawling with cops guarding barriers, redirecting traffic, and sending reluctant drivers to parking zones miles away with firm waves of the hand. Came our turn and I resigned myself to the prospect of trudging all the way back to State Street—we were so close, the music was hitting us, and revellers were spilling over to where we were.

The cop at the barrier put up his hand. Now Boy Scout stuck his head out the window and waved the bag of chips at him. 'Say, sir... George, the manager of the University Inn... he told me that if I brought him a bag of chips, he'd let us park in their lot by State. Can we go?'

Cop: You can't be serious.

Boy Scout: I am. Is what he said. "Bring a bag of chips and I'll let you park in my lot."

The cop started laughing. He couldn't believe what he was doing, but waved us through, still laughing and saying, 'There's another barrier up ahead, don't know if what you just pulled will work there.'

'It's the truth,' Boy Scout said evenly, his bag of chips ready for the next cop. It wasn't necessary. A quick right, and we were at the University Inn parking lot. George was waiting at the steps for his bag of chips. Boy Scout was telling the truth all along.

We made our way on to State Street through a labyrinth of passages in the University Inn that led to a Lebanese restaurant which opened on to the street. Although the restaurant was shut, George had the staff let us out, to mingle with the other animals. Among them were:

Roman noblemen, adjusting their wreaths
Legionaries, swords out of their sheaths
Half-naked women, in their knickers
Half-naked men, city slickers
Miss Alaska (the winner)
Miss Alaska (the runner-up)
Skulls without bodies
Heads of state
Believers, predicting Doomsday
On a slate
Gas-masked girls and astronauts
Men entertaining evil thoughts
Women in heat, courting arrest
Pleading with cops to cuff their breasts

Witches, one of whom lost her chin,
Sticking her nose in a man of tin
Batman, Spiderman, jokers
Uncle Sam, bankrupt brokers
Terrorists, Bushes, shrubs
The entire cast of Scrubs
And every known species of ghoul
Haggling with Satan, looking cool.

At dawn, having successfully given Valdez the slip, I folded my shawl and slept blissfully in the warmth of the house. Next stop: Chicago—for the big day.

✧ ✧ ✧

When I arrived in the States, back in September, my first stop was at my friend Bamby's. Bamby has a very large head, most of it occupied by a sparkling brain. He is a game theorist who now teaches in Canada. But the thing with academic life is that you can travel to, say, Chicago, to 'think'. Bamby was invited to Northwestern University, on the outskirts of Chicago, to do this. I had asked if I could come and spend a few days with him. He was staying on campus, at Garrett Theological Seminary, which looked like a church.

He wrote: 'Must warn you, very spartan acco: no AC, bed+desk+linen+dorm bathroom.'

This sounded perfect.

When I met him, he was primarily occupied with who would win the election. (When I had met him earlier in May, he was primarily occupied with who would win the primaries.) By the beginning of November, Bamby had taken to checking the betting site Intrade.com to find what the odds were on candidates who might carry Virginia and so forth, approximately every 45 minutes. ('The market always knows.')

Chicago was going to be a party. My sister flew in from Dallas, and we ditched the seminary to stay close to Grant Park. On Big Tuesday, I was stuck to the telly in the morning. Obama himself was voting, accompanied by his wife, Michelle, in a Chicago booth. On Monday, Madelyn Dunham, Obama's grandmother and the greatest anchor of his formative years, had passed away at 86. Even through this loss, the future president was able to look ahead. Late on Monday night, he had just one word for his audience at his last campaign rally in Manassas, Virginia: 'Tomorrow'.

Tomorrow had come. He was voting for himself. Taking an incredibly long time to fill up the ballot. If everyone took this long (about 10 minutes at the very least), a lot of people would be left standing.

Joe Biden, who the Democratic campaign made sure would vote in Delaware right after the Obamas finished in Chicago—when airtime freed up—got the job done real quick. For those standing in queues in booths around the country, this was more like the required speed. Some of them came to vote as early as 5.30 in the morning, spending an acceptable hour and a half to complete voting.

The polls all had Obama ahead—solid leads beyond margins of error that would result in a resounding victory, of the kind no one thought possible when he entered the race for the Democratic nomination so many months ago.

He'd done it in style.

When he stood up to give speeches, he seemed to read poetry. When he sat down to listen—to opponents in a debate, for instance—he looked like a languid jazz musician who'd set his instrument down, but was primed to pick it up and answer with notes so precise, they had to be mathematical.

The economic crisis and a bungling McCain campaign had helped him. But most of all, it was the Bush years. A large number of Americans didn't like the selfish, arrogant, consumptive, overweight—and now poor—person they saw in the mirror the world held up to them. They viewed this election as a chance to correct that.

In a personal battle, Obama had outlasted the Clintons. He'd also outspent them—which tells you what a strong idea he was selling. 'Not a red America or a blue America, but a United States of America.'

As Grant Park readied itself, you could see all of America's colours in the faces queuing up that morning. All the 'mixtures' possible, I was thinking...

So, on a November day so perfect that many were reading it as 'a sign', there were picnics to be had while waiting on the sidewalk outside Grant Park, T-shirts and new-age 'high definition' Obama buttons to be bought. The buttons were just like regular ones, except they were like Obama's message, according to the seller: sharper, clearer (and dearer).

✧ ✧ ✧

A REPORT

Grant Park, Chicago, 4 November 2008.

Just as promised, the world changed on Tuesday night. Barack Hussein Obama became president-elect of the United States. Less than two years ago, he had the wrong middle name for the job, he was of the wrong colour, and recently, it was pointed out, he had the wrong associates.

On this night, however, he was undoubtedly the right man. America voted for its first black president in a way so unequivocal that the world celebrated as it watched him ascend the stage in Grant Park, at the heart of Chicago, to accept his prize.

On Michigan Avenue, at the entrance of the park, they lined up from the morning. Those with tickets to one side, looking slightly privileged, with deck chairs laid out on the street and wearing sunglasses. Those without tickets, to the other side, with placards begging to be taken in as ticket-holders' guests since they had come all the way from Seattle or Selma for this.

Evening fell and the barricaded gates of Grant Park opened to let about a quarter of a million people in; others watched from tall tinted-glass towers. Everyone straining to find out from the big screen, or a neighbour, whether Ohio had been carried or if Florida had failed them.

But within three hours of the gates opening at 8 p.m., it was over. Ohio, Florida, Virginia, Pennsylvania—Obama had prevailed everywhere. The TV stations announced the winner.

People held their heads in disbelief. The audience, even those without the additional tear glands that Oprah Winfrey possesses, cried, hugged and whooped. The whooping did not stop for hours after Barack had come, seen and conquered (yet again). Tears rolled down Jesse Jackson's face. Jackson had wanted to be president (twice) as well. But he couldn't get the Democratic nomination because the wisdom of the time was that whites wouldn't vote for a black man. Twenty years after Jackson's second bid for a Democratic nomination, Obama was delivering his victory speech on the colour blindness of hope and aspiration.

McCain had just made his classy concession. If Obama placed the credit of victory at the feet of the electorate, McCain said the burden of loss was his and no one else's to bear. For a brief while, the power of the old man's words, spoken from a lectern in Arizona to an audience that was in despair, quietened the crowd in Grant Park. And then, Obama appeared. Presidential, even when his wife whispered 'love you' in his ear, he spoke with an awareness of both the scale and the nature of the event he was at the centre of.

'This election had many firsts and many stories that will be told for generations...' he said, going into an anecdote about a 106-year-old black woman who had stood in line to vote for him. 'Tonight, I think about all that she's seen throughout her century in America—the heartache and the hope; the struggle and the progress; the times we were told that we can't; and the people who pressed on with that American creed: Yes we can.'

He had pressed the button. That creed, or variants like 'yes we did', kept resonating through the streets of Chicago. Interspersed with cathartic whoops (mixtures of joy and bewilderment, though you couldn't tell in what proportion) from wave upon wave of supporters. There was no point trying to speak out a solicitation in the din, so the figure crouched on the pavement across the park, as swarms of people passed, merely held up a placard: 'I'm just hungry and homeless.'

—www.avirooksen.com

At two in the morning, the *Chicago Tribune* arrived: 'Obama Our Next President.'

❖ ❖ ❖

I have to say that while the occasion really hit me, I was underwhelmed by the speech. But the press wasn't. Obama's delivery is unerringly flawless, and his words unfailingly lyrical. But I had, for some reason, expected the speech to contain a new idea or two. I didn't find one. What I missed—and what the *New Yorker* didn't—which is why it is the *New Yorker*—were several important allusions and echoes.

Obama had returned to the 'more perfect union' theme (from the speech of his life), but his address, said the *New Yorker*, was 'written in a language with roots'. There were 'ghosts of Lincoln' and 'shades of Martin Luther King'.

The president-elect, the magazine said:

> Moved through time using an epic novelist's trick of a 'heroine as old as the century'. Ann Nixon Cooper, at the age of 106, had voted in Atlanta. Obama paused to imagine all that she had seen: woman suffrage; 'the despair in the dust bowl, and Depression across the land'; the start of the Second World War when 'bombs fell on our harbour'.
>
> Obama had Ann Nixon Cooper move through her American decades, then burst into world history: a man touched down on the moon, a wall came down in Berlin, a world was connected by our own science and imagination. And this year, in this election, she touched her finger to a screen, and cast her vote.

No argument at all about either the sweep or the beauty of the speech. And yet the part that I liked the most was his ambiguously delivered line addressed to those who didn't vote for him: 'I will be your president too.'

When I heard him say it, I cracked up because it sounded very much like a warning. For me, this was the first time he had indulged himself, taken a liberty, digressed slyly from 'the message'. He had not done this in years.

✧ ✧ ✧

On election day, the *Sports Illustrated* website put out a piece on who the candidates admired in the field of sports— people they thought were role models.

There had already been a lot of talk about Obama and his more than acceptable jump shot. Apparently, he had to shoot hoops with his future brother-in-law (a basketball coach) as a 'cool quotient' test when dating Michelle. Evidently, he passed.

There were pieces about how competitive he was on court. (Months later, I heard Obama, the smiling president, say: 'If you lose to Obama, you never hear the end of it.')

I could believe he was hungry for success at (and crazy about) basketball. What other type of person takes a delegation to the coach when he's not picked in the starting line-up? (He did this as a student in Hawaii.)

And yet, when Sports *Illustrated* asked which sportsman he looked up to, he didn't pick anyone from basketball. Wilt Chamberlain? Great as he was, Chamberlain also claimed to have slept with 20,000 women (or was it 30,000?). He wouldn't do. If you had to choose someone from outside basketball, could you ignore Muhammad Ali? The Greatest Of All Time? I do not know what Obama's personal opinions were, but Ali didn't fit 'the message'. He was, as the campaign put it, a 'radioactive black'.

Obama's choice was the bespectacled, studious-looking black Wimbledon champion Arthur Ashe. His reasons were as follows: 'I grew up without my dad in the house, and so I looked up to athletes like Arthur Ashe, whose influence went beyond sports, and who conducted himself with respect and dignity in a way that showed he cared about other people.'

As if to reinforce the 'decent family man' part of the message (therefore not an 'Arab', as McCain had pointed out earlier), Obama said his current favourite athlete was his soccer-playing daughter Malia. 'There is no place I'd rather be on a fall night than sitting in a folding chair watching Malia's team in action.'

I later ran Obama's choice by a man who reminded me of him. He, too, lived in Chicago's Hyde Park—the one neighbourhood in the US that can pride itself on being genuinely integrated. Hyde Park is the 'anti-ghetto'. Where middle-class blacks, focused on their careers and the education of their children, live alongside whites in large numbers.

This man, too, had dabbled in politics for a while, working at the mayor's office in Chicago—until he got disillusioned and took up a career being, as he liked to call it, 'Train Daddy'. He was probably the most intelligent, articulate conductor you could hope to find on an Amtrak train. (I overheard him use the word 'cogent' while talking to an uncomprehending bartender.)

'Arthur Ashe... hmm. From that era... Ali would make the top five definitely for me. But Jim Brown. Jim Brown was probably someone who was looked at by a lot of people as very strong on the field, and equally as active in the community.'

Trouble was, Jim Brown (he was an American football legend) wouldn't do either. The stories of the orgies at his house were legendary (and were one of the key attractions of professional sports for a young Mike Tyson, who wanted the Jim Brown life as much as he wanted to be champion of the world).

Train Daddy continued, working out Obama's choice, 'Arthur Ashe... I kind of figure... very accomplished in the game of tennis and very well spoken and very well respected off the court. That I remember. I'm not a fan of the game of tennis, but that I remember.'

For the message, Ashe was just right. Grew up in Virginia during segregation. Got the chance to play tennis because his dad was the caretaker of a sporting facility (for blacks). When he lost his mother at six, he 'latched on to books and sports as a way of defining himself'. By the time he was 12, he was the Number One black kid playing tennis in the US.

Speaking to PBS's Charlie Rose in 1992, Ashe said:

> When I was 12, my coach took me over to Bird Park, which was then the white park in the city, to try to play in an official sanctioned US Tennis Association tournament. And I was turned down. We figured we would be, but we were going to test it anyway... . That I graphically remember, because there was a very kind man, his name was Sam Woods. He said, 'No, I would like to have you play, but we just can't... the laws are the way they are.'

Ashe went on to win three Grand Slam titles. And never betrayed any bitterness. Billie Jean King, the greatest woman tennis player (and a lady with an enormous conscience), once said of her contemporary, '*I'm* blacker than Arthur.'

But it wasn't as if he was like (boxer) Joe Louis—the 'good', 'obedient' black champion for the white middle class. Ashe was one of the first sportsmen to protest apartheid and got arrested for it. He suffered similarly while marching for Haitian immigrants.

When Ashe contracted AIDS, it was because of a negligent blood transfusion. Not from 'sleeping with a thousand women' as in basketball legend Magic Johnson's case. And yet, he would say that being black in America was more painful to him than AIDS—that racism was a 'struggle, 24 hours a day', even in 1992. He said this at such a perfect pitch, however, that it freaked no one out.

As a man to embed 'the message', there was no one better than Ashe. But that's not all of it. Arthur Ashe's greatest triumph was his 1975 Wimbledon title. Billed as a nearly hopeless underdog against a rampaging Jimmy Connors, Ashe had to find a way to win. Two days before the finals, Ashe and a few of his friends sat down to work out a strategy. To win, he told Charlie Rose, he had to 'take the speed off the ball. To give him a lot of junk… . The harder you hit it, the better he likes it.'

I could now see the last few months of the presidential campaign as a tennis match. A raging McCain, swinging wildly at Obama, who just wouldn't play the game and refused to throw an unplanned punch.

The second part of the Ashe strategy was, 'Keep the ball down the middle, so he can't open up the court with wide angles.' In politics, it's called sticking to the message. Hope, Change, Unity, and no more Bush, that's how Obama defined the court. The first three were so down the centre that the only response could be one of agreement. It was the fourth, however, that caused McCain the most trouble. Instead of running the race as himself, McCain spent frustrating hours on the trail trying to convince people he was not Bush.

In 2000, running against Bush for the Republican nomination, the maverick senator was at the receiving end of the worst dirty tricks that Bush's advisers could invent. There were 'robo calls' that slandered him: he had an illegitimate black child, his wife was a junkie, and so on. McCain, a man to whom honour was everything, quit that race shattered, but never responded in kind and vowed that he never would.

But in 2008, faced with what Obama was throwing at him, his team went out and employed the same company that made the calls on Bush's behalf in 2000. Now, paid for by the McCain campaign, recorded messages went out insinuating that Obama was a 'guy of the street' who used cocaine and had 'friends who had bombed the Pentagon'.

The Obama campaign condemned these tactics, but while McCain's campaign vehicle, 'Straight Talk Express', was looking for angles and short cuts, Team Obama stuck to the plan. It was becoming increasingly apparent that McCain was playing a game that he wasn't comfortable with. It followed, therefore, that he wouldn't play very well, would get more and more frustrated, and make more mistakes.

It happened to Connors at Wimbledon in 1975. The third piece of Ashe's plan 'drew Connors to the net and lobbed over his weaker two-handed backhand'. There's a certain resignation that you can see on the faces of tennis players who lose points to the lob. Well-weighted lobs drift relatively gently overhead, but just out of reach, and all you can do is watch. By 4 November, drawn to the net in fury and frustration over the previous weeks, John McCain knew the lob had been struck.

✧ ✧ ✧

In Millennium Park, amid dazzling examples of modern architectural forms (without much function), an artist was completing an Obama portrait. On another side, in a wood that blazed yellow with the maple leaves of autumn, I saw a McCain portrait as well. It was a cut-out of his head. Shaped and pasted onto a sign, so that it replaced the first 'O' of 'DOGS not allowed'. The sight of it disgusted me. No one deserved that.

Well, maybe, one or two guys... speaking of whom, there were unconfirmed reports dating back to early October 2008 that President Bush had gone missing. Some said that he was in recovery after a month of ritual spanking administered by his mother. But this, too, could not be confirmed.

But boy, was I glad to see he was safe and sound, that day when he ducked shoes at that press conference.

14

New Orleans
LOUISIANA

Nola the Schizo

When I found a gob of spit land right next to my shoe at Jackson, Mississippi, I knew whom to expect when I looked up. Winston Salem was smiling at me. I could tell that he was slightly drunk. I was pleased to meet him.

'You get around, don't you?'

'So do you, I'd say.'

We settled down in the cafeteria on the lower level of the train, sipping Jack and Pepsi. I had boarded the train at New Orleans, where I felt I had spent too little time. I say this because the part of town that I saw, the French Quarter, seemed on a different planet from the city still wading through the never-ending wake of Hurricane Katrina.

Yet every door you passed on Bourbon Street had music coming through it. People carried their drinks out—

because, as the sellers told you, 'It's okay to drink on the street.' Jazz bars advertised low cocktail prices. Strip clubs hustled people in without a cover charge. A line of cop cars stood by, but never interfered. And members of the 'party patrol' were more like walking inquiry windows for tourists seeking daiquiris and debauchery.

The revelry teetered on the edge of unruliness, but never quite tipped over. On the street, they were selling 'big ass beers' and 'real head, real pussy' if you got close enough to hear the words spoken discreetly (by the decibel standards of Bourbon Street, that is).

I was humming, 'You will never see my shade, or hear the sound of my feet, when there's a moon over Bourbon Street', even though there was no moon. Just a lot of neon signs in the shape of martini glasses, or naked women holding martini glasses.

You could never tell that the Mississippi, whose levees had been breached, turning New Orleans into a pan* of morbid gumbo bubbling with anger three years ago, was a couple of blocks from here. For that, you would have to go to ward 9 or 13, some of whose residents still believed that the embankments had been dynamited to save the French Quarter even though it meant sinking their homes. The city, I decided, was a certified schizophrenic.

But even if there were two Nolas, I'd say that they had something in common: they both played music. If there was rap coming out of the projects, there was jazz in the French Quarter. I walked down Bourbon to Preservation

* You could make a deep-dish pizza on New Orleans. Topographically, it is a pan in the embrace of the Mississippi, with the levees as its artificial edge; the French Quarter is on very high ground, relatively.

Hall on St Peter's, where, I believe, they played the best music in town.

The hall didn't look like much. You entered a corridor with the performance area immediately to the left and a courtyard at the end. The building hadn't changed substantially since 1750, even though it had been through several avatars (a home, an inn, a tavern and a photo studio). In the early 1960s, a couple—Allan and Sandra Jaffe—took it over to begin creating the institution it is today.

This little arena without a real stage, where no more than 75 people could sit/stand comfortably, had become a sanctuary for New Orleans jazz. A place that opened at eight each night, and for just three hours had music of the kind you would only hear when everyone involved in a performance *wanted* to be there: the musicians, the audience, the usher (who had the best view in Preservation Hall), even those who just peeked in, without paying the ten dollars.

On that Sunday night, the St Peter All Stars, led by the portly Dwayne Burns, were playing to a packed house. The room had very little light and no microphones. It looked like a painting out of which dark musicians popped in and out with their horns and drums and voices—sometimes mellow, at other times raunchy ('I'm your hot dog, man'), but at all times pure.

'The fuck! Is that all you did in New Orleans?' asked Winston Salem. This was approximately true. The city's (or rather the French Quarter's) other attractions had been brought to my notice almost as I landed. A young man in his twenties needed a light outside the airport and he almost fell on me asking for it, he was so pissed. He was on his way out from a bachelor party over the weekend. 'This town just kills you, man. Kills you.'

And then, to thank me for the light, cigarette between his lips, he started digging into his pockets for something. It was a discount coupon for a topless place. He couldn't find it and said, 'Anyway, go to Barely Legal, tell them you know me. They'll take care of you.' He staggered off without telling me his name.

Winston Salem was aghast at how little I had done in the Big Easy.

'I went there with *Lattrice* and I did more than that, man.'

'So you two going out?' I asked, thinking of the stunning Lattrice and how quickly the lucky bastard had moved.

'Sort of. We like went to New Orleans a week after we met… Remember I was talking about going home on the seventh?'

I did.

'Anyway, the bitch got drunk and fell asleep. So I hit a strip club. This black chick was dancing. What a piece of ass. Firm natural boobs, nipples like raisins ready to explode, no fucking stretch marks. I had to have a piece of that. So get this, I go to the fucking VIP room upstairs with her. VIP my ass, it's got a sofa and a curtain drawn across it.'

He starts laughing, looks for a place to spit, but can't since we're on the train. So he laughs a little more.

'Cost me 150 bucks, so I'm like trying to make the most of it, feeling her up, licking, sucking, and she's supposed to do the same, right? But she says she'll just play with me first. I'm like, okay. But the fuck is that I've got the stubbornest soft-on. This thing just won't fucking listen. I tell her to get down on it, but the bitch just smiles coyly at me. Then she goes, she'll do it if *I* please *her*.

'So now, *I'm* the whore. But being that nothing's fucking happening, I say okay. So get this, she stands over me and starts rubbing herself on my face, asking me to lick. But by now, my fucking mouth's gone dry!'

'So your tongue's like a hungry baby rhino's?'

'What?'

My mind had wandered off to pick abstruse images from a foreign landscape. I shook myself out of it to offer the truthful, but convoluted, explanation. In Kaziranga, Assam, I had once had my hand licked by a hungry one-horned baby rhino called Laharani who'd been rescued from a terrible flood. It was a tender moment, but the roughest, driest lick I ever received.

'And I don't know why I thought about it,' I said, after telling him the story. Winston started laughing uncontrollably, yet again. Searching for something that he could relate to a little more easily, I told him that I found it incredible that he was out of saliva, it was like Lake Michigan drying up. He laughed even harder.

'And then like she's letting out these false moans and grinding away at my fucking face, which is pinned to the back of the sofa. My tongue's so dry I can't even fucking talk and then she like says she's coming, the lying bitch. I tell her to get down, and she just about pecks my fucking soft dick and the music stops. That's like time's up, get your shit together, don't forget the rest of your *champagne*, and get the fuck out. The bitch timed it perfect.

'So now I'm thinking like should I go and wake Lattrice to do something about my shit and then I think, I fucking shouldn't give up this easy. So I walk into another bar, where, again, there's this gorgeous black bitch. And the fuck is that she genuinely likes me. She says she's getting off work and why don't we like go for coffee and talk before we get down to it. I can't believe my fucking luck. So she tells me to go quiet and wait for her at the corner of the BBC and sure enough, she comes in about ten in a fucking Corolla. I hop in and she tells me how fucking cute I am and where we might go.

'The bitch goes, "I don't usually do this... ." And I feel compelled to let her know I don't have that much cash. Like a hundred or something at best...

'She goes, "Forget the money, I don't know, I just like you. You think I'm lying? I really do, you're so cute, and young and innocent... maybe we could get something to eat now and you could buy me breakfast or something." This was fucking complicated, it was 3.30 in the morning and how the fuck would I explain to Lattrice, when she woke up, that I'd just stepped out to buy a whore breakfast?

'But I was too fucking drunk to think, so I like kept nodding yes to whatever. Then she said, "You know what, let's forget the food right now. I've got a place close by, why don' we just go there?" I couldn't believe my fucking luck. She gave me like a peck on the lips and said, "Why don't you just wait on the sidewalk here and I'll park the car and come... it's a lovely night to walk."

'It fucking wasn't. I was freezing in my jacket, but that's hindsight. I got off the car and stood on the sidewalk. Smiling, talking to my dick, which was now like a little more open to instructions. So it was 3.45 a.m., then it was four. And four-thirty. And at fucking five I realized I'd been had once again. Fucking cold, waiting for an hour and a half, and the bitch had disappeared. What kind of sicko does that to someone?'

He was laughing again. 'Never trust whores, man,' he said, still laughing. When he was done, he said he needed another drink. There was no Jim Beam seller on board, so the bar it would have to be. On Amtrak trains, the bar is usually on the lower level, to the right of narrow stairs. Access to it is partly blocked by awkwardly placed seating, but the area to the left has more room.

As Winston approached the bar, he also sensed a quarry—a young woman with a baby, who might as well have been holding a placard proclaiming 'I'm a single mom'. She was sitting there without any food or drink in front of her. She was pretty in the way that suffering makes you pretty—it shows only when you smile.

Winston saw an opportunity. He walked past her once, walked back and asked the lady if she was okay. And then said tentatively, 'Want a drink… like a Coke?'

She smiled and declined, but Winston lingered (unnecessarily) for just a few more moments. What he hadn't accounted for was a young black guy sitting right in front of the stairs. He'd had his back to the woman, but swivelled around and asked her something very quietly, on the lines of, 'Is this guy bothering you?' The two did not know each other, but it didn't matter.

Winston overheard this short exchange. He took half a step towards the bar, then turned around and came back to where we were sitting—without a drink. The young man was back in his seat, as if on guard. You had to cross him to get to the woman or turn past him to get to the stairs.

Winston went awfully quiet. I said I was going upstairs to rest. He said he was going to hang around.

On my way up, I passed the young black man. He gave me a nod and a little once over. Then both of us looked at Winston who was trapped in his seat, it seemed, until the young man chose to leave the cafeteria, or better, the train.

Winston had the look of a man who had done nothing terribly wrong, but found himself sentenced to jail by his own guilt. Separated from the very thing that he depended on so much—his brazenness, which he could now recover only at the foot of the stairs, after passing a formidable sentry.

And that was the last I saw of Winston Salem.

✧ ✧ ✧

I took the short flight of stairs to the coach and found myself in the free world. A young teacher from Jackson had the seat beside me. She was travelling to Chicago with two charges—adolescent nieces—who sat across the aisle. There was something heart-warming about the group. The girls brought out some candy and passed the packet to me. I picked out something rubbery and blue.

The teacher then reached into a large duffel bag at her feet and pulled out a ziplock packet. It contained two apples, a tomato, and little sachets of salt and pepper.

'Would you like one?' she asked.

I dislike apples, but the offer was made with a kindness that was irresistible. I picked the smaller apple. The teacher then brought out a bottle of Germ-X, sanitized her hands, bit into the tomato just enough to create a secure landing area for the salt and pepper she dusted over it, and then took a larger bite. The whole dish, placed on a white paper napkin, looked delicious.

Across the aisle, the children were feeling hungry. I suspect that this had less to do with hunger than the fact that they had seen people eating at the inviting, neatly laid-out tables of the dining car.

'You want some chicken?' (There was home-cooked fried chicken, carefully wrapped in foil, in that duffel bag.) The girls said they didn't. I wondered whether they'd be an apple short because of me.

'Well, you're welcome to some of the tomato, provided you clean your hands.' And then to me, 'We carried our own food when we were told the prices on the train.'

'It's not very exciting anyway,' I said, knowledgeably. My Amtrak diet usually comprised microwaved spicy wings or a burger. Totally vile.

'What about in the dining car?'

'The food's not that great there either.'

'And is it expensive?'

'For what it is, I guess it is expensive. I had a steak once and it tasted like it had just been brought out of the refrigerator and heated. I think it was 22 bucks.'

'Wow. Was it big?'

Something in that question sounded incredibly sweet to me. I could almost visualize my friend the schoolteacher taking her wards to the dining car for a little treat, having checked that the steak was big enough to share.

I had seen another version of this sensibility that morning. At a convenience store across the street from the New Orleans Amtrak station, where they sold everything from liquor to lunch, I saw a man place an order for some chicken and pork stew to go. The server was about to shut the boxes and hand them over when the man said, 'Fill them up some... Iss for me and ma boy, he's 12.'

Came my turn, I wanted less than the allotted quota. 'I can't eat that much.' (This was true. If I order a full meal in the US, I can never get through it.) The lady looked at me in a strange way, almost as if it was a first. It might have been in that neighbourhood. She smiled and made the adjustment.

Neither the pork stew man nor my travelling companion was poor. All they really wanted was for the children to get the fullest value for the dollar they spent. Like parents and guardians from the middle and lower-middle classes everywhere in the world, I guess.

In retrospect, I wonder if this thought was merely trite, perhaps even sentimental. But its visual associations—the man wanting the boxes open till they were a little more full, the teacher mentally sizing up the 22-dollar steak—always make me feel that I'm leaching a bit of cynicism, getting rid of some of the vast quantities of toxins that reside in me. I can almost feel it collect at my feet.

Somewhere after Greenwood, Mississippi, an argument broke out between the conductors and a lady sitting a few rows ahead of us. The cause was this: the conductors were overcrowding our coach with passengers, while two other cars on the train hardly had any people in them.

I've spoken about individual Amtrak staff before, the unforgettable Mr Suction included. By and large they are a really good lot. Some of them, like Cherie Hanks from Salt Lake City, or 'Train Daddy', the semi-politician who used to work at the mayor's office in Chicago, are really sharp, well-travelled people. However, like in every profession, there's another (large) set. On the train, this type moves and works at a lumbering pace that is in consonance with the railroad company's promotion policy. (Some might appear really busy, rushing up and down the coaches randomly, like particles in Brownian motion, but the key word is 'appear'). This type will consistently try and make *his* job more convenient, in a way that almost always makes the passenger's journey less comfortable.

To rationalize seating and spread out a crowd on a train is really not that complicated; neither is it that difficult to reassign a seat if one is available. But no, they will not do it—and they will tell you that they will not do it, often quite rudely. As they did to the (to be fair) combative lady in front of us.

The lady wouldn't back off, so the boss conductor was called in. He was a white man who knew the rules and spat them out to the black lady, ending with: 'We know our job and we do it really well.' But there was something in his tone—he was talking down to her—that made the argument suddenly turn.

'Well sir, when you look around this car, what do you see?' the lady asked.

Slightly thrown by the question, the boss replied, 'I see passengers.'

'I think you see more than passengers.'

Now the man turned red. 'I don't know what you mean.'

There no escaping what the lady meant. If you looked around the coach, you could hardly spot a white face. This was happening two weeks after the Barack era had unofficially begun. It was a trivial, completely unrelated incident, which, nevertheless, I could not separate from the grand events in Chicago on 4 November.

The conductor left—without making any concessions to the lady, who kept murmuring that his behaviour was racist. A number of other ladies on the carriage went, 'Mmmm-hmmm'. This was a standard, if somewhat ambiguous, Southern exclamation that I found musical and interesting. It is expressed without opening the mouth (unlike the uhh-hmm). And, once you reach the 'h', there's a subtle pursing of the lips, tightening of the jaw, and through slightly flared nostrils, the exhalation of a note that could mean: Yes; okay; I understand; I agree; I wonder; and everything in between.

I began to my companion, 'The lady's really upset, you think it's a rac…?'

'Mmmm-hmmm.'

I never figured out exactly what she meant. But the lady in front kept muttering that she was going to take the matter further; that things needed to *change*.

❖   ❖   ❖

Before getting on the train that morning, I had decided to take a longish walk around New Orleans. And whom did I meet once I was past a drowsy, hung-over, trashed Bourbon Street? The guy who was selling 'big ass beers', of course. He looked fresh and ready to go, even though he was homeless and was renting a bed for six hours a day. He said he'd give me a little tour 'for my safety'. It was ten in the morning.

We saw the usual touristy things: the river, that seemed safe, but just; the horse-drawn tourist traps; street musicians making an early start.... And beyond the portico of the luxury condos at 1201 Canal Street ($159,000 to a million and a half; 80% sold), which the promoters said would herald a renaissance, we saw the footprints of Katrina.

Right behind the now repurposed historic building—it used to be the upscale Krauss Department Store—was a project where some kids were hanging out, carrying speakers. I wanted to talk to them, just ask what they were listening to, whether they went to school...

'We need to turn here. If them see that bag, one o' them'll just grab it and run,' said my guide.

New Orleans' reputation as a dangerous place predates Katrina. In the early 1990s it had become the murder capital of the United States, a reputation it is fast recovering from. (In a video on YouTube, a local blamed the guys called Smith, Wesson, Glock, Colt and others for this.)

The population of New Orleans is about two-thirds of its half-a-million pre-Katrina levels. I suspect it hollowed out from the middle. The rich and the poor have stayed— the rich because property prices fell with the flight, the poor because they had nowhere else to go. Everybody else left. The town's schizophrenia had thus become more acute.

But property developers are optimistic, hence the condos. Donald Trump has invested substantially. And through the housing collapse, New Orleans held on to values better than most cities.

It's unfair to say everyone's in it for the cash. By Christmas 2008, a number of families would have moved into homes being built by a foundation backed by Brad Pitt (they had targeted 150 homes).

Big Ass Beers and I passed Duncan Plaza, the park where thousands of Katrina victims took refuge. I asked him the 'what was it like?' question.

'I thought we was in a war,' he said. The storm had a pane-shattering sonic boom of a 'thousand fighter jets'. But there were no jets—not right away, at any rate. There was no food at the convention centre downtown where people had sought shelter for five days. The Bush administration, which had gone looking for imagined weapons of mass destruction so promptly across continents and seas, couldn't see one when it hit them in the face. New Orleans will never forgive the man.

'Duncan Plaza is Closed' said a sign, defaced to include a scrawled summary of the current situation in New Orleans: 'So we can ignore the homeless.' We went past a bus stop peopled by some who were waiting for a bus and some who were just waiting. I thought of Toledo.

15

Saginaw
Detroit
MICHIGAN

Burning Issues in Michigan

It is a long way up from New Orleans to Michigan—the length of the United States. I was to swing north of Toledo on my way to Detroit, getting off at Dearborn, thanks to a man who I could swear was Borat's twin. He and I just about made our connection at Washington DC's Union station, where I saw him run, bags flying all over the place, in his brown suit—his back freakishly straight, lifting his knees up to make a right angle every time, and saying two words: 'Michigan, Michigan'.

On the train, he said, 'No more train.' He was from Yemen, where his family owned hospitals. Here, he ran a gas station. He had very little English, but had mastered a few keywords in the right accent: 'Wassup?', 'Fuck', 'Michigan', and 'Dearborn' (where he lived). With this he had got by well enough over the last three years to be thinking of buying a second gas station, even though he was throwing people a little on the train by speaking to his family in Arabic.

I asked him how far my hotel was from the station and got: 'Wassup. Dearborn. Dearborn.'

I checked online and found that the hotel was indeed closer to Dearborn, headquarters of Ford, than to downtown Detroit. So there I was, the cold front upon me, outside Dearborn station. It was a miserable night, but tomorrow would be gloomier—it had been that way for decades in these parts.

The next morning, at the Renaissance Centre downtown, the formidable group of pillar-shaped buildings that house the headquarters of General Motors (GM), I heard someone say that the place had been burgled. Who would think of robbing the bankrupt?

'Down in the food court. Broke the register at Subway and Burger King.'

'Black guy? White guy?'

'White guy. No one's seen him before.'

It was probably just someone who thought he should take what he could get while it was there, I was thinking, as a tour guide explained the technology and cost (several million dollars) involved in the incandescent, circular jogging track within the building.

From the track's edge you could see shining old models of Corvettes and Bel Airs displayed in a circle. There was a hoarding that said: 'There are many roads to the future.' (It was safe and high, preventing vandals from adding something like: 'We chose the dead end.')

Now there was one road to the future and it led first to Washington.

Washington had a couple of months earlier bailed out banks and financial institutions with $700 billion and was now weighing the question of whether to give the Detroit 3 (GM, Chrysler and Ford) a $25 billion loan rather more seriously.

The 'main street' bailout was over real quick. No one told, say, AIG how to use the money it was given. From all accounts, it was a little like burning currency to heat the house. The bailout was supposed to (eventually) ensure that people got credit with which they could refinance their homes or perhaps buy cars and drive down main street, but there was little evidence that any of that was happening three months after the money disappeared.

With even fewer people buying cars, the automakers headed to Washington with their begging bowls. The big news which came out of that meeting was that the three Detroit bosses (Rick Wagoner of GM, Alan Mulally of Ford and Bob Nardelli of Chrysler) flew into Washington in their individual jets. A trip that cost their near-bankrupt companies $20,000 each.

This public relations disaster almost overshadowed the fact that the flying mendicants didn't have any case to make, or plan to present, and seemed to keep repeating a three-part argument: We're in trouble; it's really bad for the country; give us money.

Were they on drugs? This was not established, although Rick Wagoner did have this really weird tick, blinking and winking all the time and groping for words, which reminded me of the 1972 presidential hopeful Ed Muskie's alleged ibogaine addiction.*

The tone of the meeting was set by the mode of transport used by the car company chiefs. Representative Gary Ackerman (Democrat), New York, began a discussion that would echo across America—one that I could overhear frequently at the Renaissance Centre without trying too hard. 'There's a delicious irony in seeing private luxury jets flying into Washington DC and people coming off them with tin cups in their hands,' he said.

Representative Brad Sherman (Democrat), California, weighed in, 'I'm going to ask the three executives here to raise their hand if they flew here commercial.' (Dramatic pause.)

'Let the record show no hands went up.'

'Second, I'm going ask you to raise your hand if you're planning to sell your jet now and fly back commercial.' (Dramatic pause.)

'Let the record show no hands went up.'

Various voices chimed in.

Ackerman: There's a message there. I mean, couldn't you all have downgraded to first class or jet pooled or something to get here? It could have at least sent a message that you do get it. If you're going to streamline your companies, where does it start?

Representative Peter Roskam (Republican), Illinois: The symbolism of the private jets is difficult. You know you're talking to people that are schlepping back and forth, going through all the drama in the airports every day, along with

* Alleged, and described *only* by Hunter S. Thompson in *Fear and Loathing in Las Vegas*.

the American public. My suggestion is that those types of symbolic things, they really matter.

Representative Michael Capuano (Democrat), Massachusetts: My fear is that you're going to take this money and continue the same stupid decisions you have made for 25 years.

This wouldn't have been the script the automakers wanted. They'd seen a much bigger deal swung by the financial sector a few months previously with an equally naive pitch—and some of them, like the guys at AIG, were spending that money on spa treatments in holiday resorts.

However, now that Washington had seen $700 billion of taxpayers' money evaporate and no sign of the hoped for credit rain, they had wisened up. Suddenly, senators and congressmen wanted facts, figures, explanations, commitments, compromises—but most of all, a protection of constituents. That is really what all the quibbling was about.

Some of the facts of the automakers' case spoke for themselves. Three million jobs would be lost, directly and indirectly, if this engine of America shut down. And in some way, the American spirit would die if they stopped doing things with their hands—like making cars. They were asking for a $25 billion loan to see them through till the new financial year in spite of the following realities:

- In early December 2008, if someone wanted to buy all of the big three, it would have cost under $6 billion. That was all they were worth (Toyota's value: $130 billion).
- They spent about $5 billion combined every *month* just to keep the business going, and were asking for the loan to do precisely this.

- Through hard-fought battles in the past, the auto workers' unions had won not just higher wages (supporters said that they earned only $28 an hour, opponents said $65, an irreconcilable gap) but also benefits like getting 95% of their pay for the years they had been laid off—until they got their jobs back. In the interim, they went to the plant and played video games as some poor sod in Mexico did their job for $2 an hour.

- Chrysler, or at least the company that held 80% of its stock, had pots of money. But it wasn't willing to put another dime into the business, much like a father who cuts off the prodigal son.

Alan Geisler of Dearborn knew all of this and more. He had a jig and fixture business. Nuts and bolts, basically, but he also sold tools like ratchets and wrenches that kept cars running and assembly lines moving. He shut it down a few years ago, probably just in time, because he saw what was coming.

Geisler said, 'If you were an exhibitor at Cobo Hall downtown and you had a display booth, and you were moving materials into your booth, the union contract said that those materials had to come in with a union person doing it, if it was anything beyond a simple briefcase. I could not plug a machine into a wall without a union electrician who had to come and pick up the plug and put it in the wall.

'This was affordable as long as Detroit was selling cars. And that got to be the problem—we were selling cars and people were buying them and as long as they were buying them, this was the cost of your doing business....'

'Why do you think Detroit stopped selling cars?' I asked.

'It's very complicated, government-made mandates, you know—pollution standards, gasoline prices... if you're making SUVs and gasoline prices go up, nobody wants to buy an SUV. The people are scared by the media that it's going to get worse, and they stop buying SUVs,' said Geisler.

'Why keep building them in that case?' I asked him. Most of America's fuel supplies come from Canada, but there was an unavoidable dependence on oil from the Gulf countries. Even as we were speaking, crude oil prices were in free fall. Whereas gas was nearly $5 a gallon in parts of the country in May and June 2008, it was now down to a dollar and a half, with some people predicting a dollar a gallon in the near future. Pretty sweet if you had an SUV.

'But didn't the auto companies see that oil was, after all, a finite resource?'

'Well, yeah eventually we will run out... but we've got enough reserves till alternatives become feasible.'

I had to ask, 'So to stretch that time out, don't you need fewer SUVs and more small cars? But it's not American, is it, to have a small car?'

'No. Or be told what you have to do.'

We were speaking at the Ford Museum in Detroit, where the spirit of this thought had been captured on T-shirts at the souvenir store. Henry Ford had once said that the customer could have any colour Model-T he wanted 'so long as it was black'.*

---

* Although it appears in Ford's autobiography, *My Life and Work*, there is still a dispute whether he actually ever said it.

How things had changed. Now, the auto companies were about to get a car czar along with the loan—a government appointee who would tell them what to do.

It was as if they were going to be building Ladas, that unfortunate poster-child of Soviet automotive achievement, butt of American jokes from the good old days such as: 'How do you increase the value of a Lada? Fill up the tank.'

A part of America would rather go bankrupt than be thus humiliated. Geisler was one of those Americans. For him, the free market would eventually solve the problem, because socialism and its economics had failed time and again.

I pointed out that the free market had just pronounced its verdict on Detroit....

'In a way... yes.'

'So why is it that Detroit now wants intervention from the government?'

'There was a cartoon in our paper that showed a man in a park about to feed a pigeon a piece of bread and it was labelled "money"... and before he knew it, they were all over him! When the government starts giving out money, people will line up with their hands out.

'Our own Mitt Romney, who ran for president, said, "Let the Detroit auto industry go bankrupt." That's hard for me to say, living here in Detroit. But you know, look at the buggy whip industry, you have to face the times. Detroit is very tied to the auto industry and for a while it worked and now it's not working. You've got to move on.'

But move on to what? Everything, from the hot dog stand to the hotel, depended on car sales. There were no ready answers, only a faith in 'the system'. Geisler's education as a student of history and American politics—specializing in eighteenth and nineteenth century events and the Constitution—shaped his firm views on freedom and small government. He was a Reagan fan: 'Reagan had said when government grows, liberty shrinks.'

'Haven't the Bush years seen a conservative government that has been the largest and most profligate government in the history of the United States?'

'No, not true.'

I was thinking he was about to dive into his archives and bring something up that I wasn't aware of, but he made a completely different point.

'George Bush is not a conservative. He's a Republican. The two terms are not synonymous. The last conservative president we had was Ronald Reagan. You could come back at me and say that government spending went up in his time as well, but he had to deal with a Democratic Congress.'

'So George Bush is a religious conservative but a fiscal liberal? That sounds about right?'

'Well, not liberal, they try and use the word "moderate". Republicans today are just, in my opinion, Democrat "lite". Democrats want big government. The modern Republican Party wants not quite so big a government.'

So the automakers would get their bailout—if not quite such a big bailout—and government would take the wheel. That was what became apparent as the auto bosses headed for Washington yet again in early December 2008, their mode of transportation closely watched.

This time, they had taken care to carpool. Congressmen perversely asked if they had driven, or someone drove them.

All of them had driven. Nardelli, the man who took a $210 million severance package to quit Home Depot (his term there saw growth shrink dramatically) gave additional facts, such as he and his companions drove till midnight and then were up at 5 a.m. again to make this journey from Detroit. Heart wrenching stuff.

To be fair, they made a far better case than on the previous occasion. And Congress was generally all praise for them—relative to their discovered loathing of financial market bosses. There were compromises on the table. Ron Gettelfinger, president of the United Auto Workers (UAW), which held so firm behind the Obama ticket, was lauded repeatedly by (Democrat) congressmen who felt the union had made its sacrifices—workers had accepted lower pay, layoffs and fewer benefits.

The time came for executive compensation. This was a hot topic right after the first meeting—why should the chairman of GM take home $2.2 million ($15 million, according to Michael Moore, the not 100% credible film-maker and auto-child from Flint, Michigan) while he presides over a $39 billion loss?

It was suggested that the chiefs get paid a dollar a year. ('They mean each?' cried Jon Stewart on the *Daily Show*, saying he was keeping his dollar). Wagoner (whose tick had worsened dramatically during his second interrogation in Washington) and the others agreed to this, but were still denied the perks of martyrdom. Not much was made of their sacrifice.

A couple of weeks previously, Wagoner had told the *Detroit Free Press* that he wasn't sure about the proposed one-dollar salary: 'I have a son in college.'

✧ ✧ ✧

Broke and desperate, Detroit hangs on. You can see it in the buildings downtown. If a window isn't boarded, it's broken so you see the hollow core behind. On the walls there's graffiti at unlikely heights and angles—as if the artist wanted to fall to his death while performing his art.

The 'people mover' train, downtown Detroit's concession to mass transport, takes you in a circle around and into the buildings. On this day there are six people in the car. At least one of them is insane. He has got into the train having stepped in shit, it's all over his shoes and rims the bottom of his jeans. He keeps looking to see if it's all there. The rest of us try and look out, but the windows are sealed. We get off the train avoiding his footprints.

The magnificent former train station gets hit by the snow. It looks like a ragged beggar with holes in his coat. In the cold, windy streets, everyone looks suspicious—hunched, with their heads covered, so you can barely see their eyes. It's tough to reconcile all this with the Christmas tree on display at General Motors. But GM headquarters does look like a colony of chimneys, and who knows, Santa might come.

Even the casinos aren't making it. Detroit had three. One of them claims it's going bankrupt. A man who works in an addiction centre tells me a ridiculous little factoid that the county has only 10 registered gambling addicts. He is on his way to one of the casinos. He had received a promotional offer from one of them—coupons for $20. 'Twenty bucks of theirs... 20 of mine, who knows?'

Across the river is Windsor, Canada, where the guys who own Caesar's Palace have a seemingly vibrant gambling house going. Looks like it from this side, anyway.

Detroit wasn't always like this. Everyone here knows that, and they grit their teeth in frustration about it. There was a time when it did exactly what it pleased and people loved it. Henry Ford wanted an airplane that would fit in his office and he got the *Flivver*. In the 1930s *The Detroit News* was taking aerial pictures in an airborne jalopy, when such images would have looked incredible and marvellous.*

Long before management gurus made the word 'workflow' popular, Detroit had perfected assembly line production. Not just cars, the town even built a 'hit factory'. In 1959, just three years before Ford rolled out the Mustang and invented the 'sports car', a Korean war vet and former featherweight boxer called Berry Gordy started a record company called Tamla Records, later to become Motown Records.

Gordy had a job in the assembly line at Ford's Lincoln-Mercury plant and once said, 'My own dream for a hit factory was shaped by principles I learned on the Lincoln-Mercury assembly line. At the plant, cars started out as just a frame, pulled along on conveyor belts until they emerged at the end of the line—spanking brand-new cars rolling off the line. I wanted the same concept for my company, only with artists and songs and records. I wanted a place where a kid off the street could walk in one door an unknown and come out another a recording artist...a star!'

This highly improbable business model proved so successful that by early 1960s Motown had become the

* The autogyro wasn't an American invention; the point is that a newspaper was adventurous enough to experiment with aerial photography.

largest independent label in the country and Gordy, the owner of the country's most successful black-owned business. The Motown sound was a mixture of soul and pop that had a long love affair with the charts. Long enough for Motown to be rechristened 'Hitsville'. Smokey Robinson, Marvin Gaye, Stevie Wonder, Diana Ross, Lionel Richie, the list of Motown legends is a long one.

But this assembly line moved to California in the early 1970s and was eventually sold. This was about the time that the automakers who inspired Gordy were moving their production elsewhere and cutting jobs at home. Detroit's music was dying, and no one was listening.

❖ ❖ ❖

There were several songs that played in my head as I planned this trip. None more than *America* (Simon and Garfunkel, 1972). The fact that it took the songwriter four days to hitch-hike from Saginaw to Pittsburgh made me want to give at least the bus ride to Saginaw a shot.

The song suggested very little traffic between Saginaw and the rest of the world (in the desperation index, Saginaw is higher than Flint, which is higher than Detroit) but trust Indians to get everywhere. A group of Indian doctors chasing the American dream from places as far apart as Aligarh and Visakhapatnam had converged in the region. They were looking for permanent jobs at hospitals in places like Flint, and yes, Saginaw, having taken buses from Buffalo and Boston.

The young doctors were somewhat relieved that I wasn't an applicant. There are about 2,000 applications received for each of these gigs (the pay is $45,000 a year), and one less always helps. But they were concerned about me: 'So you are... just travelling and writing? What do you do?'

Since some of them were headed for Saginaw, I asked if they had heard of Paul Simon or *America*. None of them had. They knew Greyhound well enough, however. It was how they were destined to get around until a hospital gave them a permanent white overcoat.

Saginaw looked like it was wearing one that night. The few people who got off at the stop fled the light snow in a hurry. The Greyhound bus stop in most towns is not where you want to be longer than necessary. In Saginaw, in late November, after dark, even less.

Dineshbhai of the Budget Inn motel was kind enough to pick me up. By night, his place seemed spacious and empty, but warm. The vacancy sign kept blinking its reassurance. His wife watched a Hindi soap as he showed me to my room before retiring. I felt comfortable, even though I had no idea where I was.

I was watching the endless discussions on what to do with the Detroit 3 well past midnight when the sound of feet on the balcony began bothering me. A shuffle, a run just after, a period of silence and then the whole thing over again in a random order, repeatedly.

At about 2.30 a.m. there was a persistent knocking next door, which I had thought was unoccupied. It grew louder and then there was a long pause, as if the visitor was contemplating his next move. And then it came—a knock on my door.

I froze. Watching the door, I hesitantly enquired, 'Dineshbhai?' He was the only man I knew in town who had a reason to knock on my door. There was no answer, just more knocking.

I went to the window, drew the curtain slowly, and the negative space of two missing teeth drew itself towards the glass. It was a woman in her forties—her face the colour of expired talcum powder, with light eyes to go, and faded orange dye in her hair—working the night under a thick jacket in the dim light of the Budget Inn.

She said something unintelligible and then extended another toothless invitation—to herself—to come into my room. From behind the window, I shook my horrified head so vigorously that I thought it probably scared her. I drew the curtain and waited. There was another tentative knock, and then the sound of footsteps down the metal staircase to the parking lot.

In a few minutes, there were police cars in the lot. They lit the curtains in flashing red. There was a muffled announcement on a megaphone. And then, for some reason, loud music from a car stereo. From behind the safety of my curtain, I peeped out at the parking lot and found that the only car with life in it—the only place the music could be coming from—was the cop car.

What kind of town was this?

I called Dineshbhai and related the incidents of the past 20 minutes. He said, 'Okay.'

'Okay? What do you mean okay?'

'Okay.'

It wasn't the prospect of such a night, or some 40-year-old hitch-hiking song, that had brought me to Saginaw. The town's story had moved on from there. I was there because

Saginaw was the most flammable town in the US, and I wanted to know why.

For a town its size, Saginaw had no business having 40 cases of arson on a single night. Which is what happened on 30–31 October 2006. This 'Devil's Night' ritual had become a Halloween tradition of sorts by that year. As if the dying town was lighting flares once a year, sending out some kind of SOS.

The real explanation for the fires would reveal itself to me the next morning. It was far more mundane. First, the town was full of abandoned homes—people had left when their jobs disappeared. These houses were ripe for burning if you wanted to gut something but didn't necessarily intend to kill anyone. And second, according to Gregory Barton who was fire marshal of Saginaw for a time, you got away with it.

Barton had been a fire fighter for 18 years and the fire marshal for two years. The glut of fires which gave Saginaw its new reputation broke out within a month of his taking up the job. I couldn't tell whether the irony that most of the arson was in the vicinity of the fire department (where we met) was lost on this sincere man. He took his job far too seriously to crack any jokes about this coincidence.

Barton cleared his throat before giving me an 'introduction' to what led to the unprecedented number of fires in 2006. 'I was made fire marshal in September 2006. 30–31 October that year was our worst ever. And there was maybe a three-month window where we had *nobody* in the department. We had no fire marshal, nobody to investigate the fires or anything like that. And somehow or other, word got out onto the street.'

The fire engines at Saginaw look in immaculate shape, sparkling red and ready to go. But if you looked around on the walls, there was evidence to support Barton's claim of neglect. Each year is marked by a large framed chart, a collection of mug shots of everyone in the fire department arranged in hierarchical rows. From the late 1990s, the picture had got progressively less crowded, even as Barton's mug had moved up. By 2006, the strength of the department was down by about a third.

'So people actually thought they were free to commit arson and there was no one going to investigate them. So no one would get caught. But we were in the process of a written test, to see who comes out number one to actually take on the assignment of fire marshal,' Barton explained.

So that was it. While arsonists plotted, choosing locations, hoarding gasoline to light up the town, those who might catch them were burning the midnight oil (unavoidable cliché) studying for a competitive exam!

There were three candidates and Barton came out tops.

'Congratulations,' I said.

'Thank you. Thank you. So anyway, like I said... that October, unfortunately, people went crazy here. Now I can attribute some of those fires to a guy... over a two-year period... he may be responsible for a hundred fires. We have some court dates with him, but I don't have a case against him for all the fires. But we know that this guy was responsible for a great number of our fires. And he was a part of the fires during that whole two-week span in 2006.'

'So was he a well-known guy?'

'No, he wasn't. Well, he was known to us. We started noticing this same guy at fires. Or he was involved in some kind of way. You know—he called it in, he tried to put it out, or something like that. We know he's responsible for a lot of them. Checking his past, we found that he had a history of fires in another state. And he had moved to Saginaw and the timing was just right for him. Being that we had no one in here.'

And so to my next question: 'How do you catch an arsonist?'

'H-o-w do you catch an ar-son-ist?' he said with a lilt. 'Well, it's multifaceted, it's like a jigsaw. First you need to have an arson…'

I thought this was pretty obvious, and Barton realized I did, and proceeded to say something quite insightful about arsonists.

'I'd put it like this, how many fires have you been a witness to?'

I didn't recall any.

'None. And in my lifetime, I've been witness to maybe one—you know, riding by at night, and saw a place on fire. In most of our daily comings and goings it's very rare that we come across fires.

'Now we got some guy, this multiple fire finder. You know nobody's that lucky to stumble into fires that often,' he said of his suspected arsonist.

'Were the fires in different areas?'

'Well, they were in the areas where *he* was, I'll put it like that. It was spread across town, wherever he was, there seemed to be something going on in that vicinity. And that's unusual.'

With the prime suspect under watch, and a robust community movement called Arson Watch in place,

Saginaw was relatively fire-free in 2008; there were just eight incidents.

As in 2007, people in a lot of neighbourhoods drove around town through the night in bright orange Arson Watch sweatshirts, looking out for suspicious activity.

I took a cab to see the sites. The cabbie drove me past the Dow Center downtown, where they kept the kids engaged with 'fun activities' so that they stayed out of trouble on Devil's Night.

The Dow Center stood tall amidst the general ruin. 'This here used to be a hotel,' said the cabbie, pointing to Dineshbhai's Budget Inn where I had spent an eventful night.

'What is it now?' I asked him.

'Just a flat joint.'

He showed me vacant lots where homes once stood. 'These streets were packed with houses when I came in the early 1970s.' And on some of the forsaken, crumbling, empty homes he showed me signs that read 'This house is being watched. And so are you!' along with a toll-free 'arson tip line'.

In the Cherry Street neighbourhood, within a mile of the fire station, you could find the signs whichever direction you looked. I was driving down the street on a day the town had a big fireworks display planned—a fourth of July type of thing—as they turned on the Christmas lights in Town Hall.

✧ ✧ ✧

Leaving Saginaw was difficult. In that sense, Paul Simon was right. An outstretched hand on I-75, or annual flares, don't necessarily do it. A bus that is an hour late is a blessing, and I am on it.

The morbidity of Michigan gets more pronounced as you drive down I-75 to Detroit. The highway is lined with abandoned houses, their disrepair made starker by the new, neat caps of November snow on their roofs. Each of those houses probably represents a lost job.

Some of those jobs went to Mexico (a country Michigan isn't exactly in love with) and Mexico in turn sent back batches of fentanyl.

Fentanyl is a more potent, deadlier version of heroin, medically used as a narcotic painkiller for cancer patients. But the imports came from a lab outside Mexico City where a 'chemist' called El Cerebro (The Brain) cooked them up before they were shipped to drug houses in the Detroit area. The drug caused 300 deaths around Detroit, about a third of the national fatalities reported in the US in an epidemic between 2005 and 2007.

On a kerbside in Pontiac I saw two people who may have just survived that wave—but only just. A man with frozen tears in his eyes was trying to collect the spilled contents of a plastic bag that probably held everything he owned. A dirty sweater, a half-eaten hot dog, two open packets of crisps, some pills, a few syringes.

His companion sat on the pavement trying to hide herself, and her plastic bag, inside her jacket. The man had done about half the work when a chilly wind rose and scattered the rest of his belongings some more. He stood up tired, sighing with frustration and swaying like a boxer up from a count—faint, confused and waiting for the punch that would end the fight.

16

Malta
MONTANA

Fargo
NORTH DAKOTA

A Triceratops in the Backyard

'Chai peeyega?'

Since it wasn't the kind of question you would expect to hear at a railway station in freezing Minnesota, I looked around to see who was asking it. In fact, the question was directed at me. Tashi Wangchuk, an Amtrak conductor who had spent a bit of time in Delhi, had figured that I might need a cup.

We talked over tea as the train scythed its way through the black-and-white night. He smiled beatifically almost all of the time, allowing himself the mischievous indiscipline of a short laugh every now and then. He was a very unusual railroad employee. There was a reason for this. Tashi had had a varied career—he had metamorphosed from Buddhist monk to train conductor.

'I was at the Buddhist centre in San Francisco. I worked there for seven years as a volunteer. We get food, soap, clothes, so we really don't have to worry. And also my monk's clothes are not that expensive, because they are not fashionable,' he said.

But the time came when he needed a job—there was a family to support in Nepal.

'I have one American friend who always tells me, "Whatever you need help, I help you." "Okay!" I say, "I need job." Then he says, "Okay, what is your education?" "Tibetan Buddhist philosophy—ha, ha, ha, ha." "What is your experience?" "Tibetan Buddhist Centre."

'I apply like three or four jobs, but I never got a call. No interview, ha, ha… that was kind of funny.'

Eventually, the Amtrak interview came along. Tashi was asked a question on the lines of 'how do you deal with people?'

His answer evidently floored the panel. He told them, 'I love to care. Some people do this for a living, some people do this for a hobby. I do for hobby, you know, for elderly, sick people; it is in my culture. I do from my heart.' This, according to Tashi, was a rare response, indeed a rare attitude in the States. Very few people wore the habit of compassion under their uniforms. Tashi was hired.

❖ ❖ ❖

'Pssst. Psssst. Check it out. Fight.'

With a prod and a whisper, my dream about kind conductors was broken around midnight. A couple across the aisle was asking me to take a look at what was going on up front. I could hear it already: 'Yeah, why don't you fuckin' snap my head off.'

'I will.'

'Yeah, snap it off. Why don't you try? Fuckin' snap my head off!'

Of all the daft things I had seen on a train, this was the daftest. A tall, well-built man had locked his arm around the neck of a shorter, terrier-like adversary who, between telling his opponent to snap his head off, was attempting to bite his arm.

Why two grown-up men were doing this to each other, no one could tell. And the ridiculous deadlock continued without any solution in sight. Everybody in the coach was woken up, but nobody moved.

Procedure was followed. The train staff quietly reported the incident to marshals at the next stop, Detroit Lakes. Fifteen minutes later, four tough officers boarded, unlocked various grips and began taking statements.

'He was trying to snap my head off.'

'He was biting me.'

The two gentlemen were taken away. Net impact: I reached Fargo, North Dakota, one unearthly hour later than scheduled; Tashi, no doubt, was busy writing to the authorities proposing free on-board Buddhist philosophy lessons.

✦ ✦ ✦

For fans of classic rock, there's a specific date when 'the music died'—3 February 1959—the day Buddy Holly died in a plane crash. He was on his way to Fargo. That the demise of rock predates the Beatles and the Rolling Stones might seem odd, but that's the way some musicians saw it. Holly was 23 when he died—but already, his influence on the future of rock was apparent.

In November 2008, *Rolling Stone* magazine put out an issue on the 100 greatest singers of all time. Holly came in at a modest 48, well behind Lennon (5), McCartney (11) and Jagger (16). But during their formative years, the 'future Beatles and Rolling Stones were... trying to capture that quintessentially American vocal sound' that only Holly possessed.

Don Mclean felt something touch him 'deep inside' when he read about the crash and wrote *American Pie* many years later, in 1971. 'February made me shiver,' he sang, 'with every paper I'd deliver/bad news on the doorstep.'

This was evocative stuff, but the unforgiving Midwestern winter had something to do with Holly's death in a very literal sense. The heating on his tour bus broke down in Iowa, his drummer got frostbite, and a frustrated Holly decided to charter a small plane to Fargo. He was due to play in its twin city, Moorhead.

I got my first taste of the nut-freezing cold the moment I got off the train. It is a malevolent, white cold. It takes over the town. Licks your face wickedly with a numbing tongue. Treacherously lays transparent sheets of ice on the roads and makes the sane pavements of summer foam at the mouth in November.

I stepped onto the streets gingerly to make my way to Broadway, where Sunday night's entertainment was 'African Soul American Heart' at the Fargo Theatre (this was *not* a biography of Obama); and an evening with 'Li'l Dave Thompson and Big Love' at the Empire Tavern.

I chose the tavern, hoping to hear people say 'yaah' like they said in *Fargo* the film, but no one spoke that way. (The Coen brothers shot *Fargo* almost entirely in Minnesota, where they don't speak that way either.)

Li'l Dave and his band arrived in a small tour bus. I asked if the heating was working. It was. Dave was from Mississippi. A blues man. Hadn't heard of Buddy Holly.

'I grew up around the blues, with the blues. My father was a musician, he played the blues. He played with a band back in the day. I grew up listening to the blues all my life. So I mean, when I learned to play the guitar, the first type of music I learned to play was the blues.' And it really didn't matter that he hadn't heard of Buddy Holly. 'There's the blues in every kind of music, man. There's the blues in a heartbeat,' he said.

The tavern filled up. But for the journeymen from Mississippi, this was another not-very-well-paying gig. Li'l Dave and his band would have to split $800. It worked out to $150 each. They put in a performance to match.

It was a trying life full of mundane concerns like getting to the next gig. 'We started out at Mississippi. We hit South Dakota coming up through Sioux Falls, coming on up to Bismarck, North Dakota, we hit Fargo. Going through North Dakota. We're gonna go down back east towards Minnesota, down to Iowa, down to Illinois and Missouri and back. It's a two-and-a-half-week tour. That's a lot of travelling...

'Some of the gigs I know about and some I don't have knowledge of... Like this place, I didn't know what to expect. Never played at Fargo. Never heard of this bar...'

'Does it pay?'

'We play gigs that pays real money, you know,' Li'l Dave said, as if by way of clarification. 'We played a gig last night, one hour set, 2,500 bucks. We play gigs, three to four thousand dollar gigs. We do festivals, like I said, three to four thousand dollars for 45 minutes. When you get five or six festivals thrown in a tour, along with some of the nightclubs that will pay something like a grand or 1,500 a night... '

'What if the audience wants more than 45 minutes?'

Li'l Dave starts rubbing his thumb against his forefinger. 'If they want more and the promoter wants the band to continue, we talk more money... I mean, we can throw in an extra tune. But if they want us to just continue another hour... half an hour, we got to talk more money. So if the promoter wants it we just say, well, what's it worth?

'There's been times when we've been playin' a gig for a thousand bucks, and they've said, "Can we get another hour?" And we say, "Sure, another five hundred bucks," or something... It depends what type of evening we'd planned for.'

But tonight, there was none of that. The band packed up as scheduled. I wished them well as they boarded their van—glad they weren't flying in this weather.

I too was leaving Fargo—on a train.

❖ ❖ ❖

'Nate Murphy told me about that,' said Dennis, talking about the time his son found a dinosaur bone. 'He told me that if you want to be sure that it's petrified bone, just touch your tongue to it and it'll stick. I mean, not real hard, but it'll stick.'

Malta, in Phillips County, Montana, is where you stumble over these things when you go for a morning walk. The Koss family, for instance, had just discovered a triceratops in their backyard (backyards can be vague and vast in Montana, but nevertheless). The Bruckners had a controversial raptor on their land. The Hammonds had a hadrosaur.

It was Nate Murphy, a man with no formal palaeontology education, who opened up this rich fossil bed. A local rancher told me, 'He showed up in town 10, maybe 15 years ago. His wife is from Malta... he was quite a promoter... he promoted many weekend events during the summer. Like they had Outlaw Days... a quick draw club... .

'Then he got to finding dinosaurs. He found them every place he looked. And then we had Dinosaur Days. He was going big guns. He was on Discovery Channel a time or two, with that guy from out west... Jack Horner.'

That 'guy from out west' was a consultant for the *Jurassic Park* films and one of the best-known palaeontologists in the world. Horner, along with Murphy and company, found wagonloads of bones and as many as nine *T. rex* skeletons around Montana. Malta's amateur bone collector had hit the big time.

Murphy was the key figure in the discovery of the world-renowned 'Leonardo', a 75-year-old duck-billed dino, so perfect that it came complete with scales and wrinkles, with the remnants of a final meal of 'conifers and magnolia-like plant material' still in its stomach. Leonardo made the covers of *Newsweek* and *National Geographic* as the best-preserved fossil ever found.

He could easily have been named 'Nate', but the credit went to the unknown vandal who had carved his name on a nearby rock. However, Nate didn't stop. He helped dig out 'Roberta' and 'Elvis' and every other fossil worth a nickname that was found in the area.

He also dug up a few he didn't tell anyone about—because dinosaur bones can be worth hundreds of thousands of dollars. And he got caught doing it. A scandal of international interest exploded in 2007 when it was discovered that Malta's Murphy had stolen a turkey-sized raptor from private land with the intention of selling replicas of it. That specimen was worth anywhere between $150,000 and $400,000.

There were more bones stolen off government land. The FBI moved in. By April 2009, after changing his story several times, Murphy had pleaded guilty to all charges.

'That's where Nate lived,' said Dennis, as we passed a neat house on the outskirts of town. 'He doesn't stay there any more. Down in Billings, I think. Waiting to be tried.' Meanwhile, the globetrotting Leonardo was on show in Houston.

And Malta? Well, everyone in Phillips County had told everyone else this story of greed and subterranean wealth, so I suspect a large number of people had taken to licking any bones they found legally.

'Does it stick?' 'No. Dead cow.' But a few hundred thousand dollars can be very tasty.

For me, the famous fossil felony wasn't the town's best crime story. Surely, a full-fledged robbery with dynamite and guns and Robert Redford and Paul Newman topped that.

❖ ❖ ❖

'The old West produced some tolerably lurid gunslingers. Their hole card was a single-action model A5 Colt, and their long suit was fanning it a split-second quicker than similarly inclined gents...'

Two of the more celebrated outlaws in American history spent a few days in the vicinity of this sign at Exeter Creek, Malta—and they were certainly not there to sing 'Raindrops keep falling on my head.'

The sign went on: 'On 3 July 1901, Kid Curry and his partners, Butch Cassidy, the Sundance Kid, and Deaf Charlie, pulled off a premature Independence Day celebration by holding up the Great Northern Railway's No. 3 passenger train and blowing up the car safe near this point. Montana's most famous train robbery netted the crooks a bag of gold coins and $40,000 in unsigned and worthless bank notes...'

The text was meant as much to inform as to dissuade people from trying to look for the money. It might have been worthless, but it was never found—a killer combo for slow-learning treasure hunters. It was rumoured that Kid Curry had buried it somewhere nearby and there was a minor rush to dig for it about a century ago—before fossils became fashionable.

Why did the 'Wild Bunch' choose Exeter Creek? The topography is nondescript—a few mounds covered by dry brown grass, a narrow creek with a little bridge over it. But in Montana, this would qualify as an area with several convenient spots to hide. Usually, the only way to conceal yourself here is to cross the horizon.

'The O'Neals lived right where the train robbery was... there's nobody left of them,' says Donnie Hould, one of

Malta's oldest and most respected ranchers, pointing to a mound where a house once stood.

These people grew up with outlaw stories. 'My grandad passed Kid Curry on the street… It was either the day of the robbery or the day prior to it. He found out who he was in about 24 hours,' says Donnie's wife Kay.

I had met Kay at the Great Plains Museum, a maze of dino skeletons and (in this season) competition Christmas trees; with Kid Curry, Butch Cassidy, the Sundance Kid and the rest of the Wild Bunch looking on from portraits on the walls.

The Malta Historical Society was meeting, but its agenda was very contemporary. A fair had been held recently, and Sharon, the curator gave an account: 'We came out with sales of $787.25. That's down by about 400 from last year. Again, I think that everything is down. The economy is really making people spend less on everything. What we noticed is that the little items sold… .'

It was the economy again. But if you asked Dennis, history could help you understand, and possibly save it.

✦ ✦ ✦

'When Lewis and Clark saw those, way over there somewhere, they thought they were lookin' on the Rocky Mountains. When they got close they realized, "No, we got a way to go yet before we get to the Rocky Mountains." '

Dennis was pointing in the direction of the Little Rockies—hills of indeterminate size that stood at an indefinite distance. In the flatness of unbounded Montana, you lose your sense of scale. There are no reference points. Things can appear smaller or bigger, further or closer than they actually are. The only thing certain is the world's biggest sky. That hadn't changed since Lewis and Clark passed this way over 200 years ago.

Dennis had picked me up at six in the morning for this drive through the prairie. The object was to see 'pure' buffalo specimens that the foundation he worked for was trying to preserve. But there was a lot more to the ride.

The previous evening at the Historical Society meeting, Dennis had suggested a GPS history hunt—which I thought was a brilliant idea. He had the coordinates of most historical sites in the area—from Indian remains of tepees (animal-skin tents) to ancient Indian grave sites, to spots on the Lewis and Clark trail—which amateur explorers could find with a simple GPS gadget.

On a dead straight road, with a blinding sun flush on our faces, forcing our eyes shut, Dennis started talking about the country he had lived in for the last three decades. The story, however, began much earlier.

'When President Jefferson bought the Louisiana Purchase, he organized this expedition (Lewis and Clark's) to go through the Missouri River. The main objective was to see if they could find a waterway all the way to the Pacific Ocean. Well, that didn't happen, but they kept very detailed records of the animals, plants, and the people and conditions, soil types, the amount of moisture…'

The Louisiana Purchase (1803) was the biggest land deal in history. For $15 million, Napoleon sold the Jefferson government a swathe of land that extended from New Orleans to Montana. Today, this accounts for about a *quarter* of the USA's territory. The trouble was, no one knew anything about the land—occupied at the time by various

Native American tribes. After Lewis and Clark, they found out what a harsh country it was.

'The people in the expedition almost died of exposure and starvation, they got to the pass at the Rockies too late in the fall. They were walking through snow several feet deep—ended up killing their horses and eatin' them.'

If it was harsh country to travel through, it was even harder to live off. The land was nowhere near as productive as in the Midwestern corn belt. In the 1920s, the government provided 160 acres to farmers who wished to settle there. This was the homestead rush—farmers flocked to Montana (and other states) to take advantage of it and become self-sufficient.

'Initially, they had several years of exceptional rainfall and they got phenomenal grain crops out of that. Everybody figured "Jeez, we're gonna get rich." So they came out here and homesteaded. Then along comes what we call the dirty '30s, the Depression, and the drought... and they left the land in droves... 160 acres just wasn't enough to provide a living for a family. And gradually, they increased it in some parts of the country to 320 acres, then maybe even up to 640 acres, which is a square mile.

'But in this country, you couldn't make a living on a square mile if your land was poor and you were limited to raising livestock. One mile is nothing for livestock.'

We passed herds of cattle quietly building reserves for the winter on the infinite prairie. Their owners had a tough life. Most operated at a 3–4% profit margin and depended on bank loans for running costs.

'To make a living, you're probably going to have to have at least 500 mother cows. When you sell a calf in the fall for the slaughterhouse, you're probably gettin' 90 cents to a dollar per pound. The slaughterhouses and the retail stores, they're the ones that really make the money...

'When it comes to roundups and brandings, you can't do it yourself. You depend on your neighbours, and they depend on you. If you got a few hundred calves to round up and brand, man, that's a lot of work.'

I could barely visualize trying to round up cattle in this terrain. Mad cows could run forever in any direction they chose.

'Every now and again you might get a herd that breaks away. But they generally cooperate pretty good. This time of the year, those cows know that "we're bein' pushed towards home for a good reason, we're gonna get fed."

'See, all these cows are pregnant. Mostly, ranchers will pregnancy test their cows in the fall. And if she's dry, she's shipped to the slaughterhouse. You just cannot afford to keep a dry cow around here. If she's not producin' a calf, she's gone.

'You have to squeeze every last drop of blood out of this country to make a living. Only the toughest have stuck around... '

I believed this completely. A tiny, solitary cottage, no more than 100 square feet, stood proud, challenging the emptiness of the great grassland. This was the Prairie Union School 1943–57. In its 15 years, nine teachers had lived and taught here; 12 students had attended. Their names were listed on a board. War memorials I had seen seemed less heroic.

At a desolate crossroad, not far from the school, there were several missing pieces on a signpost pointing in the direction of farms. Dusty Emond was still around, having diversified into wild game processing. Two branches of the Blunt family were around as well, and Carrol Ereaux. Of the dozen-odd names that used to be there, some had faded on the wooden pointers. As for the others, the pointers had fallen off. Leaving slices of sky where they used to be.

✧ ✧ ✧

Phillips County is larger than a few of the states in the east, but has just 4,500 people. Life has been tough for them, but well-intentioned government intervention has probably made it tougher. Dennis has just retired from the Bureau of Land Management and knows a bit about this.

'We have a conservation reserve program (CRP),' he tells me. 'It pays farmers to take low-producing cropland and put them back into producing grasses. It keeps the soil from washing away... the same conditions we had in the 1930s (the root of the term 'dust bowl').

'But it takes 60 acres to raise one calf for sale, and you get $500 or $600 for that calf... it just makes more sense to get, say, $30 an acre to do nothing... to just keep your grass growing.'

Sounds good, except that it has hurt the local economy— since there is no produce.

'This town no longer has a farm implement dealership. If you're just growing grass, you don't need farm implements... Now, if you have to buy a tractor, you have to go to Glasgow or Havre. We used to have a very large farm dealership here, which went out of business probably five or ten years after the CRP.'

Malta's car dealership has gone as well—and several other

stores. There just isn't enough demand to sustain businesses. And there are virtually no jobs, except at the farms.

'Our largest and best-paying industry was gold mining in the Little Rocky Mountains over there.' This would have been great for the area, were it not for the fact that the mine was also the largest cyanide-leaching gold mine in the world. There's still gold up there, but it's not economical to mine it because of a lot of environmental restrictions... That cyanide can get into water... It can pool up and kill wildlife.'

So the mine went broke. Jobs disappeared. People moved out.

There was still plenty of hardy wildlife, though. 'We got rufflin' hawks, sharp-shinned hawks, got the burrowing owls that are here during the summer months, got the short-eared owl, great horned owl, long-eared owl.' There's also the prairie dog, a destructive rodent that strips an area of all its vegetation. And, of course, there's deer.

'Deer right there, got to watch out so I don't hit one,' Dennis stops as a precious white-tail lopes across the road.

'The hunting season brings in an income to this part of the country too... They stay at the motels, eat at the restaurants, buy food at the grocery store... just another thing that kind of keeps us alive.'

✧ ✧ ✧

No one ever made an easy living off this country. For generations they tried everything, until nature or the whims of the global market stopped them.

'I read a lot of books about the mountain men, the trapping period. It's just fascinating... they came out into this country and trapped beaver,' said Dennis.

In the wilds of Montana, this was a vocation fraught with hardship, frustration and danger—a life very few men could handle. It generated a good income, according to Dennis, 'for about 20–30 years... starting 1820s or so'.

'That's when the Europeans started wearing hats made from beaver skin. And then, about the time that they were running out of beaver, the style of hats changed and the market went out of that—good thing for the beaver...

'Then the world was becoming industrialized, and they needed leather and I think in South America, which used to supply a lot of the leather requirement for belts and things to run machinery, clothing, and shoes... they were having a lot of problems with disease in their cattle.

'They were no longer able to meet the needs of the European industrialized countries, so now people started killing off the buffalo in North America. It's estimated that there were 60 million buffalo in the western United States and within about 10–15 years there were less than, I believe, a thousand... a lot of those were up in Canada.

'They're slowly coming back. The only problem is, years ago, ranchers had started crossing buffalo with domestic cattle to come up with the best breed that would survive in this country and produce the most meat. So, even though an animal may look like a buffalo, it may have cattle genes in it.'

When Dennis talks about 'buffalo', he means the American bison, which is a different species. But buffalo is what everyone calls it around here. And the general populace is not that concerned with genetic purity either.

'If you were ever to be gored by a buffalo—and survived—and you walked into a cowboy bar, you could still have bragging rights in sayin' "I got gored by a buffalo" and it wouldn't matter to anybody whether it was pure-bred or a cross with a cow!'

It matters to the Prairie Foundation, however. They have got 86 'pure' specimens, most of them brought down from Wind Cave National Park, South Dakota. (Yellowstone has some as well, but those animals are victims of a blight that causes them to abort their calves.)

When I finally found myself face-to-face with one of these animals, I noticed its imperious disinterest. A bale of hay or a spot of headbutting had far greater allure.

That, and the room to roam.

The Prairie Foundation would like to give these pure-breds two million acres—which is about 10 times the size of New York. You cannot help but think they deserve it—in the cities, species far less splendid are being bailed out.

17

Seattle
WASHINGTON

Sandpoint
IDAHO

Ghettos on the Prairie

'I'm a one-eighth. Until about five or six years ago, to be considered an Indian, you had to be a one-fourth. And you got the radicals in there… and they want the reservation to be 'pure'. Which is never going to happen—there's no full-blooded *anybody* left. Transportation's been too good for too many years!'

Bill had a 2,000-acre ranch, quite close to Malta's cursed gold mine, on an Indian reservation that had 1,200 people on it. It got tight, but he said he managed to make a living off his land. He was a Vietnam War vet. A man who liked to pay his taxes—but not so much that he would pay double. That's where the talk of his ancestry came in—a Native American great-grandparent meant some pretty sweet exemptions.

We had boarded the train at Malta in the afternoon. The train came in late—following several mile-long goods trains that rattled the windows of the abandoned offices of the station. On one side of the tracks was the Sportsman's Motel and the museum. On the other, was the town— fronted by a row of little casinos. 'This is Malta...' said Bill, talking about the lack of jobs and the propensity of those who had them to routinely play the slots at lunch hour—or any other hour.

'Private sector jobs don't exist on the reservation. Because the business climate is not very good... and one of the reasons is taxes.

'If any non-Indian businesses move to a reservation, they pay all of the taxes they would normally pay. They pay for all the services they would normally get, even though they don't get 'em. Because county, state, city governments do not go on the reservations.

'But then, they are also subject to the "right to do business"—they call them fees, the Indians don't use the word tax—they subject the same business and all the non-Indian employees to fees.

'Then there's the other fee for tribal employment rights. And that can be anything they want it to be—it's a percentage of your gross income. Lot of these businesses run 3–4% profit margins. If they want to tax it at 3–4%, there's no object in being there. So private industry on the reservations in Montana is almost non-existent.'

Bill's views weren't very popular on the reservation. And by his own admission, he had hardly endeared himself to the chiefs who ran the place.

'I was subject to all these double fees and stuff for a lot

of years. The state and the county felt they could tax me because I wasn't "enrolled" in an Indian tribe. The tribe felt it could charge me fees because I wasn't enrolled. So I fought 'em both.

'And then, about five or six years ago, and I'm not making a racial comment, they went, "Holy Christ, we're runnin' outa' Indians." They draw 98% of their budget on federal money. And they draw it on body count. So they started enrolling (the one-eighths). I say they lowered their standards!'

'How different is reservation life?' I asked.

Bill looked out the window into the grassy nothingness of Montana, spotting settlements that only he could see, and said, 'There's New Town and Rodeo Drive and Half Town. They're housing developments in the middle of nowhere with no business around them... ghettos on the prairie.

'The vast majority of the Indians that don't have jobs is by choice. There are jobs available for those who want 'em, but they're almost all government jobs.

'And the government has this idea that... say, if you got a construction job building this highway here, they pay you special wages, and it's $32 for an hour of labour. That's real good money.

'To me it makes more sense, where there's 70% unemployment, to employ twice the number of people at $16 an hour. But by law they can't...'

'How do people get by?'

'Live on welfare... I would say, probably $900 a month. But medical is free. Most of the housing is free or next to free. Commodities are provided free or greatly subsidized, food stamps and stuff. Heating, utilities, are usually subsidized.

If anyone in a household is on general assistance, it can have a free telephone—local and emergency. So the $900 is deceptive. I would say it's more like $2,500, which in this country is a pretty good job.

'I got a son. He works as a mechanic, 40 hours a week. Makes about $32,000 a year and no benefits.'

Bill pointed in the general direction of more little towns along the way. Ghettos on the prairie.

'There's Harlem. The agency is up there, but you can't see it... there's the little community of Dodson... that's the high school, the brown building right there.

'On Indian reservations, there's nothing more important than high school basketball. There's a school in Hays, big building, cost millions of dollars 30 years ago. Looks like a jailhouse with big steel bars on the windows... it'd get broke into every night otherwise.

'Hays has had a couple of state championship teams, which is a terrific feat. However, a majority of that team would not have been eligible any place but Hays.

'The last time, they kept them all eligible by putting them in alternative school. You know what that is? It's a joke. They don't even go to school. So what they do in Hays, they put them all in alternative school, they put them all in the gym and they shoot baskets. And they get passing grades.'

Bleak as this education system sounded, I found it a little less depressing than the talk of confined, welfare-funded lives that had preceded it. High school teams, however well or badly they did, at least had colourful names. These provided a welcome diversion. Malta had the Mustangs; I remembered the Atoms (well, they couldn't call themselves the 'Bombs' now, could they?) from Oak Ridge...

But the Sugarbeeters? This very well-rooted name belonged to the team from Chinook, an area where sugar beet was abundant. It was funny, nevertheless. (I mean, think of, say, the Palamu Parvals, or the Bikaner Bhujias running up and down a basketball court in India.)

Chinook had a little more history, though. 'There's the Chinook Bear Paw battlefield. It's only about 12 miles south or something. There's the museum sign right there. There are markers of who fell here, or whose tent was pitched there. It's nicely done. Not all commercialized.'

✧ ✧ ✧

Of all the stories of battles that the colonizers fought with the Indians, the story of Bear Paw is the most moving. In the late 1870s, after more than a hundred years of bloody campaigns involving hundreds of tribes, the Indian wars were drawing to a close. The colonizers were clear winners, but felt there were still a few irritants that needed removal.

The Nez Perces of Oregon, led by Chief Joseph, were one such. They were what was called 'non-treaty' Indians—those who hadn't forged any agreements with the government. But in 1877 they were asked to leave their beloved Wallowa Valley and move to a reservation so that white farmers could settle on their rich homeland.

Chief Joseph, a statesman rather than a warlord, weighed his options. But soon, the Nez Perces received an ultimatum: pack up in 30 days or it's war. The chief and his men had little choice—war was suicide. They set off towards Idaho.

But on the way, bitter and angry over the theft of their land, they killed four white men in a skirmish. This set off a chain of events typical during the Indian wars—the fighting escalated and the government called up the full might of its forces to hunt the Indians down.

What followed was a three-month chase over flats and mountains, rivers and valleys, with both hunters and quarry braving inhuman conditions. Chief Joseph's plan was to get to the safety of Canada, where his band of 800 men, women and children would be out of reach of the US forces. And where, surely, another great chief, Sitting Bull, would give them shelter.

They were cut down just 40 miles short of the border, at Bear Paw. His fallen tribesmen around him, Chief Joseph surrendered to the one-armed, Bible-carrying General Howard, saying: 'I am tired of fighting. Our chiefs are killed. Looking Glass is dead. Toohoolhoolzote is dead. The old men are all dead. He who led the young men (Chief Joseph's brother Ollokot) is dead. It is cold and we have no blankets, no food. The little children are freezing to death... I want to have time to look for my children and see how many I can find. Maybe I shall find them among the dead. Hear me, my chiefs! I am tired. My heart is sick and sad. From where the sun now stands, I will fight no more forever.'

Herded off to a reservation in strange Kansas with some surviving tribesmen, the chief spent years requesting that he be allowed to return to his valley. He wouldn't see Wallowa again. He died in 1904.

'Happened right there...' said Bill, a little wistfully. 'This is not a very popular line of thought. If they were to go back to the original treaties, the way they were written up... the reservations would have imploded in a hundred or two hundred years, the Indians would have been absorbed by society and they'd have been better off. And maybe it wouldn't be right, but where would you rather raise your family?'

What Bill referred to was the policy of forced assimilation that the United States adopted once it had successfully confined the Indians. By the mid-1880s there were reservations on 181,000 square miles of territory (about 5 per cent of the land). Administered by agents who gave the residents handouts—almost always after keeping a substantial cut for themselves.

There was a supporting cast of bureaucrats, traders, farmers, teachers and missionaries. All of them tried to wean the natives away from hunting, fishing and making war—their lifestyle—towards white goods, white crops, white books and a white God.

One commissioner of Indian affairs noted: 'To domesticate and civilize wild Indians is a noble work... to allow them to drag along... in their old superstitions, laziness and filth... would be a lasting disgrace to our government.'

Translation: 'Now that we've put the animals in a game park, let's train them for the circus.'

I was shortly to meet someone who thought exactly that way.

✧ ✧ ✧

In the viewing car, there were raucous groups of people playing a card game called Moose. An American Idol hopeful—a girl in a yellow T-shirt that was struggling to wrap itself around a waist as wide as the Missouri—was putting in a bit of practice. A pair of intellectuals discussed the fate of America under a black man. A lost gent with long hair was looking for something. And I was in the clutches of a benign evangelist trying to sell me the idea of conversion—a free Bible thrown in.

'If I gave you something, would you accept it?'

'Sure.'

Out came a copy of Gideon's Bible. 'An Australian edition. Rare. Just have one of these.'

I took it and thanked him. Then, quite without thinking, I asked, 'If I gave you the Koran, would you read it?'

'I don't need to. All I need is in that book.' He was pointing to the pocket edition he had just handed me.

He was a kind man. Large, pink and tonsured, with a full smile that revealed large, rather endearing gaps between his incisors.

I offered a mild riposte, 'So, what happened to do unto others…?'

He smiled brightly again. 'That's in the book too!'

I think he sensed the slight frustration I was feeling.

'Town of Shelby. Do you know about the town of Shelby, Montana?'

We were about to make a stop there. 'Actually, I do. It's where a Jack Dempsey fight was scheduled in the 1920s. The promoter sold tickets and ran off with the money. Large banks went down as a result…'

'You knew that?'

'Yes. It wasn't in the book you gave me, because it happened later. It was in this…' I handed him an Amtrak brochure and made for the exit quickly. I had to smoke.

Down on the platform, a man asked me for a light. I offered him my matchbox and said, 'Say, weren't you on the train a few days ago?'

'Don't even talk about it. I've been on this trip for the last five days…'

Thing is, I knew why it had taken him this long. He was hauled off the train at Detroit Lakes for an injudicious armlock. He had a black eye, which I now noticed. Suddenly, it dawned on him that I knew this. It freaked him out. He threw the matchbox back and ran off.

✧ ✧ ✧

I sat near a group of Amish when I hopped on again, partly to avoid the persistent evangelist. The Amish speak a Germanic tongue among themselves. They're one of the few early settlers who have retained their linguistic roots. You will always find them on trains, because they don't travel by motor vehicles unless absolutely necessary. They don't own cars—as a matter of faith—preferring horse buggies instead.

I had been told this, but never quite believed it. So I asked, 'Do you own a horse and buggy?'

'Oh yes,' said Andy Yoder, promptly, but casually. He was a fine gentleman from a small community in north-west Montana.

'If we start driving cars, we'll drift into the world of worldly fashions… as long as we can get by like this, we will.'

The Amish don't believe in too much education either.

'We have our own private schools and generally they go to the eighth grade, and that's as far as they go. Then they stay home and help. I got a little wood shop and a store, my children help with whatever there is to do around there.'

I thought it fascinating that kids stayed on to make or sell furniture—considering the allure of the world that they saw every day.

'A few leave, but mostly they stay. The bond is love. The family, neighbours, but love in general. From a very young child on up, we believe this and choose to stay with it. What we see on the outside doesn't really impress us. We don't really see what we gain by leaving.

'We aim to advance, but slowly… so no Internet for the kids—they can learn whatever they want from newspapers. They know what's going on. And no television. What would we want with it?

'You want to know the difference between an Amish and a non-Amish? I'll tell you the biggest difference that I know. There was some kind of a meeting—you know, different people asking questions. So this Amish man got up and said, "Everybody in this room that owns a TV raise your hand." So everybody raised their hands.

'The next question was, "Everybody that thinks they'd be better off to not have the TV raise your hands." So, kind of slowly, quite a few people raised their hands.'

I was enjoying this. I said I could understand their hesitation—even though this was only a story, the question was deep and existential.

'So the next question was, "How many are willing to get rid of it, if it's best to not have it?" Nobody raised a hand. That's the difference between an Amish and a non-Amish.

'We live kind of simple… most of our stuff is plain… you spend on all the little fancy knick-knacks. We just have a plainer lifestyle. I'd feel guilty if I saw a movie. Most of anything that comes along, my question is, would Jesus want me to do this, or would he not want me to do it?'

The difference between Mr Gideon and Mr Yoder was that the Amish gentleman never insisted that he was right. Leave alone try and make me offer morning and evening devotions in some Germanic tongue.

His concerns were simple: Jesus and the family of ten (Amish don't believe in contraception either) that He provided for.

'Wouldn't it be easier to raise a family of four?'

'Don't know. Never tried it.'

Touché.

✧ ✧ ✧

Back in the viewing car, I settled in with a bootlegged Jack and Coke. The lost long-haired man sat across. I realized that all he was doing earlier was looking for someone to talk to.

'Where you headed?' he asked.

'Sandpoint, Idaho.'

'You got to watch out at Sandpoint. They're a bunch of racist bastards. They don't like people of our colour… they'll take you up into the woods and fucking fuck you up.'

His name was Timothy, and he was of Indian stock.

'My brother, your best bet would be to jump off at Spokane. Don't get off at Sandpoint.'

This was a bit excessive, I thought. 'Unsafe? At an Amtrak station?' I asked.

'There ain't no Amtrak station. They drop you off at a fuckin' gas station. And it's dark… I wouldn't wanna be there by myself.'

We were joined by an angry young man, a 24-year-old welder and pipe fitter. His name was Cody Charboneau. Cody was also of Native American descent, but he had a name that recalled a past. There was a controversial Frenchman with that last name who accompanied Lewis and Clark. One of his wives, a Native American, was a translator for the expedition. Cody began a monologue that was at once homey and high-flown.

'Regardless of whether night or day, Sandpoint is regarded as highly racist. And that's about it, man. Person of dark-coloured skin or anything like that is looked down upon. Looked at in every other way—besides the good way.

'It is the way that people look at you, the way they treat you. You know you have a sense that they're not lookin' at you, they're lookin' at the colour of your skin. Where you came from. And what you're doin' here. The whole question of where you should be and where you're not. It's not even who.

'I walk around in stores... people follow me around. In my experience in this life, the Indian country has the highest racial tension—besides the South—in the United States. Indian country is North Dakota, South Dakota, Minnesota, Montana, Idaho and some parts of Washington. It seems like the further you get away from the reservations, the more respect they have for Native Americans.'

'Why is that?'

'It is, within straight definition, ignorance. The absence of knowledge. If they would take their time to know me, they would know I have a good job and that I support my family, pay my child support, pay my dues and do what I have to do in order to live in this society.

'But they don't. They see the colour of my skin and they automatically think "drunk", "alcoholic", "thief", "shouldn't be in my community."'

I thought it seemed logical that people who lived near Native Americans would know them better. But he was saying the opposite. He sounded frustrated when I said this. I tried to calm him down with a Jack and Coke...

'Of course you're going to be angry if your ancestors have been oppressed, their lands taken away. Put on a 70 mile square and told, "don't leave".

'Take our religion away from us. The very foundation that America was built on—freedom of religion, that's why they came to these lands. And 120 years into their little escapade over here, they take away our right to practise our religion. We had to do it underground for years—till 1970, it wasn't legal to practise Native American ways—anywhere in the United States.*

'I know my history. That's why I'm so angry. See, in the 1910s and 1920s, they put us in boarding schools. My great-grandmother went to a boarding school and she was whipped 'coz she spoke her native tongue. How's that word... they *beat* it out of us.'

And now, he was left with no choice but to join his ancestors' tormentors.

'I just can't go out and shoot a buffalo and put food on the table now, can I?'

'Is it really that bad?'

---

* The American Indian Religious Freedom Act was passed in 1978. While the religious freedom of various groups, including the Native Americans, are now protected, the Act acknowledged that rights were routinely violated in the past.

'You wouldn't understand. We're on different journeys.'

Just then, everyone on the train felt their ears go pop. The train was crawling up the mountains between Whitefish and Libby. Cody and I both gulped and rubbed our ears. It wouldn't be long before we entered the Idaho Panhandle.

No one dragged me off into the woods in Sandpoint. That's because no one was around to do this—it was a miserable, wet night.

✧ ✧ ✧

I woke up the next morning in Sarah Palin's birth town, to this story in the *Bonner County Bee*:

> The US Secret Service is being asked to review a sign a Bonner County landowner put up which suggests a 'free public hanging' of president-elect Barack Obama and several other political figures.
>
> The handmade cardboard sign also features a noose fashioned from a length of nylon rope. 'That's a political statement. They can call it whatever they want, a threat or whatever,' said Ken Germana, who installed the sign on his property off Golden Gate Road in south-western Bonner County....
>
> Germana said he posed absolutely no threat to Obama, but admitted he would not lose any sleep if harm did come the president-elect's way. He said he made the sign to protest hypocrisy in two high-profile incidents involving effigies of Republican vice-president nominee Sarah Palin and Obama.
>
> The Palin effigy was erected in Los Angeles and the Obama effigy was put up at the University of Kentucky campus in Lexington. Both incidents made headlines

in the run-up to the general election, but Germana maintains they were treated differently by authorities and the press.

In Germana's view, nothing was done to the creators of the Palin effigy, while those who were involved with the Obama effigy were arrested.

'If other people can make political statements, so can I. Just because I don't live in California doesn't mean I don't have my rights, too,' he said.

This was about what I expected to find in the town that had brought Sarah Palin into the world. Besides, somebody had to put those homo-loving commies in California in their place. If the job's left to a politically-inclined nutcase from far off Idaho, so be it. Bring on the secret service!

But did they really need to move in on Paradise?

Sandpoint was one of the most scenic towns I had seen in the United States—a settlement in a wooded valley around the shimmering blue waters of the lake Pend Oreille. It even had a beach and lots of fish, including, I learned, the 'cut-throat trout' and the 'crappie spiny ray fish'.

This called for some investigation, so I walked into Craig Gildersleeve's Flying Fish Company. It reminded me of the little school on the prairie. It was 96 square feet, built on the sidewalk, and was open only two days a week, during which Craig sold 300 pounds of fish—cut-throat, crappie and all the rest. It was also the neatest fish shop that I had seen.

Craig's big day was Friday. 'Catholics… in fact, all Americans, eat fish on Fridays.' This was a faith thing about which there are many conspiracy theories—like some Pope had a cousin in the fishing business, and made a rule. But this expression of religion worked very well for Craig. About a few other religions practices, he wasn't so sure. He was a liberal to the core.

Idaho was the reddest state in the Union—two of every three voters had supported the McCain–Palin ticket. And here I was, meeting the odd one of every three. It was frustrating.

'Have all the conservatives gone into hiding after the election? Where can I find one?' I asked.

'This part of Idaho (the narrow sliver of land in the north) is different. We're kind of more independent than conservative—we don't even grow potato! You could try their headquarters—220 Pine,' said Craig.

So off I went. The address belonged to 'Rainbow Realty', but it served as the Republican Party headquarters for the county. Two weeks after the election was done, it looked like a campsite that had been ransacked. Posters and yard signs lay on the ground, and but for a young Rainbow Realty executive, no one was around.

Dan Young, the firm's proprietor and the big Republican organizer for the area, came by in a bit. He showed not a trace of bitterness about the result, nor offered any excuse. He explained it instead by saying, with appreciation rather than resignation, 'How do you stop somebody like Obama anyway?'

He then went on to dismiss the nut who had made the paper that day as ignorant and irrelevant. 'The election is over. And he is my president now.'

Dan wasn't being correct. He was just being himself.

Later that evening, I had a few beers with Craig at Eichardt's—a bar that liberals frequented—and I wondered if I was in the right town after the primer I'd been given about Sandpoint earlier.

From the racism point of view, in the two days I spent there, the town was a total washout. I fell asleep at the allegedly terrifying station waiting for the train to Seattle that night. A concerned white man woke me up just in time to board the train.

✧   ✧   ✧

I reached Seattle fairly early the next morning. When I'd put the city on my list of destinations, I thought I'd do a chapter titled 'Looking for Asok'—the slightly dysfunctional, hopelessly unathletic Indian geek who never gets promoted in the 'Dilbert' cartoon strips.

The idea was to try and find a suitable candidate—and my friends at Microsoft had told me there was no Asok shortage. But I was tired. Over months I had looked for lots of things that I thought I might find in America. At times I found them, at other times they found me. Maybe Asok would find me too—right here at Pike Place market, as I listened to the buskers and ate buttered crab. After all, that's the kind of luck I'd had on this trip.

I gave Asok two hours, but he did not arrive. He must have just got promoted and taken his colleagues out for a vegetarian lunch.

Acknowledgements

I have a long list of people to thank for this book. First my family. My wife, Suparna, whose patience I so often tested (and still do), for loving me and believing in me. My parents, Nitibrata and Gouri Sen, and my father-in-law, S.K. Sharma, all of whom offered their unflinching support.

My sister, Indrakshi, and her husband, Basudeb. I had the luxury of a home in the USA, their house in Dallas, to which I could come back whenever being on the road got to me. My friends, Ankur and Ashwini, opened their home to me in the wonderful town of Madison. I received constant encouragement from my dear friends, Poonam Saxena and Tushita Patel, who read the manuscript. I doubt if I'd have been able to complete it without their help.

Sheema and Karthika, my editors at Harper Collins, it was a pleasure working with you. And finally, to all the strangers I met during my travels—this book would not have been possible without their kindness.